*Father Figures*

# Father Figures

## GENEALOGY AND NARRATIVE STRUCTURE IN RABELAIS

Carla Freccero

*Cornell University Press*

ITHACA AND LONDON

First published 1991 by Cornell University Press.


International Standard Book Number 0-8014-2554-9
Library of Congress Catalog Card Number 90-55728
Printed in the United States of America
*Librarians: Library of Congress cataloging information*
*appears on the last page of the book.*

To my father,
precursor poet,
and to my mother,
who taught me how
to translate
empires

# Contents

# Prologue:
# The Author's Excuse

Rabelais scholars continue to be divided into camps: those who use contemporary theoretical insights to understand his difficult text and those self-designated historicists who feel that to do so violates the text, preferring to invoke Renaissance theoretical debates as their sole analytical tools in reading Rabelais. The latter course is impossible; no amount of erudition can re-create the historical context in which Rabelais wrote and contemporary literary theorists debated. Furthermore, in attempting to re-create Renaissance approaches to the text, the scholar risks merely perpetuating myths that their Renaissance producers created for themselves and for posterity. Thus, for example, the imperialist bases of humanism have yet to be fully confronted. They constitute a blind spot in the Renaissance's articulation of itself, felicitously (and not unpredictably) preserved in nineteenth-century historical constructions of the period.

My own use of current theoretical writing stems in part from a desire to estrange Rabelais's text from a history of institutions and ideas we may think we understand— humanism, for example—and to disrupt the notion of the imagined continuity of the canon that European literary history proposes, whereby the Renaissance constitutes the birth of the values and ideals of twentieth-century academic institutions and Rabelais becomes illustrative of the Renaissance. At the same time, by resisting the text's representations of its own coherence, I question those values and institutions that claim their genesis in "Renaissance thought."

A related debate concerning Rabelais's books involves the text's coherence or unity. Those who read Rabelais as an erudite evangelical humanist continue to find a basic Christian hermeneutic at work, whereby the text itself becomes a brilliant allegorical surface with a hidden, privileged meaning beneath its linguistic veil. Others, postmodernists, insist that textuality always goes beyond any conscious meaning imposed upon it and find in Rabelais a consummate example of such linguistic play. I find myself partially convinced by both approaches. On one hand, scholars who have shown ideological coherence in the work have argued their case ingeniously and produced readings that enlarge the possibilities for understanding difficult and mysterious places in the text. On the other hand, passages can almost always be found that resist, if not oppose, these impositions of ideological coherence. Both and neither: the history of Rabelais's reception itself tells us which is correct, but this approach of course is to argue against the notion of any definitively correct reading of any text. It is always a question of interests, as my discussion of genealogy in this book suggests.

François Rigolot, in *Le Texte de la Renaissance*, suggests that the relationship between Dante and Rabelais has yet to be fully investigated, taking his cue from Victor Hugo, who declares, "Dans l'ordre des hauts génies, Rabelais suit chronologiquement Dante: après le front sévère, la face ricanante" (*Oeuvres complètes: Critique*, 12:278: "In the chronology of great geniuses, Rabelais follows Dante: after the stern brow, the derisive face"). The canonic paradigm of filiation he proposes suggests an oedipalized complicity that carries personal resonance for me, and indicates in part why father figures and filiation are the narratives I am concerned with in Rabelais. Many male critics of this text (and this tradition) have regarded filial succession as the inheritance of a revered and rival paternal legacy that will in time be surpassed. Thus they have read Rabelais as triumphantly realizing and improving upon the legacy of ancient Rome and Greece. In doing so, they are also speaking about themselves and their inheritance of the European Renaissance as it is mythically idealized in literary history. Psychoanalysis permits a skeptical reading of this view of sons and fathers, as does a differently gendered relationship to the question of inheritance in all its forms.

A retrospective reading of this book suggests to me further explorations of the Rabelaisian text that follow changing critical currents in the academy and have not, as yet, been fully charted. The place of "woman," as figure and as referent, is here alluded to but not analyzed in depth. My own subsequent work on Rabelais moves in this direction, yet more needs to be done to analyze the murder of the mother in this narrative of filial succession and in the construction of Renaissance humanism itself. Current scholarship on Rabelais and on the Renaissance too often colludes in the deliberate elision of this other half of humanity. Furthermore, the emergence of what is called the novel in France is not a matter of fathers and sons at all, but one of mothers and daughters, if *La Princesse de Clèves* is to be regarded as its starting point.

Another suppressed dimension of Rabelais's text—suppressed, that is, by both the text and its critics, and for different reasons—is its homoeroticism. The emergence of scholarship in gay studies and the history of sexuality suggests that such an analysis may soon be possible.

Finally, I am convinced of the necessity for further studies of the relation between Rabelais's narratives and the infrastructure of early modern European social formations, particularly insofar as Renaissance (and other) canonical texts are currently being conscripted in the academy's canon wars and its debates about the merits of humanism.

Throughout this study I have used the Textes Littéraires Français editions of Rabelais's first four books; for the fifth book I have employed the Classiques Garnier edition edited by Pierre Jourda. Long passages are given in both French and in English, using J. M. Cohen's translation in the Penguin Classics edition, supplemented and corrected, when necessary, by my own translations (in brackets). Other passages and secondary sources are presented in translation, except where the French original is absolutely necessary to convey the sense of the passage. Some of those translations are my own, but I have used standard ones wherever possible; these are listed in the bibliography along with the original editions.

Parts of this work have appeared elsewhere in condensed or revised form: "Damning Haughty Dames: Panurge and the 'Haulte Dame de Paris'," in *Journal of Medieval and Renaissance Studies* 15 (Spring 1985): 57–67 and "The 'Instance' of the Letter: Woman in the Text of Rabelais," in *Rabelais's Incomparable Book: Essays on His Art*, ed. Raymond La Charité (Lexington, Ky.: French Forum, 1986), 45–55 (see chap. 2); "Rabelais's 'Abbaye de Thélème': Utopia as Supplement" in *L'Esprit Créateur* 25 (Spring 1985): 73–87 (see chap. 4).

The writing of the book was aided at its earliest stage by a grant from the Mrs. Giles Whiting Foundation; a Dartmouth College Junior Faculty Fellowship later relieved me of teaching responsibilities so I could rewrite and revise.

The idea for this book emerged from many conversations about Rabelais with Paolo Valesio, whose teaching and writing have deeply influenced me. I thank Thomas Greene, who oversaw its early development, and Margaret Ferguson, whose valuable criticisms shaped later revisions.

Friends and colleagues at Dartmouth and elsewhere have been helpful and supportive during my years in Hanover. I am grateful to Terry Viens, who made the manuscript electronically accessible to me, and to Gail Vernazza, who also helped me to prepare it for publication. I owe the title to Nancy Vickers's inspiration.

Less tangible, but equally essential, support was provided by the women's community at Dartmouth College, both the women who have left and those who remain. Their brilliant minds, courage, friendship, and ardent feminism have sustained me. Through graduate school and beyond, Antonella Ansani, Rachel Bowlby, Nancy Harrowitz, Stephanie Jed, Marcelle Mekiès, Marilyn Migiel, Ann Mullaney, Jill Robbins, and especially Barbara Spackman helped to shape me through their writings and their persons.

I am grateful to Thomas Trezise for dialogues about Thélème, to my colleague and friend Walter Stephens, whose work on Rabelais I admire, and to the Dartmouth French and Italian department medievalists whose support and criticism improved my understanding of Rabelais and of the Middle Ages. David Rollo also generously helped with last-minute details.

Finally, I thank the midwives of this project: the student activists at Dartmouth, who challenge my thinking daily; Kelly Ireland; and James Breeden, *pateros*.

CARLA FRECCERO

*Hanover, New Hampshire*

*Father Figures*

# Introduction:
# Allegories of Filiation

Recent Rabelais scholarship has for the most part taken a decidedly conservative turn, continuing the important archaeological work of uncovering this encyclopedic author's classical sources. Other critics have sought to read Rabelais as a Christian philosopher and have provided increasingly coherent interpretations of the first four books. Many alternative approaches—psychoanalytic, feminist, poststructuralist, Marxist—have proved fascinating but partial in their scope. My approach differs from all these first in that it contextualizes the narrative structure of the work in terms of an overall Renaissance thematics. It also takes all five books as its object of study, not to affirm the authenticity of the fifth book, but to demonstrate the text's affinity with and inheritance of medieval quest literature and to explore the connection between the questions of the text and its outcome, or closure, in the arrival at Bacbuc's temple of the Holy Bottle.

In a general sense, the return to origins implies a concern for ends. A genealogy, as a work of fantasy or fiction, represents the desire to locate and fix (spatially, as on a heraldic tree, as well as temporally) one's lineage, and thus it indicates a certain anxiety about legitimation. This "recollection," inspired by a desire in the present, actively works upon the future in the Nietzschean sense of a "workshop where ideals are manufactured," projecting a continuum of descent that is to be carried out.[1] Legitimizing or "authorizing" what exists by tracing it to its origin constitutes not a discovery, as Nietzsche points out, but an interpretation, a creation, the appropriation of something for "new" purposes: "Whatever exists, having somehow come into being, is again and again reinterpreted to new ends, taken over, transformed, and redirected by some power superior to it; all events in the organic world are a becoming master, and all subduing and becoming master involves a fresh interpretation, an adaptation through which any previous 'meaning' and 'purpose' are necessarily obscured or even obliterated" ("Genealogy of Morals," 513). Renaissance genealogy—from the construction of family trees for the petty nobility of the Italian courts and the investigation of royal lines of descent from Charlemagne in France to the narration of "histories" for the great cities of Europe (and the parodies of these)—is thus a political gesture. On the one hand, this step in the process of ideological solidification is taken by an aristocracy seeking to justify its existence when confronted with the threat of change; on the other, it is the means by which a nascent bourgeoisie composed of parvenus seeks to legitimize its newfound wealth. Finally, in the Renaissance it is also the means by which "nations" (defensively) construct for themselves an ancient and venerable history to justify their present policies and their goals. Noble lineage ensures nobility, divine descent, divine right.

The books of Rabelais begin by demystifying the legitimizing function of genealogies; the story of the son inaugurates the new and repudiates the past. But only in part, for

[1]Friedrich Nietzsche, "The Genealogy of Morals," in *The Basic Writings of Nietzsche*, ed. Walter Kaufmann, 439–603.

the story of the son turns to the father to find both its origin and the terms of its difference. The confrontation with paternal imperatives in *Pantagruel* occasions the father's death, but already, in incipient form, it implies the son's obedience to those imperatives in the chapters where Panurge substitutes himself for Pantagruel as the force of transgression and domination in the tale. The narrative thus engenders a repetition of the story of succession it sought to escape: *Gargantua* follows *Pantagruel* and inherits its narrative structure, though the metaphors that govern it underscore its constructedness as a book. The Gargantuan afterthought is itself a story of filial succession, though retrospectively it cannot seem so, for it is the story of the father. Its culmination, Thélème, figures the impasse of the historical predicament, not as solution but as symptom.

In chapters 2 and 3 of this book I analyze the narrator's articulation of the genealogical problem and its relation to the question of literary inheritance and the authorship of the book. *Pantagruel* presents itself as an outgrowth of other chronicles and romances, organically related to its literary origins and to the teller of the tale. *Gargantua*, with its parody of genealogy, presents the story as deliberately constructed from an ancient and illegible book, requiring transcription and, by implication, invention. My analysis of the successive prologues and editions of Rabelais's books focuses as well on the author's *prise-de-conscience* as author and on some of the material conditions informing it. Related to this is the thematic father-son relationship in *Pantagruel*, which I analyze through readings of selected chapters. Here the appearance of Panurge in conjunction with the question of woman in the text marks an initial displacement of filiation that finds its fullest realization in the *Tiers Livre*.

Chapter 3 also examines paternal-filial relations and shows how, in the book of the father, potential conflicts are repressed. As the story of the father in the Rabelaisian corpus, the *Gargantua* must be originary. Its story of filial succession is effaced, as is the demystificatory force of the parody of genealogical inheritance in its thematic enactment as a story of father and son.

In a reading of chapters 8 and 9 of *Gargantua*, I analyze the relation between language and meaning explored by the narrator's lengthy digression on the significance of the colors blue and white. I concur with Richard Waswo's observation that a paradigmatic shift is under way during this period in the area of language theory, from language as referential to language as relational, but that the shift is never theorized as such.[2] Rather, there is expressed a persistent nostalgia for the belief that signs point beyond themselves to the divine, to a fixed meaning beyond language. This belief too is an issue of filiation, for what is at stake in these chapters is the father's capacity to impose his meaning arbitrarily on a sign, while the connection between language and the divine figures in itself "man's" problematic relation to his (symbolic) Father.

Thélème is the narrative of the escape from temporality and history and the arrival at the ideal place, utopia. Thus, within the terms of *Gargantua*, filial succession reaches its goal. Yet Thélème's rhetoric of culmination, which produces it as a Renaissance ideal for posterity, confronts its own deconstruction in the enigma of its very foundations. Chapter 3 thus concludes with a discussion of the issue of closure in the first two books and introduces the question of Thélème's place in the story. Thélème—its relation to the chapters that precede it and its connection to the thematics of filiation—is the subject of chapter 4. The end of *Gargantua* and Thélème also raise the question of the political unconscious of Rabelais's text and connect the issue of paternal domination to the imperialism that supplements the "Abbaye." I discuss the logic of the supplement and how it informs the enigma that deconstructs the foundations of the abbey, opening the text up to the impossibility of closure and resolution. The debate

[2]Richard Waswo, *Language and Meaning in the Renaissance*.

between Gargantua and Frère Jean reiterates this inconclusiveness and connects it to problems of meaning and interpretation.

The *Tiers Livre*, *Quart Livre*, and *Cinquième Livre* no longer employ the family metaphor in their titles, and the subject or agent of the quest they delineate—Panurge—completes the process of displacement begun in *Pantagruel*. Thus chapter 5 proceeds somewhat differently, analyzing the overall narrative structure of the last two books and their relation to the continuator's *Cinquième Livre*. Here I explore the differences between the first two books and the last two in generic terms as the relation between epic, embodied in the heroic son Pantagruel, and romance, figured in Panurge, the antigenealogical protagonist of the quest.

The Prologue to the *Tiers Livre* foregrounds the writer as author of his book and describes the activity of writing as an ironically useless gesture not entirely under the author's control. Instead of acting out his promised role as national chronicler of the deeds and exploits of his epic heroes Gargantua and Pantagruel, Rabelais turns to the question of Panurge's marriage and explores the problem of the romance quest. Through a comparison with medieval romance and with François Habert's *Songe de Pantagruel*, I analyze the allegory of father and son in the *Tiers Livre*, where Gargantua is resurrected and forecloses the possibility of the story's continuing in the mode of filial succession. Correspondingly, the theme of nostalgia for an absolute, inaccessible, and ideal past emerges in several chapters of the *Tiers Livre* and *Quart Livre*. The text articulates its anxiety around filiation in the (displaced) question of Panurge's cuckoldry, in the discussion of woman, and in the gods' response to the threat of Pantagruel's progeny. All these converge to suggest a rationale for the configuration the Rabelaisian novel assumes.

The ironic unfolding of the book's predicament takes the form of the medieval motif of the romance quest because it is the genre that enacts and puts into question narrative's movement toward and digression from closure as revelation. Thematically, the story of filial inheritance reaches a standstill; father and son reenact their complicity in rejecting the future—figured as the question of the hero's marriage—for a nostalgic loyalty to the past (and to the father). What chapter 15 of *Pantagruel* implies, the *Tiers Livre* realizes: the son desires to be the father, rather than to become one. Panurge, instead, becomes the motivating rationale for the quest—he who, the text implies, will not accept the answers he is seeking. He inherits, through displacement, the obsession with genealogical succession the earlier books assign to the son.

The writing subject of the *Quart Livre* allegorizes the failure of the quest as a failure to escape from the predicament of teleology and as the impossibility of arriving at a revelation that will also be a redemption. The book describes a series of fragmented episodes—occasions for satire, islands of discursive play in an endless voyage with no particular direction. Yet though the text playfully mocks the inability of any sign to deliver a universal and transparent meaning to its questers, Bacbuc's admonition, "Be, yourselves, the interpreters of your enterprise," resolves in the direction of individualistic solutions the ironic ambivalence of the allegory of the quest.

In my readings of selected episodes in the *Quart Livre*, I show how the split between the writing subject and the thematic content of the narrative makes ironic the text's predicament: the tending of the tale toward a telos and a revelation in spite of the superfluity, not to say impossibility, of any meaningful "arrival." I argue that the continuator parodically resolves the predicament, comparing the final chapters of the *Cinquième Livre* with Teofilo Folengo's *Baldus* and the similarly "failed" closure of that parodic quest.

Thus a predicament of filial succession structures Rabelais's narrative, even as it constitutes the themes: of the writer as author of "his" book, of the narrator as royal historiographer, of the son Pantagruel and his gigantic father Gargantua. The predicament is theological and linguistic as well: many chapters enact the search for and the impossibility of finding a transcendent guarantee or reference outside language that will authorize meaning, at the same time that the text seems to celebrate the very contingency implied by the failure of such a search.

The end of the quest exposes the fictions of the text's own narrative process—that beginning and ending are the arbitrary but necessary boundaries of an "espace littéraire."[3] But whereas in this Renaissance text the authority of tradition casts its genealogical shadow upon the origins of the work, the failure of its end opens a space for a "new," fatherless genre, that "school for orphans" that is the novel.[4]

My suggestion throughout this book is that the question of filiation, and Rabelais's narrative enactment of it, informed the shape the novel was to take in the next century and beyond. A submerged suggestion of my work is that the triumphant individualism critics have read into the quest for the word of the Holy Bottle is not triumphant at all; it is the result of a predicament—indirectly related, I think, to nation-state consolidation in sixteenth-century France, the beginnings of imperialism, and nascent capitalism—whose negativity the Rabelaisian corpus, for all its parodic serenity, does not entirely conceal.

[3]Maurice Blanchot, *L'Espace littéraire.*
[4]R. Howard Bloch, *Etymologies and Genealogies: A Literary Anthropology of the French Middle Ages,* 107.

# *Pantagruel*: Genealogy
# and Filial Succession

R abelais's text thematizes genealogy in several ways. The sequence of publication of the first two books immediately renders doubtful, on the material level, the level of the book's production, the "issue" of filial descent. Although Pantagruel is the son of Gargantua, his book precedes that of the father.[1] In this respect the work claims for the present a certain priority over history. This anxious move to usurp the authority of the past is later retracted in the appearance of *Gargantua* and its assumption of an anterior position in the fictional chronology of the narrative.[2]

[1]*Pantagruel* appeared sometime in 1532, whereas *Gargantua* was published in 1534. The order was later reversed, so that *Gargantua* appears to precede and anticipate *Pantagruel*. See *Oeuvres de François Rabelais: édition critique*, ed. Abel Lefranc, vol. 3, *Pantagruel*, chap. 1.

[2]I use the term "anxious" here to refer to Harold Bloom's study of the anxiety experienced by poets in relation to their predecessors in *The Anxiety of Influence*. See also Edward Said, *Beginnings: Intention and Method*. Whereas Said bases his idea of beginnings on the modern assumption that a novel seeks to emphasize its difference from, and its uniqueness in relation to, other works driven by that "anxiety of influence" that all modern writing is familiar with, I shall take as my point of departure the Renaissance desire to inscribe the literary work in a line of textual descent (tradi-

On the textual level, the narrator articulates the uneasy equilibrium between the present work and the rest of its family. The greatness of the *Chronique Gargantuine* lineage is playfully asserted in at least two explicit comparisons to the Bible: "Les avez creues tout ainsi que texte de Bible ou du sainct Evangile" (Saulnier ed., 3) ("You have believed them just as you believed the text of the Bible or of the Holy Gospel" [Cohen ed., 168]), and "Il en a esté plus vendu des imprimeurs en deux moys, qu'il ne sera achepté de Bibles de neuf ans" (6) ("More copies of it have been sold by the printers in two months than there will be of the Bible in nine years" [168]).[3] The Prologue separates this family chronicle from other "related" texts:

> Bien vray est il que l'on trouve en d'aulcuns livres dignes de mémoire certaines proprietez occultes, en nombre desquelz l'ont mect *Robert le Diable*, *Fierabras*, *Guillaume sans paour*, *Huon de Bourdeaulx*, *Monteville*, et *Matabrune*; mais elles ne sont pas à comparer à celuy dont nous parlons. (6)

> It is very true that one finds in some books [worthy of memory] certain occult properties; and among these are counted . . . , *Robert the Devil*, *Fierabras*, *William the Fearless*, *Huon of*

---

tion) whereby it is perhaps only in the process of writing that its difference (and distance) from antiquity is realized. It is almost as though an "anxiety of originality" was at work that required a textual endeavor to have the sanction, the authorizing model, of an ancient source. For a study of anxiety as it affects Renaissance culture, see William J. Bouwsma, "Anxiety and the Formation of Early Modern Culture."

[3]Page numbers refer to the Textes Littéraires Français edition of *Pantagruel*, edited by Verdun Saulnier, throughout this chapter unless otherwise indicated. Throughout the book, English translations will be taken from the Penguin edition of *Gargantua and Pantagruel*, trans. J. M. Cohen, except when the translation is inadequate or does not correspond to the French editions I work with. My changes are inserted in brackets. Page numbers refer first to the French text, then to Cohen's translation. Translations that have no page numbers are my own.

*Bordeaux*, *Mandeville*, and *Matabrune*; but they are not compar-
able to the book of which we speak. (168)

The references to the Bible, though playful, nevertheless
border on the aggressive: the text becomes a sort of counterpart pertaining to the realm of darkness, with its "occult
properties," its power to instill belief, its gigantic origins
(giants usually being enlisted on the side of evil), its parentage in the *romans de chevalrie* (condemned by the church as
heretical in the sixteenth century), and finally its offspring
Pantagruel, the little devil of the fifteenth century *Mystère des
actes des Apôtres*.[4] It is as though the text were inscribing itself
playfully and ironically within a tradition of rebellious and
guilty sons.

A gesture of filial indebtedness toward the parent text is
made: "Wishing therefore still further to increase your enter-
tainment, I, your humble slave, offer you now another book
of the same stamp" (6; 168), culminating in a modest boast,
"though one a little more reasonable and credible than the
last." The narrator's position vis-à-vis this previous work
(and tradition), however, is evidently more ambiguous. In a
curious passage that has been considered a jibe at Sorbonne
censorship, he claims:

> Et à la mienne volunté que ung chascun laissast sa propre
> besoingne, et mist ses affaires propres en oubly, affin de y
> vacquer entièrement sans que son esprit feust de ailleurs dis-
> traict ny empesché jusques à ce que l'on les sceust par cueur,
> affin que, si d'aventure l'art de imprimerie cessoit, ou en cas
> que tous livres périssent, au temps advenir ung chascun les
> puisse bien au net enseigner à ses enfans. (4)

[4]See *Pantagruel*, Saulnier ed., chap. 12. For the church's condemnation
of romance literature and of Rabelais, see Henri Busson, "Les Eglises
contre Rabelais." On the genealogy of giants in the Renaissance and
Rabelais's transformation of the meaning of giants, see Walter Stephens,
*Giants in Those Days: Folklore, Ancient History, and Nationalism.*

I would have every man put aside his proper business, take no care for his trade, and forget his own affairs, in order to devote himself entirely to this book. I would have him allow no distraction or hindrance from elsewhere to trouble his mind, until he knows it by heart; so that if the art of printing happened to die out, or all books should come to perish, everyone should be able, in time to come, to teach it thoroughly to his children. (167)

The narrator's anxiety is as much a function of the attempt to justify appropriating the narrative as of concern about the suppression of books; there is a contradiction, since the narrative had not, before the publication of *Pantagruel*, had any trouble surviving in oral form.[5]

The gesture toward the parent text is repeated on the thematic level and reveals itself to be intimately connected to the existence of the *Pantagruel*. Alcofrybas Nasier declares:

C'est des horribles faictz et prouesses de Pantagruel, lequel j'ay servy à guaiges dès ce que je fuz hors de page, jusques à present, que par son congié m'en suis venu ung tour visiter mon pays de vache, et sçavoir s'il y avoit encores en vie nul de mes parens. (7)

It tells of the horrific feats and deeds of Pantagruel, whom I have served for wages since I grew out of my page-hood till

---

[5]Barry Lydgate discusses the tension between the oral and the written in Rabelais in "Going Public: Rabelais, Montaigne and the Printed Word." He takes this passage seriously, however, as a concern about censorship: "The narrator of *Pantagruel* proposes that if printing is suppressed the Gargantua stories contained in the *Grandes Cronicques* will be circulated and preserved by word of mouth—that is, he prescribes oral structures of preservation for narratives endangered by the disappearance of books" (14). For a more general survey of oral versus textual traditions and practices, see Elizabeth Eisenstein, *The Printing Press as an Agent of Change: Communications and Cultural Transformations in Early Modern Europe*, and Walter Ong, *Interfaces of the Word: Studies in the Evolution of Consciousness and Culture*.

today, when by his leave I have come to visit my pastures and discover if any of my kindred survives there. (168)

Here the metaphor of a return toward origins, genealogical investigation, explicitly creates the text—it is the pretext by which the narrator achieves presence. The discourse, however, is metacritical: the narrator, not Pantagruel the hero or protagonist, is on a parental quest. Whereas classical and medieval traditions provide the foundation for the hero's genealogical exploration, notably the search for the father, Rabelais transposes the discourse, from the start, to the level of the narrative itself, to the level of writing. His work parodically links the Renaissance action of literary re-creation to the desire to find and revive a lineage and the desire to usurp or triumph over the authority of the parent culture. The latter move, with its burden of guilt, engenders a compulsive repetition of genealogical themes in the text.[6] Walter Ste-

---

[6]In referring to Freud's term "repetition-compulsion," from *Beyond the Pleasure Principle*, I am talking about repetitions in Rabelais's text that are both thematically and structurally overdetermined. Thus the pseudohistoriographer's gesture of genealogical anxiety contaminates the rest of the text, the ambivalence about the relation between past and present structuring the elaboration of the work as a whole. Aspects of the compulsion to repeat include the repeat performance in *Gargantua* of *Pantagruel* with a more precise structuration, the apparent alteration of *Pantagruel* through the introduction of chapter 9 (see Gérard Defaux, "De Gorgias à Socrate: L'Itineraire de Pantagruel," and his "Au coeur du *Pantagruel*: Les Deux Chapitres IX de l'édition Nourry"), and the return of the father at the threshold of the quest; as in the case of Freud's child, the goal is to master a situation (the genealogical predicament) over which the text (Rabelais) has no control. The second aspect of repetition, as the reenactment of an experience in which the repressed psychic material is "forgotten" (*Pleasure Principle*, 12), can best be understood textually through Lacan's revision of the notion as having its basis in "the *insistence* of the signifying chain." Here what is repressed, unconscious, in the text becomes the will to truth, since the text as such can articulate only the signifier and has no connection with the real. Thus the text is compelled to repeat the signifying process, manifesting "its capture in a *symbolic* dimension." See Jacques Lacan, "Seminar on the Purloined Letter," 39, and his *Ecrits: A Selection*, trans. A. Sheridan, "Translator's Note," ix.

phens has brilliantly argued (*Giants in Those Days*) that the obsession with genealogy is a function of Rabelais's deliberate parody of the pseudohistoriographer Jean Lemaire de Belges and his *Illustrations de Gaule et singularités de Troye*, so that in the case of Alcofrybas the compulsion is overt and parodic. But the gesture is not confined to the narrator; the problematics of filiation haunt this text at every level.

Chapter 1 of *Pantagruel* serenely mocks biblical genealogy with its list of Old Testament, Greek, Roman, and medieval giants. The race itself is born of the surplus created by the death of Abel. Most of the giants are in the legion of the devil, monstrous figures defeated by the heroes of myth, legend, and history. At this time Pantagruel is perhaps one whose deeds of prowess are in fact "horrible," but this anti-hero of Rabelais's rival myth, taking his cue from the *Illustrations* of Lemaire and the *Grandes Chroniques*, becomes not only the servant of the good king Arthur but also a humanist giant, a Christian hero in his own right, reversing the medieval and Renaissance dictum "we are dwarfs sitting on the shoulders of giants."

In a parody of the philologist's concern for verisimilitude, the narrator claims, as evidence for his own history, the authority of exegetes:

Je vous allégueray l'auctorité des Massoretz, interprès des sainctes lettres hébraicques: lesquelz disent que sans point de faulte ledict Hurtaly n'estoit point dedans l'Arche de Noë. . . . mais il estoit dessus l'Arche à cheval, jambe deça, jambe delà, comme les petitz enfans sus des chevaulx de boys. Et en ceste façon, saulva ladicte Arche de périller: car il luy balloit le bransle avecques les jambes, et du pied la tournoit où il vouloit, comme on faict du gouvernail d'une navire. (15–16)

I will cite the authority of the Massoretes, [interpreters of Hebraic holy letters], who affirm that in fact Hurtali was not in Noah's Ark. . . . But he sat astride of it, with one foot on each side, as small children do on hobby-horses, [. . .] In this fashion, by God's aid, he saved the said Ark from danger. For he kept it balanced with his legs, and with one foot turned it whichever way he wished, as one does a ship with the tiller. (174)

Hurtaly guides Noah's ark and establishes truly gigantic dimensions for the members of Pantagruel's family.[7] Rabelais, through the persona of the narrator, rewrites the Holy Book, imposing an origin and a genealogy that in turn create a justified, mock-legitimate space in history for his text.

The two levels of genealogical (re)construction in the Prologue and chapter 1 of *Pantagruel* perform different functions. The first, textual genealogy, legitimizes the repetition of the Gargantua narrative for the present work and situates its point of origin, nevertheless conveying a discreet challenge to the tradition. The second, a genealogy of Pantagruel, proceeds more playfully, less anxiously, and yet poses the greater, more subversive threat. This chapter rewrites biblical history, thus setting itself up alongside, perhaps in opposition to, divine truth. As the previously unwritten continuation of divine history the narrative, much like the New Testament in relation to the Old, assumes greater authority than the *Chroniques*, the writing of the history of the giants becoming a more worthy enterprise than the "frivolous" medieval legends suggest.

At the same time, the inscription of gigantic history in the teleology of Christianity creates a present and a future for these Rabelaisian characters. If indeed their origins can be traced to that first founding moment (the murder of Abel by his brother) and their story can be told alongside that of Noah and his descendants, then it is likely that giants, like men, have their role to fulfill in the scheme of divine providence. Rabelais's text occupies that unwritten space in histo-

[7]In a later episode that is also linked to divine intervention at sea (*Quart Livre*, chaps. 18–22), the giant's dimensions are considerably reduced. Pantagruel, the son, serves as a mast for the storm-tossed ship, but he is small enough to fit on board.

ry, the as yet unuttered phoneme in the Augustinian sentence leading inexorably to its fulfillment in the Word.[8] Finally, Rabelais makes possible the creation of a humanist myth; by imposing an ancient lineage on Pantagruel (and Gargantua), he sets a temporal precedent that lends authority to the otherwise ephemeral figurative gigantism he will define, whether or not the intention is parodic.[9]

The Prologue and chapter 1 of *Pantagruel* ironically figure the genealogical gesture and the tensions that accompany the situating of the self and the text in a line of descent. Another set of chapters in *Pantagruel* figures this filial relationship in a different way. The characters are again invoked, but this time as biological father and son rather than as emblematic personages on a family tree. These chapters, 8 and 9, have been the subject of debate for years.[10]

The two most problematic points of dispute concern the

[8]For the Augustinian articulation of theology and rhetoric and its influence on the Middle Ages, see Kenneth Burke, *The Rhetoric of Religion: Studies in Logology*; David Quint, *Origin and Originality in Renaissance Literature: Versions of the Source*; R. Howard Bloch, *Etymologies and Genealogies: A Literary Anthropology of the French Middle Ages*; Dennis Costa, *Irenic Apocalypse: Some Uses of Apocalyptic in Dante, Petrarch and Rabelais*; and John Freccero, *Dante: The Poetics of Conversion*.

[9]Gérard Defaux, in "Au coeur du *Pantagruel*," suggests the figurative nature of the giant's dimensions: "The attitude of this linguistic Hercules—destined, as well, to purge the world of its monsters and tyrants and to clean the stables of Augias—this precociously affirmed will to independence (he breaks his cradle) . . . naturally invites interpretation, since it seems so symbolic of a certain moment in the history of the sixteenth century" (94). Walter Stephens, as I mentioned, argues that Rabelais's initial intention in constructing biblical genealogies for the giants was to parody Jean Lemaire's pseudohistorical genealogies. He admits, however, that Rabelais succeeded in lending authority to his gigantic figures in a way that Lemaire never did.

[10]See, for example, the following articles: Charles A. Béné, "Erasme et le chapître VIII du premier *Pantagruel*"; Gérard Brault, "'Un Abysme de Science': On the Interpretation of Gargantua's Letter to Pantagruel"; Ver-

tone of Gargantua's letter to Pantagruel in chapter 8 and the presence of a chapter 9 and a chapter 9 bis in the first edition of *Pantagruel*.[11] Chapter 8 has been considered both as a glowing homage to the "new" humanist learning and as a parody of a medieval and gargantuan thirst for knowledge at the expense of evangelical humility before the mysteries of divine wisdom. More recently, Edwin Duval has convincingly demonstrated how far the course of study outlined in the letter specifically and hyperbolically parodies a medieval curriculum ("The Medieval Curriculum, the Scholastic University, and Gargantua's Program of Studies").

The debate on these chapters is itself cast in terms of succession and inheritance. Much of the discussion responds to the question: Is *Pantagruel* a medieval or a Renaissance work? In other words, is Pantagruel a Sophist or a humanist giant? On the one hand, the letter enacts a transition from a parent to an offspring culture. Gargantua sanctions the son's efforts and exhorts him to strive for mastery in the famous command, "In short, let me find you a veritable abyss of knowledge" (47; 195). In a sense he (and so the Gargantuan tradition) authorizes a continuation and an amelioration of what he, "[reputed] to be the most learned man of the century" (44; 194), has begun. This is explicitly stated in repeated references to a Neoplatonic perpetuation of the self:

dun Saulnier, "Le Doute chez Rabelais?" Gérard Defaux, "Un 'Extrait de haulte mythologie' humaniste: Pantagruel, *Picus Redivivus*"; and Edwin Duval, "The Medieval Curriculum, the Scholastic University, and Gargantua's Program of Studies (*Pantagruel*, 8)."

[11]This is the subject of Defaux's study in "Au coeur du *Pantagruel*," where he also provides a (somewhat sarcastically inflected) survey of the opposing interpretations of the letter (61–63); see also his book *Pantagruel et les sophistes: Contribution à l'histoire de l'humanisme chrétien au XVIème siècle*. The Saulnier edition of *Pantagruel* reproduces the first (1532) edition and is used here.

"L'humaine nature . . . . peult, en estat mortel, acquérir une espèce de immortalité, et, en decours de vie transitoire, perpétuer son nom et sa semence." (41)

"We can, in this mortal state, acquire a kind of immortality and, in the course of this transitory life, perpetuate our name and seed." (193)

" Doncques non sans juste et équitable cause je rends grâces à Dieu, mon conservateur, de ce qu'il m'a donné povoir veoir mon antiquité chanue refleurir en ta jeunesse ." (42)

" Not without just and equitable cause, therefore, do I offer thanks to God, my Preserver, for permitting me to see my grey-haired age blossom afresh in your youth." (193)

"Je ne me réputeray point toutallement mourir, mais plustost transmigrer d'ung lieu en aultre, attendu que, en toy et par toy, je demeure en mon ymage visible en ce monde, vivant, voyant, et conversant." (42)

"I shall not now account myself to be absolutely dying, but to be passing from one place to another, since in you, and by you, I shall remain in visible form here in this world, visiting and conversing." (193)

Just as in the Prologue *Pantagruel* represents a continuation and an amelioration (6), so here Pantagruel is to continue and improve upon the image of his father without, it seems, any conflict of will. What have changed, drastically, are the "times." This point is also subjected to repeated references in the text and characterized by the metaphor of light dawning on a dark age:

"Le temps estoit encores ténébreux et sentent l'infélicité et calamité des Gothz, qui avoient mis à destruction toute bonne littérature. Mais, par la bonté divine, la lumière et dignité a esté de mon aage rendue ès lettres. . . . "Maintenant toutes disciplines sont restituées, les langues instaurées." (43–44)

"Indeed the times were still dark, and mankind was perpetually reminded of the miseries and disasters wrought by those Goths who had destroyed all sound scholarship. But, thanks be to God, learning has been restored in my age to its former dignity and enlightenment. . . . Now every method of teaching has been restored, and the study of languages has been revived." (194)

This celebrated Renaissance theme, first articulated by Petrarch in a reference to the preceding dark ages and then elaborated upon by others who added the notion of a rebirth, sets the tone for a reading of the letter as a contrast between medieval and Renaissance learning.[12] Pantagruel will be, in this interpretation, a humanist giant.

Gérard Defaux uses the tone of the letter to support postulated changes in the text that explain the presence of two chapter 9s. Although the comic or serious nature of chapter 8

[12]Although the French term "Renaissance" was not coined until much later, metaphors of rebirth and restoration were applied as early as the mid-fifteenth century to developments in Italian culture. Matteo Palmieri (1406–75) is often quoted: "Sculpture and architecture, for long years sunk to the merest travesty of art, are only today in the process of rescue from obscurity. . . . It is but in our own day that men dare boast that they see the dawn of better things. For example, we owe it to our Leonardo Bruni that Latin, so long a bye-word for its uncouthness, has begun to shine forth in its ancient purity, its beauty, its majestic rhythm. Now, indeed, may every thoughtful spirit thank God that it has been permitted to him to be born in this new age" (*Della vita civile*; translation from W. H. Woodward, *Studies in Education during the Age of the Renaissance*, p. 67). Wallace Ferguson, in *The Renaissance in Historical Thought*, points out "how frequently the humanists of both Italy and the northern countries employed metaphors of rebirth, revival or resuscitation, all of which imply a previous death, or the contrasting metaphors of darkness and light, to denote their conception of the history of literature, learning, and the fine arts from antiquity, through the Middle Ages, to their own time" (2).

is not of primary concern here, it is interesting to see how this node of uncertainty (chaps. 8, 9, 9 bis) inspires Defaux to construct an allegory of filiation for the text.[13] In Defaux's view, most of the educational and moral precepts outlined in the letter are medieval commonplaces as well. Furthermore, Gargantua's exhortation to Pantagruel to become "an abyss of knowledge" remains morally ambiguous in a humanist value system, for it fails to acknowledge the limits of human understanding before God.[14]

The recurrence of phrases such as "It is my earnest wish that you shall become a perfect master of languages" (45; 195); "Keep your memory well stocked with every tale from history" (46; 195); "I would have you learn the best texts by heart," "Let nothing be unknown to you" (46; 195); and "Gain a perfect knowledge of that other world" (46; 195) suggests a will to power in the letter and recalls the antibiblical threat posed by this "devil's" story in the Prologue. The concession made to God's power—"'Mais par ce que, selon le sage Salomon, Sapience n'entre point en âme malivole, et science sans conscience n'est que ruyne de l'âme, il te convient servir, aymer et craindre Dieu'" (47) ("'But because, according to the wise Solomon, Wisdom enters not into the malicious heart, and knowledge without conscience is but the ruin of the soul, it befits you to serve, love, and fear God'"

[13]Defaux, "Au coeur du *Pantagruel*," 61: "Through the complicitous opposition between the divine Pantagruel and the sophist Panurge, Rabelais inscribes the dilemma and grandeur, the hopes and the failures, the entire parable of Erasmian Evangelical Humanism."

[14]"For the humanist never assumed himself capable of knowing all. He is one who walks in the shadows searching for a light, who never ceases to repeat, following Democritus, that the truth is hidden at the bottom of a well too deep for the human spirit ever to hope to discover it" (Defaux, "Au coeur du *Pantagruel*," 75). See also Defaux, "De Gorgias à Socrates," where he compares the Renaissance debate on knowledge versus wisdom with the Platonic polarization of Sophist and Socratic learning. The Middle Ages are seen as incarnating the Sophist capacities, whereas Socrates becomes the emblem of the Renaissance.

[196])—rests on the level of commonplace advice, its importance equal to that of "Respect your tutors, avoid the company of those whom you would not care to resemble" (47;
196). Henri Busson points out in fact that "knowledge without conscience" was a traditional Scholastic dictum ("Rabelaisiana: 'Science sans conscience,' *Pantagruel* Ch. VIII,"
238).

Gargantua's self-glorifying obsession and the reference to
the disputation of theses prove, in Defaux's view, the over-
whelmingly sophistical, and so medieval, nature of the father's letter ("Au coeur du *Pantagruel*," 71–72). From this
point of departure, the critic generates the allegory that attempts to explain the presence of two chapter 9s and the
friendship between Pantagruel and Panurge. In order for the
giant to become a true hero and the *porte-parole* of Christian
humanism, which he seems to have become in contrast to his
father's Scholasticism, Panurge has to be introduced, as
"shadow," or evil double of Pantagruel.[15] The story of Pantagruel and Panurge thus becomes a personified dialogue between Renaissance humanism and its powerful predecessor,
medieval Scholasticism, and is couched in the language of
oedipal failure, a son's desire and inability to free himself
from paternal authority ("Au coeur du *Pantagruel*," 91).

Such critical reactions testify to a locus of tension in the
letter. Defaux's account fails to take into consideration the

---

[15]Defaux, "Au coeur du *Pantagruel*," 91. For the concept of the shadow
see Carl G. Jung, *Aion*. The shadow is basically the demonic double who
emerges as a result of ideological pressures that repress rather than integrate the demonic in the divine. See Paolo Valesio, "Il seggio e l'ombra: Da
un romanzo spagnolo del quattrocento," 80: "The crucial problem . . . is,
in brief, the following: the concentrated pressure to integrate chivalry
completely into a religious, specifically confessional system . . . releases
the counterpressure of the collective shadow—which emerges in short
bursts, awkward . . . and ambiguous. That is to say that the sanctifying,
confessional, edifying pressure evokes *a contrario* the violence and cruelty
that from the beginning are an intrinsic part of the knight's profession."

striking contrast between past and present the letter insists on and locates the parody in the character of Gargantua rather than in the text of the letter itself, whereas the other accounts, including Duval's, do not explain the father's narcissistic and oppressively dictatorial position. Both views, however, signal that inheritance is rendered problematic here, even as they seek alternative explanations to "solve" the conflict.

No overt rivalry occurs in this father-son relationship. Yet the very absence of an oedipal moment seems to generate multiple thematic and structural displacements of rivalry and resistance within the text and in critical assessments of it. The potential for oedipal conflict is eradicated at the very outset by the death of Badebec, Pantagruel's mother, which if anything guarantees the absolute obedience of the son.[16]

The letter sets forth the "law of the father." As striking as any nuance of "content," Scholastic or humanist, is the paternal domination the letter imposes on Pantagruel. Gargantua insists that Pantagruel is but a *reflection*, the *image* of his father: "in you, and by you, I shall remain in visible form

[16]*Pantagruel*, chap. 2, 17: "Il ne peust venir à lumière, sans ainsi suffoc-quer sa mère" ("he could not be born without thereby suffocating his mother"). Pantagruel's relationship to Gargantua is antioedipal (in the Freudian sense of the term) in that it is a relation of mimetic desire. This could also be said of the Renaissance as a whole, in its relation to classical antiquity. René Girard, in *Violence and the Sacred*, discusses the son-father relationship in these terms: "There is a clear resemblance between identification with the father and mimetic desire; both involve the choice of a model . . . the identification is a desire *to be* the model that seeks fulfillment, naturally enough, by means of appropriation; that is, by taking over the things that belong to his father" (170). The strength and clearly authoritative position of the father short-circuit the potential rivalry in this text. See Girard, 188: "The Oedipus complex appears most plausible in a society in which the father's authority has been weakened but not completely destroyed." The elimination of the mother, however, may be a symptom of the anxiety that such potential rivalry might be realized were there an object of desire.

here in this world" (42; 193); "just as, in you, lives the image of my body"(42); "to leave you, after my death, as a mirror representing the person of me your father" (43; 194).[17] In fact the letter circumscribes Pantagruel's life: the circumstances of his birth are explained to him, and his destiny (in the service of his father) is determined: " 'Car, doresenavant que tu deviens homme et te fais grand, il te fauldra issir de ceste tranquillité et repos d'estude: et apprendre la chevalerie et les armes, pour défendre ma maison' " (47) (" 'For, later, when you have grown into a man, you will have to leave this quiet and repose of study, to learn chivalry and warfare, to defend my house' " [195]. Unlike the knight in many of the medieval romans whose father is unknown, unnamed, or wounded and whose quest therefore consists, among other goals, in finding, naming, or healing the father, Pantagruel matures in the presence of a powerful (and present) father/king, thus rendering unnecessary the quest for an identity.[18] Pantagruel, like Aeneas, must reach heroic fulfillment through obedience—yet unlike Anchises (who must be carried by

[17]The narcissism expressed in these images points once again to Gargantua's "delusions" and to the anxieties about sameness and difference in the son. Jacques Lacan's discussion of the Imaginary, in describing a narcissism truer to its namesake than Freud's, opens the way for a suggestive interpretation of the father-son relationship in Rabelais. See "Le Stade du miroir comme formateur de la fonction du Je," in *Ecrits*, 1, translated in *Ecrits: A Selection*. For Lacanian interpretations of Rabelais, see Ellie Ragland-Sullivan, "The Myth of the *Sustantificque Mouelle*: A Lacanian Perspective on Rabelais's Use of Language"; also Lawrence Kritzman, "Rabelais's Comedy of Cruelty: A Psycho-allegorical Reading of the Chiquanous Episode."

[18]Chrétien de Troyes's *Perceval le Gallois, ou Le Conte du Graal* is especially concerned with this quest for the father, which is also the quest for an identity. See Bloch, *Etymologies and Genealogies*, 206: "Perceval's quest for knighthood is, at bottom, a quest for the father that is indistinguishable from a quest initially for the proper names of the father's profession and, ultimately, for his own proper name."

Aeneas), Gargantua remains a dominant and dominating force in the life of Pantagruel.[19] Chapter 8 thus repeats, on the level of character, the testimony of the Prologue to *Pantagruel*, which declares that the book is of the same material as the father, the *Chroniques Gargantuines*, although (as Gargantua also indicates in chap. 8) "a little more reasonable and credible than the last" (6; 168), if only because it occurs later in time. Paternal authority met with filial obedience and homage remains a constant in the books of Rabelais. Pantagruel, originally a devil's advocate, as indicated by the early chapters of the book, becomes enlisted in the services of the king, as his father was in the chronicles that preceded Rabelais's work.[20]

The subversion of authority manifests itself more subtly. The parodic aspect of the letter undermines the declarations of power it contains. Gargantua's false modesty—"'De présent à difficulté seroys je receu en la première classe des petiz grimaulx, moy qui, en mon aage virile, estoys (non à tord) réputé le plus sçavant dudict siècle'" (44) ("'Nowadays I should have difficulty in getting a place among little schoolboys, in the lowest class, I who in my youth was reputed, with some justification, to be the most learned man of the century'" [194])—remains an implicit critique of the giant (all the more since it is followed by such an expression of *philautia*) and indicates the limits of his wisdom within the present frame. The chapters preceding the letter also prepare the way for a skeptical attitude toward this authoritative discourse, particularly chapter 3 which, as Defaux has shown, turns the death of Badebec into an occasion for sophistical

[19]Gargantua reappears to take control of his son's destiny in the *Tiers Livre*, chap. 48.

[20]See *Les Grandes et Inestimables Cronicques du grant et enorme geant Gargantua* (1532), where Gargantua is "created" in order to rid King Arthur of his enemies. The work is published in *The Tale of Gargantua and King Arthur by François Girault*, ed. Huntington Brown, "Appendix," 105–28.

argumentation ("Au coeur du *Pantagruel*," 68). Gargantua's lineage supports this position too, since the giants he is descended from are in general monsters, not one of the cultivated beings he claims to be. Finally, the *Chroniques* themselves limit, a priori, a serious treatment of the giant as responsible father and *homme de lettres*.[21]

The final paragraph of chapter 8 also raises the question of the son's resistance through the use of a simile employing one of Rabelais's most ambivalently valorized elements, fire:

> Ces lettres receues et veues, Pantagruel print nouveau courage, et fut enflambé à proffiter plus que jamais, en sorte que, le voyant estudier et proffiter, eussiez dit que tel estoit son esprit entre les livres, comme est le feu parmy les brandes, tant il l'avoit infatigable et strident. (48)

> After receiving and reading this letter, Pantagruel took fresh courage and was [inflamed to profit more than ever]. Indeed, if you had seen him studying and [profiting], you would have said that his spirit among the books was like fire among the heather, so indefatigable and ardent was it. (196)

Pantagruel's enthusiasm for books is compared to the way fire consumes heather; elsewhere in Rabelais's books consumption by fire poses serious threats to "pantagruélisme" and to Alcofrybas himself in the 1542 prologue. The repetition of Gargantua's injunction to "profit," with its economic connotations, also suggests a certain resistance to that injunction.

The ambivalence toward authority is expressed, in a displaced manner, on the thematic level as well. Pantagruel never directly rebels against the commands of his father, in word or deed. Panurge, rather, assumes the role of subverting the

[21]Walter Stephens argues that the character of Alcofrybas can be seen as a limit too, since he is the object of Rabelais's parody.

forces of law and order. It is no surprise, then, that Panurge makes his first appearance after the chapter where Gargantua both legitimates Pantagruel by defining him and oppresses him by determining his role. If a motivation is to be sought for the presence of two chapter 9s, for a "split" in a single heroic protagonist or for the union of two apparently contradictory characters in an indissoluble bond of friendship, it is in the ambivalence toward authority that the motivation must be found. This ambivalence haunts, thematically and metadiscursively, most of the books of Rabelais.

Panurge appears when the *enfances* of the hero have ended and the *exploits* are about to begin. He seems initially to be a more characteristic quester—he has just come from the East, escaping Turkish captivity, and he already boasts a list of adventures:

> "Mon vray et propre nom de baptesme est Panurge, et à présent viens de Turcquie, où je fuz mené prisonnier lors qu'on alla à Metelin en la male heure. Et voulentiers vous racompteroys mes fortunes, qui sont plus merveilleuses que celles de Ulysses." (chap. 9, 54)

> "My true and proper baptismal name is Panurge, and just now I have come from Turkey, where I was taken prisoner during the ill-fated attack on Mytilene. I'll gladly tell you my story. For I have had adventures more marvellous than Ulysses." (201)

Both the narrator of the episode and Pantagruel insist upon Panurge's nobility in spite of his pitiful appearance. The identification of a hero takes place in this repetition of a common medieval and classical topos of recognition:

> Ung homme, beau de stature et élégant en tous lineamens du corps, mais pitoyablement navré en divers lieux. (48)

> A man of handsome build, elegant in all his features, but pitifully wounded in various places. (196)

"Par ma foy, il n'est pauvre que par fortune: car je vous asseure que, à sa physionomie, Nature l'a produyt de riche et noble lignée." (49)

"On my faith, he is only poor in fortune. His physiognomy tells me for certain that he comes of some rich and noble stock." (197)

Pantagruel's first address to Panurge includes the epic echo that identifies the latter as a quester: "'Qui estes vous? Dont venez vous? Où allez vous? Que quérez vous? Et quel est vostre nom?'" (49) ("'Who are you? Where do you come from? Where are you going? What are you looking for? And what is your name?'").[22]

The final stage in the preparation of a heroic substitution between Pantagruel and Panurge occurs when the giant declares the future inseparability of the two:

"Car, par ma foy, je vous ay jà prins en amour si grande, que, si vous condescendez à mon vouloir, vous ne bougerez jamais de ma compaignie, et vous et moy ferons ung nouveau per d'amytié, telle que fut entre Enée et Achates" (54)[23]

"I've taken such a liking to [you], I swear, that if I have my way you'll never stir from my side. Indeed you and I will make such another pair of friends as Aeneas and Achates." (201)

[22]Gérard Defaux, *Le Curieux, le glorieux et la sagesse du monde dans la première moitié du XVIe siècle: L'Exemple de Panurge (Ulysse, Démosthène, Empédocle)*, 31–32. Defaux notes that this series of questions derives from both Homer and Virgil. Note also the allusion in chapter 9 (49) to *Aeneid* 1.203 ("forsan et haec olim meminisse juvabit"): "'Das die Gedechtnus des Ellends unnd Armuot vorlangs erlitten, ist ain grosser Lust.'"

[23]The homophony in "per d'amitié" points to the homelessness and fatherlessness of Panurge, which constitutes another reason for the substitution.

Pantagruel invokes Aeneas, the obedient son. Panurge, while responding in kind, uses the name that evokes an essential incompatibility between two versions of the heroic: Ulysses. The Greek quester, though assimilated through tradition into the panoply of epic wanderers passing through the medieval and Renaissance corpus of quest narrative, necessarily acquires, at least since Dante, an ambivalent status in the Christian world. He is in Dante's imagination one who abjures patriotic and domestic responsibilities in order to "divenir del mondo esperto" (*Inferno*, 26.98) ("become expert in [knowledge of the] world").

Erasmus's guidebook to Christian living unceasingly reiterates the sinful implications of the quest for worldly knowledge and the necessity to rely on God rather than on oneself: "For, as Paul says, in the eyes of God there is no more profound folly than worldly wisdom: it must be unlearned by one who wishes to be truly wise. . . . Dare to trust yourself to Him with all your heart; dare to distrust yourself; dare to transfer every care you have to Him. Stop relying upon yourself; cast yourself with complete confidence upon Him, and He will receive you" (*Enchiridion*, chap. 4, 60; chap. 11, 88).[24] Pantagruel, as representative of the Christian humanist discourse in the chapters following his meeting with Panurge, repeatedly draws attention to this topos of Christian humility, first in the encounter with Thaumaste: "'Sir, of the graces which God has given me there is none that I would refuse to communicate to anyone, to the extent of my powers. For all good comes from Him'" (chap. 13, 104–5; 231), then again, more playfully, during the battle with Loupgarou:

"Car tu est le Tout Puissant, qui, en ton affaire propre, et où ta cause propre est tirée en action, te peulx défendre trop plus

---

[24]See also Francesco Petrarca's "The Ascent of Mont Ventoux," in Ernst Cassirer, Paul O. Kristeller, and John H. Randall, eds. *The Renaissance Philosophy of Man.*

qu'on ne sçauroit estimer, toy qui as mille milliers de centaines de millions de légions d'anges, duquel le moindre peust occire tous les humains, et tourner le ciel et la terre à son plaisir . . . en toy seul est ma totalle confiance et espoir." (chap. 19, 153)

"For thou art the Almighty, who in thine own affairs, and where thine own cause is called into question, can defend thyself a great deal better than man can conceive. Thou who hast thousands and thousands of hundreds of millions of legions of angels, the least of whom can slay all mankind, and turn the heavens and earth upside down at his pleasure, . . . in thee alone is my whole trust and hope." (262)

Panurge and Pantagruel exhibit contrasting versions of the heroic, analogous to the nuance inscribed in the text by the use of two names, Aeneas and Ulysses. Pantagruel, like Aeneas, obeys a patterned destiny; the letter of the father in chapter 8 documents an inheritance whereby Pantagruel will obediently execute the wishes of his father. Panurge, on the other hand, is characterized by Ulyssean *curiositas* and becomes, in the later books, the subject of a kind of quest for knowledge. The limits of human knowledge, recognized by Pantagruelian discourse from chapter 9 onward, clash with the will to subversion (of existing norms) and the will to power (represented by the quest or voyage toward the unknown and the attempt to master it) in the form of Panurge. Yet the couple establishes a pact. In chapter 9 Pantagruel asks Panurge never to leave his side, and the latter swears to follow:

"Mais, puis qu'il vous plaist me retenir avecques vous, et que je accepte voulentiers l'offre, protestant jamais ne vous laisser, et allissiez vous à tous les diables, —nous aurons en aultre temps plus commode, assez loysir d'en racompter." (chap. 9, 54–55)

"But since it is your wish to keep me with you—and I gladly accept your offer, and swear that I'll never leave you even if you go down to the devils in hell—we shall have leisure enough to speak of them at some more convenient time." (201)

The compatibility rests upon a shared heroic knighthood. The opposing characteristics of the two bind them in a functional relationship that renders possible the substitution of Panurge for Pantagruel, leaving undisturbed Pantagruel's obedient relation to authority (both Gargantua's and God's). Panurge, a "negative hero," assumes the responsibility for a rebellion rendered necessary by the father's oppression (the oppression of censorship and limitation, in all its forms).[25]

The chapters that follow chapter 9 reinforce the presentation of Pantagruel as an exemplary figure and further delineate the opposing qualities of Panurge, those that link him to the archetypal trickster figure.[26] This is done partly by asso-

[25]For the concept of the negative hero see Carl G. Jung, "On the Psychology of the Trickster-Figure," 255, in *The Archetypes and the Collective Unconscious*. Henri Busson, in "Eglises contre Rabelais," discusses the problem of censorship in connection with Rabelais, which I will also discuss in chapter 4. See also F. M. Higman, *Censorship and the Sorbonne*. Panurge's opposition to limitation also takes a linguistic form; he incarnates the slippery, unstable, elusive aspects of language. Claude-Gilbert Dubois's *Mythe et langage au seizième siècle* provides an excellent study of this question. See also François Rigolot, *Les Langages de Rabelais*.

[26]Jung's formulation concerning the trickster figure helps explain the substitution effect of the couple and sheds some light on the claim of Defaux and others that Panurge is in fact a "splitting off" of certain aspects of Pantagruel: "The split-off personality is not just a random one, but stands in a complementary or compensatory relationship to the ego-personality. It is a personification of traits of character which are sometimes better than those the ego-personality possesses" ("On the Psychology of the Trickster-Figure," 261–62). Paolo Valesio makes a remark concerning the romance *Tirant lo Blanc* that could also apply here: "In effect, it deals with nothing less than an attempt to *materialize and externalize its own shadow*—in the terms of a medieval code" ("Il seggio e l'ombra,"

ciating him with his alchemical counterpart Mercurius, another trickster figure, as his genealogy (from Hermes, god of thieves) suggests. Panurge, like Mercurius, is associated with fire (as part of a Turkish rotisserie) and suggests that this spirit may have come to his aid in escaping the Turks, by means of a trick that once served that spirit's malicious purposes: "'Le routisseur s'endormyt par le vouloir divin, ou bien de quelque bon Mercure, qui endormyt cautement Argus qui avoit cent yeulx'" (chap. 10, 76–77) ("'The turnspit fell asleep, by the will of God—or else by the virtue of some good Mercury, who cunningly put Argus to sleep, with all his hundred eyes'" [214]). Finally, in a chapter that leaves no doubt concerning the dubious character of Panurge, he is said to resemble a "dague de plomb," a mercurial material whose elusiveness lies paradoxically in its resistance to the attempt to disguise its nature (chap. 12, 89, n.4).

As trickster figure or shadow to Pantagruel, Panurge often functions as a substitute for the hero in passages where the text's ambivalence prevents his *prise-de-position*, as in the famous Scholastic debate by signs between Thaumaste and Panurge. Here the exhibitionist aspect of knowledge becomes the quality of the giant's companion rather than appertaining, as previously, to the hero himself.[27] A more ambiguous substitution (because answering to a greater threat) occurs in chapters 14 and 15, one that is further complicated by the announcement of Gargantua's death. This time, how-

79). One of the most thorough studies of Panurge's character is Ludwig Schrader's *Panurge und Hermes. Zum Ursprung eines Charakters bei Rabelais*; see also his "Panurge: Théories récentes—observations méthodologiques—conséquences possibles."

[27]See, for example, chap. 9 bis, 55–56. Here Pantagruel's skills are turned away from Scholastic prowess and channeled into the service of justice. The Baisecul-Humevesne resolution rejects the rhetorical flourish of the earlier debates and is characterized by brevity and common sense rather than eloquence and erudition.

ever, the text does not point to the action of displacement, as it did in chapter 9 bis ("'Retire and sleep at your ease. For in the morning I will answer and argue against Master Englishman, and if I don't reduce him to speechlessness, then abuse me as you will,'" says Panurge [106; 232]). Instead, chapter 14 depicts Panurge's courtship and degradation of an "haulte dame de Paris." The ensuing dialogues between the lady and Panurge enact a parody of courtship. The substitution of Panurge for Pantagruel in this chapter is deeply overdetermined, thematically and intertextually. It demonstrates the extent to which the father reigns over Pantagruel and prefigures, as well, the final substitution of Panurge for Pantagruel in the erotic quest of the *Tiers Livre*.

The chapter begins with the familiar equation between rhetorical power and erotic persuasion and playfully calls attention to the analogy between rhetorical contest and the project of seduction: "Il entreprint venir au dessus d'une des grandes dames de la ville" (116) ("He set out to conquer [or top] one of the great ladies of the city" [239]). Although being a lover (according to popular versions of Capellanus and Jean de Meung) consists in literalizing the figurative "venir au dessus" of verbal struggle, Panurge does not take the metaphorical leap. Rather, the fear that always agitates the environs of the feminine in Rabelais's text (and becomes the ruling obsession of the *Tiers Livre*) surfaces here as Panurge proceeds to literalize, brutally, the figurative conquering by resorting to an *argumentum ad baculum*.

In mock oratorical style, Panurge appeals to the welfare of the republic, then hastily dispenses with words, proposing to show the lady that it will be good for her to be "covered by his race." She, in a ferociously aggressive move, threatens to cut off all his appendages except one, rendering him, ironically, more like that phallus that is the signifier of his discourse. At this point she has already "lost," for the comically displaced castration she threatens enables Panurge to insist all the more on his purpose (116).

From this point on the narrative discredits the lady; her next threat is far less powerful: "'If you say one word more, I'll call the people and have you beaten on the spot'" (116; 240). Panurge then dilates his theme, rhetorically drawing out the seduction in proportion to the softening of the lady's resistance. He ends his panegyric, of course, with a sudden change of register: "'O dieux et deesses celestes, que heureux sera celluy a qui ferez ceste grace de vous accoller, de bayser bayser, et de frotter son lart avec vous'" (118) "'O ye celestial gods and goddesses, how happy will be the man to whom you grant the favor of embracing this woman, of kissing her, and rubbing his bacon with her'" [240]). The sudden shift in tone produces the humor, which is then reinforced by a narrative commentary that continues to compromise the lady's resistance: "Et la vouloit embrasser, mais elle fist semblant de se mettre a la fenestre pour appeller les voisins a la force"(118) ("And he would have embraced her had she not [pretended to go] to the window and call on the neighbours for help" [240]).

Panurge continues to expose the lady's weaknesses in several more ways before the final humiliation. He demonstrates to the reader her willingness to listen to his obscene wordplay; he extracts from her a *gage*, her "patenostres," cutting it off her belt with his knife in a gesture of symbolic rape, then offering the knife as another occasion to bring the phallus into play. She refuses, but her thoughts, which revolve around the stolen rosary and the explanation she must provide her husband for its disappearance, serve to highlight the hypocrisy of one more woman who has said no when she means yes. Her devoutness is assaulted too; she reveals herself as hypocritical and interested in Panurge by the evasive response she gives to the question of which loves the other more: "'For my part, I do not hate you. For, as God commands us to, I love all the world'" (120; 241). After her threat to cut off Panurge's limbs, this answer rings patently false; at the same time it evades the question by changing what is meant by love. Finally, it is a way of not saying no.

Panurge's final stripping away of the lady's layers of false virtue consists in seducing her with jewels and money. Here again the narrator tells us she is tempted: "By virtue of these words he made her mouth water" (121; 242). Nevertheless, she refuses. Panurge makes one more attempt to get to the point, and the text comments once more on the lady's near capitulation: "But she began to shout, although not very loud" (121; 242), at which point Panurge takes off his disguise ("tourna son faulx visaige") and reveals the true object of his game, physical humiliation and degradation. Thus Panurge's "courtship" consists of despoiling this noblewoman of all her pretensions to virtue: she yields to flattery, she lies to her husband, she is hypocritically devout and capable of succumbing to greed for material possessions. Panurge knocks her off her pedestal with his verbal wit. He has indeed won.

Panurge's emblematic chastising of the noblewoman of Paris follows the pattern of comic punishment in the *Fabliaux*: through Panurge's artifice the lady becomes a dog in heat ("chienne en chaleur") and receives the attention of more than six hundred male dogs. The irony of the gesture provides the humor, for not only is her hypocrisy punished but, according to the logic of the joke, the lady does get what she really wants, but from unexpected admirers. Meanwhile, Panurge kills a female dog in the lady's stead (the reference to the dog's being in heat and to the lady's assumption of its sexual scent suggests the connection), while sexual interest becomes equivalent to urinating and defecating upon the desired object. Finally Pantagruel is called in, as the figure for the reader, to witness the spectacle and approve: "Pantagruel very gladly accepted this invitation and went to see the show, which he found very fine and original" (124; 244).

Given the dialogic structure of the episode, however, one cannot help but notice that Panurge fails in one dimension of the enterprise defined as "venir au dessus." When the lady speaks, it is to express a consistent no. As I have argued elsewhere, the gap between the narrative (which invites complicity with Panurge) and the dialogue permits a reading of

Panurge that already prefigures the anxieties he will have in the *Tiers Livre*.[28] In the context of the rest of *Pantagruel*, the episode loses some of its traditional humor and becomes instead an enigmatic and significant moment in the substitution of Panurge for Pantagruel.

Juxtaposed to Panurge's defilement of the Parisian noblewoman, Pantagruel's Virgilian leave-taking is a set piece for portraying piously heroic behavior with regard to Eros. The first mention of a lady in connection with the hero occurs after his departure from Paris, when the company is about to set sail: "Auquel lieu, attendant le vent propice et calfretant leur nef, receut d'une dame de Paris (laquelle il avoit entretenu bonne espace de temps) unes lettres inscriptes" (chap. 15, 127) ("And as they were waiting there for a favourable wind, and caulking their ship, Pantagruel received from a Parisian lady, whom he had kept as his mistress for some time, a letter" [245–46]). Although Pantagruel asks her name she, like the "haulte dame de Paris," remains nameless, the request being forgotten in the ensuing frenzy of interpretation initiated by Panurge. Once more the rhetorician dominates, erasing the question of "woman" from the text.[29] Pantagruel's blameless departure is tacitly given approval by the disparaging portrait of the lady in chapter 14. There is almost perfect complicity: Panurge demystifies the lady and frees Pantagruel to assume a heroic stance, untroubled by that enigma of otherness, that force of digression that prolongs the adventures of the medieval knight as well as the prose of the *roman*.

The text also eliminates the potentially self-compromising moment to which the hero is submitted in *Aeneid* 4. Pan-

---

[28]See my "Damning Haughty Dames: Panurge and the 'Haulte Dame de Paris'" (*Pantagruel* 14); and "The 'Instance' of the Letter: Woman in the Text of Rabelais."

[29]Panurge submits the lady's message to similar degradation by covering and disfiguring it with a variety of substances intended to decode the invisible message.

tagruel puts Aeneas to shame, since his departure is un-premeditated and, when he is accused of betraying his lady, he is contrite: "This depressed him, and he would gladly have returned to Paris to make his peace with her" (chap. 15, 130; 247). Epistemon's reply makes explicit the comparison with Aeneas:

> Mais Epistemon luy reduyt a memoire de department de Eneas d'avecques Dido, et le dict de Heraclides Tarentin, que, a la navire restant a l'ancre, quand la necessite presse, il fault coupper la chorde plus tost que perdre temps a la de-slyer. Et qu'il debvoit laisser tous pensemens pour survenir a la ville de sa nativite, qui estoit en dangier. (130)

> But Epistemon reminded him of Aeneas's conduct towards Dido, and of Heraclides of Tarentum's saying that when the ship is at anchor and the case is urgent it is better to cut the cable than to waste time untying it. He advised his master, therefore, to put aside all other thoughts in order to assist the city of his birth, which was in danger. (247)

In this restaging of the arms/love conflict, Rabelais redefines Pantagruel as the heroic son whose quest is a return to redeem the homeland. By means of this locus classicus from Virgil, Pantagruel comes to be retrospectively defined as a (burlesque) romance hero, dawdling with his lady. Pantagruel now turns from errance as digression, as directionless wandering, toward a goal.

In these chapters the woman's defiled body (that of the noblewoman and of Utopie, the motherland) becomes the pretext for male bonding, the ground upon which their friendship is cemented. "Woman" in these chapters constitutes a pretext for the tighter bonding of Pantagruel and Panurge in their shared project. Yet woman and the erotic phase of the knight's career produce sufficient tension to require the substitution of Panurge for Pantagruel in the courtship process. The feminine constitutes a threat both indirectly, as the cause of war (the invasion of Utopia), and directly, as a potential source of distraction for the hero. Pantagruel remains untouched—a chaste hero who avoids contact with the "lower" or "shadowy" aspects of intercourse for the sake of some higher purpose, such as the war against the Dipsodes. The substitution of Panurge for Pantagruel in the courtship scene eliminates woman so that the epic narrative may begin; it also ensures Pantagruel's absolute filial obedience.

Chapter 15 opens with the topical death or wounding of the king in romance literature: Gargantua has been "translated into Fairyland by Morgan" (125; 245). The disappearance of the father and the son's assumption of his responsibilities had already been outlined in Gargantua's letter; in chapter 15 they are first suggested by the references to Old Testament figures, Enoch and Elijah (Elie), as fathers who disappear and by the name of the town, Hommefleur, which marks the flowering of Pantagruel's manhood. Utopia, the mother's territory (chap. 2, 16–17), has been invaded and is referred to in characteristically romance terms as "gasté" or "wasted" (chap. 15, 126).[30] Pantagruel is charged, then, with perpetuating his father's name, threatened here by an encroachment upon the mother. Even the message on the lady's ring, with its echoes of Christ's words to *his* father, "LAMAH HAZABTANI," signals the primacy of the son's relation to the father, but in a way that suggests the son's desire rather than the paternal imperative. The conflict that would exist in the oedipal configuration has been displaced onto a father substitute, the enemy, while the father has been conveniently removed from the scene. The *Tiers Livre*'s return to the ques-

[30]In almost all the Grail romances there is a maimed king whose wound or illness also affects the kingdom, which becomes barren and desolate; it is referred to as the "terre gaste." See *La Queste del Saint-Graal*; also Eugène Vinaver, *The Rise of Romance*, Charles Méla, *Blanchefleur et le saint homme*, and Bloch, *Etymologies and Genealogies*.

tion of woman will bring with it a symptomatic resurrection of the father that once again forces a displacement from Pantagruel to Panurge—a displacement that brings the narrative of epic succession to a halt.

*Pantagruel*'s final suggestion that the "castrated" son (because subordinated to the father) requires Panurge in order to resolve conflicts with figures of authority throughout the text occurs in chapter 19, where Pantagruel conducts a kind of displaced struggle with the father in the form of the giant, club-wielding Loupgarou.[31] In a moment of weakness Pantagruel cries, "'Ho, Panurge, where are you?'" (156; 263), after which he succeeds in defeating the giant, as though the name itself sufficed to reinvigorate the hero.

Throughout the first book the text enacts a process of self-definition, exposing as it does so a scene of conflict (*Pantagruel*, chap. 8). The confusion resulting from this generational struggle seems thematized in the hesitation between the two chapter 9s: a split occurs whereby the discourse of errance becomes categorized into much more rigidly separate entities: the discourse of heroism (the speech of Pantagruel as epic hero) and that of its subversion, an errance without quest, error (Panurge). These categories remain incipient in *Pantagruel*, as the final chapter's indecisiveness suggests. There the text returns to its origins in romance and popular literature (as defined in the Prologue). But the naming of a

[31]The "wolf," psychologically read, is often a figure for the father, while the phallic implications of the massive club, wielded by Loupgarou and nearly killing Pantagruel, hardly need mentioning. For a reading of the battle in the tradition of Christian allegory, see Edwin Duval, "Pantagruel's Genealogy and the Redemptive Design of Rabelais's *Pantagruel*." Duval's interpretations, while usually shedding welcome light on concrete interpretive difficulties in this text, also belong to the *Rabelais moralisé* tradition I discuss later in the book. Walter Stephens, examining the question of why Loupgarou is a giant, offers a suggestive interpretation of the battle as fratricide. See *Giants in Those Days*, 218–22.

new character, Panurge, sets up an initial duality that will more clearly define itself in the third and fourth books. The splitting off that produces Panurge prefigures the thematic (and generic) impasse of the later books. This impasse traces the failure of an epic paradigm for sixteenth-century France; the subject of future narratives will be not the exemplary epic hero Pantagruel, endowed with an ancient and illustrious lineage, but the fatherless and wayward protagonist of the novel, Panurge.

The Prologue sets the theme of an inheritance, in which the genealogy of the text and of the characters are coextensive. The vacillation between textual positioning in a line of inheritance and the claim to autonomy occurs indirectly, through the reinscription of a "new" genealogy into the authoritative history of the world, mimicking in this very procedure the strategy by which the New Testament inherits, succeeds, and thus supersedes the Old. The chapters analyzed stage this conflict, again indirectly, as the human drama of inheritance. Through this struggle a successor, the hero, is defined, who perpetuates (through obedience) a lineage, yet who renders the text, as epic, capable for the moment of creating a new history, a literary world. The final chapter retreats, however, returning to the (romance) world of aimless erring and anonymous continuation of a succession of literary gestes.

The Prologue and the first two chapters of *Gargantua* redefine the genealogical problem recurring obsessively in *Pantagruel* and testify to changes in the concepts of textual autonomy and narrative authority in the work. Whereas the Prologue to *Pantagruel* presents the book as an anonymous, quasi-oral continuation of the *Chroniques*, the narrator of *Gargantua*'s Prologue clarifies the relationship between the books and retrospectively confers an independent status even on *Pantagruel* ("the pleasant titles of certain books of our invention, such as *Gargantua, Pantagruel, Toss-pint, On the Dignity of Cod-*

*pieces, Of Peas and Bacon, cum commento, &c"* [Calder, Screech, and Saulnier ed., 11; 37]).[32] The first works mentioned assume their places as the "inventions" of Alcofrybas (and perhaps the author), rather than being, as was *Pantagruel*, "another book of the same stamp."

The narrator of *Pantagruel* presents it interchangeably as an oral and a textual narrative, both in the Prologue (*Pantagruel*, 4) and in chapter 1, where the genealogy of giants receives a guarantee of truth. The Massoretes hand down the genealogical account whereby it becomes plausible not only because transmitted by an authority, but also because some part of it has been, in a sense, witnessed (*Pantagruel*, chap. 1, 16). The Prologue to *Gargantua*, however, presents as unambiguous the work's status as a written text: "Most noble boozers, and you my very esteemed and poxy friends—for to you and you alone are my writings dedicated" (9; 37). *Gargantua*, here as elsewhere, is manifestly text.

The different elaborations of genealogy in *Pantagruel* and *Gargantua* depend in part upon different metaphors that structure the book. The self-consciously adopted metaphor of the Italian Humanists, *rinascita*, undergoes, in the transition between Rabelais's first two books, an "overdetermined" revivification couched in the thematics of genealogy.[33] As critics have often noted, Rabelais's text combines, in this metaphor, the notion of biological reproduction with verbal productivity in iconic gestures of repetition and regeneration.[34] The term "genealogy" encompasses these various as-

[32]*Gargantua: édition critique*, ed. R. Calder, M. A. Screech, and V. L. Saulnier. Subsequent references to *Gargantua* will be from this edition unless otherwise indicated.

[33]On the metaphor of rebirth and its thematic developments in Renaissance literature, see Thomas M. Greene, "Resurrecting Rome: The Double Task of the Humanist Imagination."

[34]See Raymond La Charité, "Gargantua's Letter and *Pantagruel* as Novel," for the thematic intermingling of biological reproduction and textual creativity. Lawrence Kritzman approaches the question psychoanalyt-

pects, foregrounding issues of inheritance and continuation. Although it might be expected that such a metaphor should structure a literary work of the Renaissance, it nevertheless seems important to note the way genealogy, as a metaphor and as a theme, mimes its own action through repetition and differentiation. The *way* the text calls this action into question points to specifically Rabelaisian concerns.

As I have suggested, the structuring metaphor of *Pantagruel* (that of genealogical succession) creates an "organic" world for the chronicle. The narrator finds occasion to present the story through a return to his birthplace. Although there is a punning awareness of textuality ("since I grew out of my page-hood"), the explicit conceit is that of a return to one's birthplace. The narrator's return to origins constitutes the renewal of the Gargantuan Chronicles in the form of the story of Pantagruel. Although it is a continuation ("another book of the same stamp"), the book also represents an amelioration of past efforts ("a little more reasonable and credible than the last"). This metaphor of renewal through successive generations (where the present is a continuation and perfection of the past) creates an organic genesis for the text and repeats itself, on the character level, in chapter 8, where textual parentage is animated as a father's address to his son.

The organic quality of the figure of speech that brings this "first-born Chronicle" to life seems to confirm M. A. Screech's contention: "The printed page is above all the vehicle for conveying to us an account of the spoken word. Many forces were at work on Rabelais and some of his contemporaries encouraging them to look upon writing and printing as primarily the recording of speech. And Rabelais's Chronicles are works which derive their greatest comic effects from the

---

ically, as a kind of will to power through the deferral of closure, in "The Allegory of Repression." See also Terence Cave, *The Cornucopian Text: Problems of Writing in the French Renaissance*, especially 183–223.

spoken tongue" (*Rabelais*, 27). He goes on to speculate whether Rabelais actually intended his work to be recited aloud, citing historical evidence to support the argument for "orality." Many references in Rabelais's text to the *Grandes et inestimables Chronicques* point toward recitation as the primary mode of transmission. Furthermore, the narrator presents himself as speaker in the Prologue. The discourse, however, rather than aspiring to speech as Screech suggests, seems to pose, rhetorically, as a living voice. Walter Ong describes this in Renaissance texts as resulting from the advent of print, which brought a kind of overdetermination in the rhetorical structures of a literary work. In the absence of an oratorical context, where a living speaker can directly address a living audience, rhetorical structures must compensate to create and control a fictional audience for the "speaking" voice.[35]

Problems of audience control and the growth of a print culture perform crucial roles in restructuring the metaphorical conceptualizations of Rabelais's first two books. Script and oral culture presuppose an intimacy between narrator and audience that printed dissemination undermines. Elizabeth Eisenstein warns against adducing too immediate a change from the growth of the printing industry in the six-

---

[35]Ong, *Interfaces of the Word*: "The Writer's Audience Is Always a Fiction," 71. Unfortunately, Ong continues to relegate rhetoric to a part of diction, thus describing it as if it were something one could choose whether to employ. In an important revision of Aristotle's definition of rhetoric, Paolo Valesio adjusts this assumption: "Rhetoric is the functional organization of discourse. . . . In other words: rhetoric is *all* of language, in its realization as discourse" (7), and "*every discourse in its functional aspect is based on a relatively limited set of mechanisms— whose structure remains essentially the same from text to text, from language to language, from historical period to historical period— that reduce every referential choice to a formal choice* . . . the choice is only between what mechanisms to employ, and these mechanisms already condition every discourse since they are simplified representations of reality, inevitably and instrinsically slanted in a partisan direction" (*Novantiqua: Rhetorics as a Contemporary Theory*, 21).

teenth century (*Advent of Printing*, 1:26). Nevertheless, *Pantagruel* seems to articulate a hesitation between the two, with the narrator perpetuating the fiction of a living presence and the structuring metaphor sustaining the "biological" body of the text, while certain obstacles, both textual and contextual, to such an "organic" conception force a return, in *Gargantua*, to seek out new premises on which to found a conceptualization of the book.[36]

One way to perceive this hesitation between the narrative as organic outgrowth and the book as constructed textuality focuses on the interaction between narrator and reader in the Prologue to *Pantagruel*. Narrative seems most sensitive to the changes in this relationship as it moves from an oral medium, to script, to the printed book. The Prologue to *Pantagruel* creates a context mimicking the oral situation (in the first of a series of such gestures occurring throughout the five books). The existence of a fictional narrator, the textual "jongleur," fulfills several functions: one is to suspend the reader's disbelief for the duration of the narrative by referring to the

[36]On the question of printing as it relates specifically to Rabelais, see Barry Lydgate, "Going Public: Rabelais, Montaigne, and the Printed Word," especially 12–14: "*Pantagruel*, published in 1532, is the first significant work of imaginative prose narrative in French written specifically to be disseminated via the printed page. But it is tensely poised between the new and old modes of production and consumption. This printed text has deep roots in oral traditions of folklore and popular mythology. . . . *Pantagruel*, like its predecessor, supposes a received tradition of narrative and a community of traditional belief, collective experience and collective memory." Perhaps the very genre of folktale elicits this metaphor of organic birth and development. It is interesting that Northrop Frye describes the process in this way: "Folktales by themselves, at least at first, lead a nomadic existence. They travel over the world through all the barriers of language: they do not expand into larger structures, but interchange their themes and motifs at random. . . . But as literature develops, 'secular' stories also begin to take root in the culture and contribute to the shared heritage of allusion" (*The Secular Scripture: A Study of the Structure of Romance*, 9).

living situation, whereby the reader can play the part of audience or spectator, itself an explicitly fictitious role. This suspension of disbelief allows the reader to participate in the experience of the textual world, with the narrator as guide. François Rigolot describes the textual contract upon which this suspension of disbelief, "undisbelief," or verisimilitude depends:

> Rabelais chooses to confer on the notorious Alcofribas, this strange character of arabist physiognomy, the duty of establishing the readerly contract, within the fiction itself, with a delegate of the reader, constituted from the outset at the very threshold of the Prologue by Alcofribas himself. . . . One could not confuse him with the "true reader" (if such an abstraction had any meaning), not even with a supposed typical reader of the sixteenth century whom Rabelais could have had in mind while composing his novel. He is a kind of virtual reader . . . a "narrataire," the narrator's interlocutor, separable and indeed separated from any reader implicated by the act of reading. ("Vraisemblance et Narrativité dans le *Pantagruel*," 55–56)[37]

The detachment of the reader from the "narrataire" permits the suspension of disbelief without compromising the reader's sense of truth value, so obviously excluded from the Prologue. The narrator, in employing the organic trope of continuation for the story, makes no authoritative claim; furthermore, the distance between the reader and the narrator's addressee undermines any such claim. The existence of two distinct orders of reading, as Rigolot points out, effects this "critique of credulity" and warns the reader against accepting the word of the text.

The fictive speaker serves another important distancing

---

[37]For the term "undisbelief" see Norman N. Holland, *The Dynamics of Literary Response*. Rigolot develops this argument at greater length in *Le Texte de la Renaissance: Des rhétoriqueurs à Montaigne*.

function, this time for the author. So long as the narrator remains the vehicle for the story, the author can evade implication. The Prologue achieves this purpose both from the point of view of the inheritance of a tradition and from that of a narrator whose hyperbolic claims and imprecations situate the narrative in the realm of the fantastic and control the reader's responses. Walter Stephens explains this division between narrator and author as an effect of Rabelais's deliberate parody of the hyperbolic claims to "gospel truth" on the part of the pseudohistoriographer Alcofrybas (*Giants in Those Days*, chap. 6).

But *Pantagruel* seeks to impose itself with greater authority than the narrator claims. Paradoxically, this is in part effected through a playful degradation of the Bible to the level of the *Chroniques*. The early edition of the Prologue compares the two directly, whereas the 1542 edition replaces the phrase "les avez creues tout ainsi que texte de Bible ou du sainct Evangile" ("you have believed them as you would the text of the Bible or the holy Gospel") with "les avez creues gualantement" (3) ("[you] have nobly believed them" [167]). The second comparison to the Bible remains uncensored, although its implications convey a more aggressive challenge (6). Barry Lydgate argues that sacred and secular narratives are similarly received: "The sacred scripture and the secular must have seemed roughly analogous as narrative, equally independent of any concrete text, and rooted in a tradition whose spoken and written manifestations were similarly authoritative" ("Printing, Narrative and the Genesis of the Rabelaisian Novel," 365). Yet in such a comparison the biblical text suffers. Printing implies construction, as the narrator's motive for writing *Pantagruel* suggests (*Pantagruel*, 4). The narrator playfully implies that it was necessary to write the story so it would be memorized; the *Chroniques* themselves, somehow, do not suffice, nor does the oral tradition guarantee life for the fable. The justification for the existence of *Pantagruel* is that it will aid the (oral) preservation of the tale. What is at work is an authorial act of appropriation: the "natural" growth of the narrative is being arrested and fixed in print—the rhetoric of reconstruction and creation, which *Gargantua* does not disguise, emerges in the Prologue to *Pantagruel* in conflict with the metaphor of the text as biological continuation. Similarly, introducing the biblical text into the arena of marketplace competition suggests that it is subject to the same process of construction and production as other printed books and exposes it to the possibility of plural versions, each with varying degrees of authority, much like the Chronicles themselves.

In relation both to the *Chroniques* and to the Bible, the problem of authority appears associated with the printed book (the word "livre" appears six times in the Prologue, four times in close succession). In the case of the Bible, problems of authorship (and so authority) and interpretation have potentially far-reaching consequences. For example, Erasmus, in the 1514 letter to Martin Dorp, finds it necessary to defend his work on the Bible against the accusation of authorial intervention in a text whose ideological usefulness depends (for the established church) upon the existence of a single authoritative version. In this letter Erasmus reveals just how conscious the humanist is that his intervention may be construed as interpretation, or invention, which carries consequences for the author:

> What you write about the New Testament makes me wonder what has happened to you. . . . You do not want me to change anything, unless perhaps something is expressed more meaningfully in the Greek; and you deny that there are any defects in the edition we commonly use. You think that it is impious to undermine in any way an edition that has been sanctioned by the consensus of so many centuries and approved by so many councils. I beg you, most learned Dorp, if what you write is true, why do Jerome, Augustine, and Am-

brose so often quote Scripture in a different form than the one we read? Why does Jerome censure and correct many scientific errors, which we still find in our edition? . . . Neither is anyone asserting that there is any falsehood in Holy Scripture, since you also brought up that charge. . . .

. . . Who promotes the cause of falsehood, the person who restores the correct reading or the one who would rather see an error added than one taken away? For it is the very nature of such corruptions for one to breed another. And most of the changes I have made pertain to the emphasis rather than the meaning itself, although the emphasis often constitutes a large part of the meaning.[38]

The extent to which an author claims responsibility for the secular narrative also carries consequences, as the evolving authority of the writer in Rabelais's work makes apparent. Rigolot claims that, in the course of *Pantagruel*, the distance between narrator and author collapses, causing the reader to become more directly engaged than in the former distancing role as "narrataire" ("Vraisemblance et Narrativité," 66). Verisimilitude, so carefully suspended by the rhetoric of the Prologue, becomes reestablished, on the level of narrative intent, through the collapse of narrative voices in *Pantagruel*. Stephens, on the other hand, sees this collapse occurring in the course of *Gargantua*, where the relation to authority has definitively changed: "Whereas *Pantagruel* often flaunts a disrespect for authority that can be superficially reconciled with Bakhtin's vision of class-conscious popularism, *Gargantua* displays an equally blatant respect for many forms of authority" (*Giants in Those Days*, 291–92).[39] In effect, it seems that

[38]Desiderius Erasmus, *The Praise of Folly*: "Erasmus' Letter to Martin Dorp, 1514," 167–68. This document, it seems to me, is crucial in any study of the relationship between philology, hermeneutics, and structures of power in the Renaissance.

[39]There is currently in Rabelais studies what could be called a "Bakhtin debate," centering on the extent to which Rabelais sided with popular culture against "high" culture. See Richard Berrong, *Every Man for Him-*

the parody of Alcofrybas and the author's suspension of veri-similitude are, from the very beginning, ambivalent gestures. The author and narrator contaminate each other so that it becomes impossible to distinguish between the parody of Alcofrybas and the gestures of the author.

The insistence upon the "natural" growth of *Pantagruel* from the *Chroniques* persists through the final chapters of the book to the "excuse of the author." In a last ironic appearance of the expanded metaphor of the work as organic entity, Pantagruel and *Pantagruel* merge into a single "world" from which the narrating voice emerges to address the *lecteurs*. As in the Prologue, a return from another world is enacted before the address to the readers begins anew.

In the final chapter, the narrative is described as a "commencement," whose ending takes the form of arrested growth or, more precisely, premature harvest; for as the Lefranc edition notes, the "purée de septembre" refers to new, and thus "troubled" wine (4:344, n. 2). The competing discourses of historical transcription and authorial construction alternate once again as the speaking "voice" abruptly cuts off the narrative ("here I will make an end of this present book" [177; 277]), mock defensively pleading a headache and imperatively demanding pardon from the audience (178). The theme of perpetuation or continuation is projected and sustained over the forthcoming interruption by a catalog of

---

*self: Social Order and Its Dissolution in Rabelais*, and his *Rabelais and Bakhtin: Popular Culture in "Gargantua and Pantagruel."* Berrong's claim is that Rabelais's attitude toward popular culture changed in the time between *Pantagruel* and *Gargantua* in concert with the sixteenth-century upper classes' repression of the people consequent upon the peasant uprisings and popular rebellions. Walter Stephens concurs with the observation concerning *Gargantua*, and Gérard Defaux offers a different rationale for the change, in "D'un problème l'autre: Herméneutique de l' 'altior sensus' et 'captatio lectoris' dans le prologue de *Gargantua*." For a defense of Bakhtin's reading of Rabelais, see Mary McKinley, "Bakhtin and the World of Rabelais Criticism."

episodic formulas from the genre of romance, to which *Pantagruel* was likened in the Prologue.[40]

The 1532 Nourry edition ends with the phrase, "Bonsoir, Messieurs. *Pardonnate my*: et ne pensez pas tant à mes faultes que vous ne pensez bien ès vostres. FINIS" (178) ("So goodnight, gentlemen. *Perdonate mi*, and do not dwell so much on my faults as not to give good thought to your own" [277]). Its title page announces that the "faictz et prouesses" ("feats and deeds of prowess") of Pantagruel have been "composez nouvellement par maistre Alcofrybas Nasier" ("newly composed by Master Alcofrybas Nasier"). The "nouvellement," while signaling the work's difference from the *Chroniques*, also seems to suggest the repetitive gesture that constitutes the renewal of the Gargantuan Chronicles. Later editions of chapter 34 include a long passage attacking the "men who peer from under a cowl," which concludes with the following phrase: "Fin des chronicques de Pantagruel, roy des Dipsodes, restituez à leur naturel, avec ses faictz et prouesses espoventables composez par feu M. ALCOFRIBAS; abstracteur de quinte essence" (179) ("End of the Chronicles of Pantagruel, King of the Dipsodes, drawn in their natural colours, with his terrible deeds and exploits, composed by the late Master Alcofribas, abstractor of the quintessence" [278]). Several changes have occurred that indicate a strategy of authorial appropriation at work. First of all, whereas in the first edition the narrator resumes his role as performer before a fictive audience, enlarging once again the gap between author and narrator/reader and "narrataire" and forcing readers to criticize their own suspension of disbelief, the 1542 version attacks an extra textual party. This diatribe binds

[40]Northrop Frye argues that romance itself, as a genre, is structured according to patterns resembling the natural cycle of seasonal change; see *The Anatomy of Criticism: Four Essays*.

together the formerly divided author/narrator and reader/ "narrataire" against a common scapegoat.[41]

The author lays more specific claims on his work as well. The addition to chapter 34 refers to the work as "livres pantagruélicques"(178) ("Pantagruelic books"), and the postscript makes no mention of Gargantua (whereas the 1532 title page names Pantagruel as the "son of the great giant Gargantua"). *Pantagruel* assumes its status as autonomous creation, barely conserving its links with its Gargantuan predecessor. The phrase "restituez à leur naturel" does not refer, as did the "composez nouvellement," to the oral body of narrative restored from potential disappearance by the chronicler Alcofrybas Nasier, but alludes to the early version of the "chronicques de Pantagruel" itself, as composed by the "author" Alcofrybas. The latter has become an alchemist, with the ability to transform substance into something new (rather than to renew or restore), to abstract essence or create meaning from raw material through the agency of fire (perhaps that Platonic "étincelle" or *furor divinus*). Furthermore, the "feu" or "late," signals the death of the narrator Alcofrybas and makes way for Rabelais eventually to assume his position as author of the book (Stephens, *Giants in Those Days*, 299).

Contextual events clarify many of the changes between the early and later editions of the text and legitimate, from a historical point of view, the Foucauldian aphorism that "the author is the principle of thrift in the proliferation of meaning" ("What Is an Author?" 159). Rabelais's works became

---

[41]"Rabelais later adds an epilogue where, doubling Alcofrybas, he attacks his slanderers. This added ending can be interpreted as a *pro domo* plea and, on the poetic level, as yet another turn from the improbable toward verisimilitude, or, to put it differently, as the ultimate search for a 'discourse that resembles the real,' where verisimilitude would have us think it is another name for truth" (Rigolot, "Vraisemblance et Narrativité," 67–68).

extremely popular but suffered from numerous "unauthorized" reprintings.[42] Possible economic benefits were not the
only reasons for designating the authoritative Pantagrueline
text, as the addendum to chapter 34 energetically demonstrates. The danger of accusations of heresy, as with the
Erasmian edition of the New Testament, made it necessary
to assign specific authorship to a work:

> Rabelais' reputation was growing in the "wrong" circles. Since
> he did not have a privilège until 1545, and because his books
> had a widespread popularity, many editions from various
> printing ateliers followed. With the lack of a privilège, "Al-
> cofrybas Nasier" must have been powerless to stop the pirat-
> ing of his work, and by 1533 many copies of *Pantagruel* were
> in circulation. . . . With ever increasing popularity, it was
> not long before the book came to the attention of the Sor-
> bonne. Along with the Pantagrueline prognostication for
> 1533, it was judged obscene, condemned, and placed on the
> Index in October of 1533. (Michael B. Kline, "Rabelais and
> the Age of Printing," 15)[43]

---

[42]Michael B. Kline, in *Rabelais and the Age of Printing*, describes the
situation: "Since the time of the first publication of *Pantagruel* in 1532,
Rabelais' works had been extremely popular, but had suffered from many
unauthorized reimpressions of his texts. From 1553 to 1542 there were at
least seven known pirated editions of *Pantagruel* published in Paris and
Lyon; three editions of the Pantagrueline prognostications, and one edition of *Gargantua*. There was obviously a demand for these books, and the
slight modifications in the titles were probably a means of implying something new on the market, thereby arousing the reader's interest and possi-
bly reopening his pocketbook" (18).

[43]See also Michel Foucault, "What Is an Author?" 148: "Texts, books,
and discourses really began to have authors . . . to the extent that authors
became subject to punishment, that is, to the extent that discourses could
be transgressive." He goes on to say that this occurred at the end of the
eighteenth century and the beginning of the nineteenth, which in my
opinion is manifestly not true, as demonstrated in the case of Rabelais.
Defaux discusses the problem of Rabelais's reception in "D'un problème
l'autre." See also Marcel de Grève, *L'Interprétation de Rabelais au XVIe siècle*.

This danger was dramatically illustrated in Rabelais's time when, subsequent to the publication of an expurgated edition of Rabelais's works in 1542, Etienne Dolet, a man well known for his heretical connections, published a version of the works taken from previous editions and containing certain dangerous attacks against the Sorbonne.

Thus, retrospectively, Rabelais revises the notion of authorship and of the book: after *Gargantua*, *Pantagruel* assumes a legitimate place in the genealogy of the works of Rabelais, protected by the authority of its (his) father.

*3*

# *Gargantua*:

# Inheriting the Father

Whereas during the earlier phases of humanism the metaphor of rebirth conserved a relatively simple relationship with its "reality reference," the Rabelaisian text explicitly complicates the connection.[1] The organic trope of rebirth or even exhumation and resuscitation that continues to make its appearance in *Pantagruel* (on the level of subject matter as well) gives way to archaeological and architectural metaphors of excavation and reconstruction in *Gargantua*, where a self-consciousness of the text as written discourse dominates. This is in part a political gesture, a polemic against the pretentious genealogies constructed in the sixteenth century to justify national chauvinism, as Walter Stephens has pointed out with regard to Rabelais's parody

---

[1]Paul Ricoeur, *The Rule of Metaphor*, 137: "Discourse, mainly as sentence, implies the polarity of *sense* and *reference*, that is, the possibility to distinguish between *what* is said . . . and *about what* something is said. To speak is to say something about something." The term "reality reference" refers here to "the power of discourse to apply to an extralinguistic reality *about* which it says what it says." Stephens's thesis is that Rabelais is parodying the entire nationalist enterprise of constructing genealogies for France in the Renaissance.

of contemporary historiography. It is also thematically and structurally symptomatic of the predicament of authorship and genealogical succession in this sixteenth-century prose narrative on the threshold of novelistic discourse.

The creation of meaning through metaphor (and so fictional narrative) is an authorial process, a work of construction rather than a "natural" growth.[2] And discourse as text is appropriation. Throughout *Pantagruel*, the theme of organic renewal and succession comes into conflict with a recognition of the book's textuality, and thus its arbitrariness—the way a constructed work, an invention, does not follow the natural laws of biological reproduction.

The metaphor that structures *Gargantua* (published only a short time—one and a half to three years—after *Pantagruel*) is a metaphor of structuring. The text delineates a return to the past to seek out origins. This time, however, the vehicle is an archaeological act of excavation, reconstruction, construction and, in chapter 58, excavation once again. Thomas M. Greene notes: "At the opening stand the unearthing of the book and the chaotic 'Fanfreluches': at the end stands the institution of the Abbey of Thélème. Disinterment and construction frame the volume" (*The Light in Troy: Imitation and Discovery in Renaissance Poetry*, 237). The narrative foregrounds the artificiality of its created world.

In noting the differences between the two works, M. A.

---

[2]For definitions of metaphor, see Aristotle, *Poetics*, chap. 21: 1457b, 251, and I. A. Richards, *The Philosophy of Rhetoric*. More recent discussions of the subject which pertain to my use of the term can be found in the writings of Jacques Derrida, particularly "White Mythology: Metaphor in the Text of Philosophy" in *Margins of Philosophy*. *Critical Inquiry*'s Special Issue on Metaphor provides a useful survey of the problem. Another work on the subject is Paul Ricoeur's *The Rule of Metaphor: Multi-disciplinary Studies of the Creation of Meaning in Language*, trans. Robert Czerny. Ricoeur and Derrida are often opposed as "constructionist" versus "deconstructionist." With regard to the critique of philosophy this may indeed be so; insofar as literary or poetic texts are concerned, I do not find them radically incompatible.

Screech comments: "*Pantagruel* in all its versions starts off
with a reference to the *Grandes et inestimables Chronicques* and
succeeds in getting right to the end of its Prologue without a
single classical allusion. *Gargantua* on the other hand plunges
the reader straight into Alcibiades's praise of Socrates in the
*Symposium.* . . . It is much more clearly the work of a humanist
with lessons to convey" (*Rabelais*, 125). This impression is
partially conveyed through a discourse of construction. The
text, a text of "symboles Pythagoricques," resembles a Silenus box containing drugs, not the organic substance of the
Prologue to *Pantagruel.* The process of interpretation ("by
diligent reading and frequent meditation," 14; 38), and composition (17) are invoked, divorcing the book from its previous connections with oral transmission. Barry Lydgate
illustrates how this difference is declared from the very beginning of the Prologue:

> "Beuveurs tresillustres et vous, Verolés tresprecieux"—the
> initial words of the Prologue to *Gargantua* signal the reader
> from the start that this is to be the world of a private fiction.
> In *Pantagruel* the imitation of epic formulas ("Trèsillustres et
> trèschevaleureux champions") evokes familiar patterns of col-
> lective response, if only to discredit them more tellingly. In
> *Gargantua*, however, the grouping is purely symbolic from the
> outset, and refers to a context of reception that the Rabelaisian
> *oeuvre* itself alone creates. ("Printing, Narrative and the Gene-
> sis of the Rabelaisian Novel," 398)

Not only do the "beuveurs" and "veroléz" (the latter a
Rabelasian coinage) refer specifically back to those for whom
*Pantagruel* was intended, but even the title page (except in the
first edition, where it is missing) identifies Gargantua
through his Rabelaisian progeny.[3] The author's coming into

---

[3] Rabelais, *Oeuvres complètes*, ed. Guy Demerson, 33–35: "La Vie très
horrificque du Grand Gargantua père de Pantagruel." Fernand Hallyn
appropriately remarks: "Isn't Rabelais making an accommodation in

his own occurs simultaneously with the admission of the work's textuality, its constructedness. There are many references, in the Prologue and in the first chapter, to *Pantagruel* and *Gargantua* as works belonging to the same corpus. The Prologue does not foreground the narrator's role as character, his voice remaining indistinguishable from that of the author throughout the references to Rabelais's books: " my writings" (9); "certain books of our invention, such as *Gargantua, Pantagruel*" (11; 37); "for I never spent—or wasted—any more—or other—time in the composing of this lordly book, than that fixed for the taking of my bodily refreshment" (17; 39); "my books" (17).[4] Chapter 1 returns to the fictional narrator but cites *Pantagruel* twice as sole subtext for the present book: "For knowledge of the Gargantua's genealogy and of the antiquity of his descent, I refer you to the great Pantagrueline Chronicle" (19; 41). The second mention constitutes, according to Lefranc, one of the most important clues that *Pantagruel* did, in fact, precede *Gargantua*: "You may see in your pantagruelizing: that is to say, as you drink to your heart's desire and read the fearsome exploits of Pantagruel" (*Rabelais: Oeuvres*, 1:24, n. 47; Calder, Screech, and Saulnier, 24; Cohen, 42).

*Gargantua* is not an entity with "roots." It has been obscured, entombed: it refers back, but not to nature:

---

choosing Gargantua for the hero of his second volume: what better way to introduce a paternity of meaning, belatedly reclaimed, than by having the story of the son followed by that of the father?" ("Le Paradoxe de la souveraineté," 343).

[4] I do not entirely agree with Floyd Gray's assertion that in the Prologue the narrator's voice is clearly distinguishable from the author's, whereas in chapter 1 it seems to me that a narrator *is* present. But, I also do not think the distinction is crucial in order to posit the parodic distance that Defaux seems to think depends heavily on the presence of a narrating persona who remains distinct from the author. See Floyd Gray, "Ambiguity and Point of View in the Prologue to *Gargantua*," and Gérard Defaux, "Rabelais et son masque comique: *Sophista loquitur*."

Et fut trouvée par Jean Audeau en un pré qu'il avoit près l'arceau Gualeau, au dessoubz de l'Olive, tirant à Narsay, duquel faisant lever les fossez, toucherent les piocheurs de leurs marres un grand tombeau de bronse, long sans mesure. . . . Icelluy ouvrans en certain lieu, signé, au dessus, d'un goubelet à l'entour du quel estoit escript en letres Ethrusques: HIC BIBITUR, trouverent neuf flaccons en tel ordre qu'on assiet les quilles en Guascoigne, des quelz celluy qui on mylieu estoit couvroit un gros, gras, grand, gris, joly, petit, moisy livret, plus, mais non mieulx sentent que roses. (22–23)

It was found by Jean Audeau, in a meadow of his near the Arch Gualeau, below l'Olive, on the way to Narsay. Here, as they were cleaning the ditches, the diggers struck with their picks against a great tomb of bronze, so immeasurably long that they never found the end of it. . . . Opening this tomb at a certain place which was sealed on the top with the sign of a goblet, around which was inscribed in Etruscan letters, HIC BIBITUR, they found nine flagons, arranged after the fashion of skittles in Gascony; and beneath the middle flagon lay a great, greasy, grand, grey, pretty, little, mouldy book, which smelt more strongly but not more sweetly than roses. (42)

The book is surrounded by signs of an absolute past, including obscure symbols that function like hieroglyphs, so as to be undecodable by a noninitiate. Rabelais will return to the question of hieroglyphs and the opacity of signs in chapters 8 and 9 on the meaning of the colors blue and white. For now what is foregrounded is the excavational endeavor and the "discovery" of the book as artifact of the past. Nor is the genealogy transmitted orally, as it is in *Pantagruel*, chapter 1. Here it consists of a parchment requiring transcription (as in the illegible symbols of chapter 2's facsimile), decoding ("[practicing] that art by which letters can be read that are not apparent" [23; 42]), and translation. There is an acute awareness of temporal distance: the title page of one of the variants announces that the book was "composed, of old, by

M. Alcofrybas" (4), the book's appearance harks back to another age—"The first editions of *Gargantua* are tiny books,
badly printed in those gothic characters that the French humanists despised" (*Gargantua, édition critique*, xxiv)[5]—and the
genealogy itself is found in a coffin. *Gargantua* is an archaeological artifact, reconstructed and irrevocably severed from
its past.

The gap between past and present widens in the transition
from *Pantagruel* to *Gargantua*. Whereas *Pantagruel* exists as a
work of the present, seeming to evolve from a recent past,
*Gargantua* extends further back into antiquity, the difference
between the time of the story and that of its composition (or
transcription) providing the thematics of chapter 1. The anxiety of the Prologue to *Pantagruel*, resulting from the uneasy
coexistence of a claim to sameness and a will to differentiation, seems resolved in *Gargantua* by the explicit acknowledg-
ment of an archaeological, reconstructive endeavor.

The narrator justifies his enterprise in the opening pages
of chapter 1:

> Ne vous faschera si pour le present je m'en deporte, combien
> que la chose soit telle que, tant plus seroit remembrée, tant
> plus elle plairoit à vos Seigneuries; comme vous avez l'autorité
> de Flacce, qui dict estre aulcuns propos, telz que ceulx cy, qui
> plus sont delectables quand plus souvent sont redictz. (19)

> Do not take it amiss, therefore, if for the moment I pass this
> over, though it is such an attractive subject that the more often
> it were gone over the better it would please your lordships.
> For which fact you have the authority [. . .] of Horace, who
> says that there are some things—and these are no doubt of

---

[5] See Defaux, "Rabelais et son masque comique," 100: "The handwrit-
ing of Master Alcofrybas is striking for its archaïsm, it is deliberately
conceived in order to reveal a character historically belated with regard to
his period in time."

that kind—that become more delightful with each repetition. (41)

He invokes authorities on "the pleasure of repetition," citing Plato (in the later edition) and Horace, and masks to some extent a motive for his own repetition "with a difference." By rewriting the story of Gargantua, Rabelais not only repeats but appropriates it.

If the motives of repetition are concealed, those that underlie the genealogical impulse are not. In Nietzschean fashion, the narrator hints at the origins of aristocratic genealogies, demystifying the determinism of origins with a joke about himself:

> Pleust à Dieu qu'un chascun sceust aussi certainement sa genealogie. Je pense que plusieurs sont aujourd'huy empereurs, roys, ducz, princes et papes en la terre, lesquelz sont descenduz de quelques porteurs de rogatons et de coustretz. . . . Et, pour vous donner à entendre de moy qui parle, je cuyde que soye descendu de quelque riche roy ou prince au temps jadis. Car oncques ne veistes homme qui eust plus grande affection d'estre roy et riche que moy, affin de faire grand chere, et pas ne travailler, et bien enrichir mes amis et tous gens de bien et de sçavoir. (20–21)

> Would to God that everyone had as certain knowledge of his genealogy, from Noah's ark to the present age! I think there are many today among the Emperors, Kings, Dukes, Princes, and Popes of this world whose ancestors were mere pedlars of pardons and firewood. . . . And to give you some information about myself, who address you, believe that I am descended from some wealthy king or prince of the olden days. For you have never met a man with a greater desire to be a king or to be rich than I have, so that I may entertain liberally, do no work, have no worries, and plentifully reward my friends, as well as all worthy and learned men. (41)

The narrator comments upon the arbitrariness of the connection between the past and the present, thus diverting attention from the rewriting of Gargantua's story while at the same time hinting that, just as the narrator's aristocratic origin is arbitrarily a function of his desire for wealth, so too *Gargantua* inherits fictitiously, merely by the will of its author. The lineage claimed for the book (the retelling of a well-known tale) in one passage is denied in the next by the assertion that genealogies may disguise rather than reveal origins ("Would to God that *everyone* had as certain knowledge of his genealogy"). *Gargantua* may be, then, at the same time a "lordly book," descended from obscure and lowly origins, and also one of the "almshouse beggars—poor, suffering wretches—who are descended from the blood and lineage of great Kings and Emperors"(20; 41), suffering present ignominy while awaiting a greater destiny in a future world: "Mais en ce je me reconforte que en l'aultre monde je le seray [roy or riche] voyre plus grand que de present ne l'auseroye soubhaiter" (21) ("But I comfort myself with one thought, that in the other world I shall be all this, and greater still than at present I dare even wish" [41]). Finally, this passage, which for the first time in the text confronts the "issue" of genealogy as a result of construction, delineates on a microcosmic level that temporal sequence from past to future that informs the macrocosm of the Rabelaisian quest.

Although the letter to Pantagruel in *Pantagruel*, chapter 8, attempts to retrace the passage of time from Dark Ages to Enlightenment, it does so at the level of biological reproduction, the natural perpetuation of humanity through time.[6]

---

[6]*Pantagruel*, chap. 8, 41: "'Mais, par ce moyen de propagation séminale, demeure ès enfans ce que estoit de perdu ès parens, et ès nepveux ce que dépérissoit ès enfans, et ainsi successivement jusques à l'heure de jugement final, quand Jésuchrist aura rendu à Dieu son père son royaulme pacificque hors tout dangier et contamination de péchée'" ("'But by this method of seminal propagation, there remains in the children what has perished in

*Gargantua*, chapter 1, adds a historical dimension. The past becomes a construct of the present—a "genealogy"—that, though human, needs to be interpreted from a book. Furthermore, whereas Gargantua's letter assumes a linear progression of time toward perfection, chapter 1 both questions the progressive view of history and suggests a transformation of "vertical" time to horizontal or spatial time (the time of narrative unfolding). Time may produce regression, as in the case of the "almshouse beggars" or the prophesied disasters preceding final retribution in the Christian view of history presented by the "enigma" of chapter 56. *Translatio imperii* and its analogue *translatio studii*, the principles of inheritance cited in chapter 1, proceed by location, in a nonlinear, occasionally retrogressive drift westward:

> des Assyriens es Medes,
> des Medes es Perses,
> des Perses es Macedones,
> des Macedones es Romains,
> des Romains es Grecz,
> des Grecs es Françoys. (21)[7]

from the Assyrians to the Medes, from the Medes to the Persians, from the Persians to the Macedonians, from the Macedonians to the Romans, from the Romans to the Greeks, from the Greeks to the French. (41)

---

the parents, and in the grandchildren what has perished in the children, and so on in succession till the hour of the Last Judgement, when Jesus Christ shall peacefully have rendered up to God His Kingdom, released from all danger and contamination of sin'" [193]).

[7] See Douglas Kelly, "*Translatio Studii*: Translation, Adaptation, and Allegory in Medieval French Literature." Although the movement from the Romans to the Greeks to the French has been explained as referring to the Holy Roman Empire, which, succeeding Rome, becomes the ancestor of France (see *Gargantua*, ed. Lefranc, 1:21, n. 16), I wonder if it is not also Rabelais's interpretation of the inheritance of French humanism. See the stress on Greek learning in Gargantua's letter to Pantagruel, *Pantagruel*, chap. 8.

In chapter 2, time is depicted graphically, in the reproduction of the incomplete (because damaged) "Fanfreluches antidotées," "out of reverence for antiquity" (24; 42), as the narrator says. Historical distance resulting in loss or decay (however playfully presented) sets the tone for the beginning of Gargantua's story. The vaguely apocalyptic "nonsense" of the "Fanfreluches" points backward to an obscure, undecodable origin from which *Gargantua*, as narrative extension, emerges. Mystery lies at the origin of signification—semiotic confusion in the present, which becomes a theme in *Gargantua*, finds its source here, in an enigmatic text.

The end of *Gargantua* will return to the idea of enigma, in the form of the "Enigme en prophétie," which lies at the foundation of one of the seemingly most serene detailed and rationalistic Renaissance constructions, the "Abbaye de Thélème." Throughout the book, questions of origin and signification—of the origins of signification—are explored, while that exploration occupies a space between two mysteries, at the beginning and at the end.

In this second book, which situates *Pantagruel* in a line of descent and provides it (him) with a history in the form of a father whose authority determines the outcome of the son, the problem of genealogy (and so authority) is linguistically played out. Having been formulated in terms of a problem of construction, the question of authority arises in connection with the text's symbolic edifice, its system of signs.

The Prologue first introduces the question of interpretation that will return again and again throughout *Gargantua*, specifically in relation to words as signs, to symbols, and to emblems.[8] Until recently, critics argued about the narrator's

[8]For a study of how emblems function in Rabelais's text, see François Rigolot and Sandra Sider, "Fonctions de l'écriture emblématique chez Rabelais," and Rigolot's article "Cratylisme et Pantagruélisme: Rabelais et le statut di signe." For the literary historical treatment of symbol in relation to allegory, see Paul de Man, "The Rhetoric of Temporality, in *Blind-*

position on allegorical reading in the Prologue, citing the famous "turning point" that seems to contradict the injunction to find a "higher meaning."⁹ Edwin Duval has convincingly argued that it is not necessary to consider the turning point a contradiction, that Alcofrybas is merely pointing out that authors do not intend all the meanings that can be found in their texts. Cathleen Bauschatz demonstrates how the debate about allegory in the Prologue exposes the tension between author's and reader's interpretation that informs *Gargantua*, attributing this in part to the loss of authorial

---

*ness and Insight: Essays in the Rhetoric of Contemporary Criticism.*" In focusing on the difference between Rabelais's treatment of symbols and the use of allegory in the text (see chap. 6), I understand their difference to be that discussed by de Man: "Whereas the symbol postulates the possibility of an identity or identification, allegory designates primarily a distance in relation to its own origin, and, renouncing the nostalgia and the desire to coincide, it establishes its language in the void of this temporal difference" (207). See my discussion of hieroglyphs in the *Quart Livre*, chap. 25. I discuss the use of symbols and emblems in Rabelais in "The Other and the Same: The Image of the Hermaphrodite in Rabelais."

⁹"Croiez vous en vostre foy qu'oncques Homere, escrivent l'*Iliade* et *Odyssée*, pensast es allegories lesquelles de luy ont beluté Plutarche, Heraclides, Ponticq, Eustatie et Phornute, et ce que d'iceulx Politian a desrobé? Si le croiez, vous n'aprochez ne de pieds ny de mains à mon opinion, qui decrete icelles aussi peu avoir esté songéez d'Homere que d'Ovide en ses *Metamorphoses* les sacremens de l'Evangile. . . . Si ne le croiez, quelle cause est, pourquoy autant n'en ferez de ces joyeuses et nouvelles chronicques, combien que, les dictant, n'y pensasse en plus que vous" (*Gargantua*, 15–17) ("But do you faithfully believe that Homer, in writing his *Iliad* and *Odyssey*, ever had in mind the allegories squeezed out of him by Plutarch, Heraclides Ponticus, Eustathius, and Phornutus, and which Politian afterwards stole from them in his turn? If you do, you are not within a hand's or a foot's length of my opinion. For I believe them to have been as little dreamed of by Homer as the Gospel mysteries were by Ovid in his *Metamorphoses*. . . . If you do not believe [that Homer had in mind these allegories], what reason is there that [you should not do the same] with these new and jolly chronicles, [even though] as I dictated them I gave no more thought to the matter than you" [38–39]).

control occasioned by print and the wide dissemination of works in the sixteenth century and to the very real possibility of hostile readings.[10]

François Rigolot and Richard Regosin have shown how the Prologue nevertheless remains problematic because it interrogates the inside/outside polarization in interpretation through a series of container/contained images: the Silenus boxes, the cover and the contents of a book, the monk and his "habit," the bone and its "substantial marrow," the bottle.[11] The proverb "the habit does not make the monk" (11; 37) reverses the hierarchy of privilege granted to the inside in the rest of the series, destabilizing the traditionally valorized superiority of inner truth over surface. Regosin argues, in relation to allegory, that "scriptural exegesis provided the model of reading and while its approaches and methodologies might have been discussed, its difficulties debated, its extensiveness disputed, the text itself, by guaranteeing the integrity of its meaning and justifying (necessitating) the endless quest for its significance, validates the paradigm of container and contained, and the privilege of secreted truth" ("Ins[ides] and Outs[ides] of Reading," 69). This paradigm continues to inform the debates on meaning in Rabelais's text, for example, in the heated exchange between Cave, Jeanneret, and Rigolot on the one hand and Defaux (speaking also for Duval) on the other.[12] Bauschatz nicely characterizes the debate as one be-

[10]Edwin Duval, "Interpretation and the 'Doctrine Absconce' of Rabelais's Prologue to *Gargantua*." Cathleen Bauschatz approaches the question by comparing author-oriented and reader-oriented approaches to reading and gives a critical overview of the debate from this perspective in "'Une Description du Jeu de Paulme Soubz Obscures Paroles': The Portrayal of Reading in *Pantagruel* and *Gargantua*."

[11]François Rigolot, *Le Texte de la Renaissance: Des rhétoriqueurs à Montaigne*, "Parémiologie," 123–35; Richard Regosin, "The Ins(ides) and Outs(ides) of Reading."

[12]Cave, Jeanneret, and Rigolot respond to Defaux's article, "D'un problème l'autre," and Defaux in turn responds to their response, in the *Revue d'Histoire Littéraire de la France* 86, 4 (June–July 1986), "Débats."

tween author-centered paradigms of reading (Defaux, Duval)
and reader-centered ones ("'Description du Jeu de Paulme
Soubz Obscures Parolles,'" 71). Even Regosin, however, attributes authorial triumph to the undermining of the in-
side/outside paradigm of reading: "The parodic destruction
of the 'sacred word' and of the forces it supports begins with
the undermining of its own word and the challenges to that
hermeneutic process which pretends to reveal the mysteries
it hides. But most significantly, the prologue demonstrates
that neither voice nor text is original or autonomous; each is
open to intrusions from the outside, each indeed is constituted by the very interaction of what it would claim as *self*
and what is *other*" (70). Rather than a triumphant unmasking
of the "sacred word," there is throughout *Gargantua* a hesitation between paradigms, an interrogation of the bases of
meaning related to a crisis of the sign that Richard Waswo
sees as informing the "relational semantics" of Lorenzo Valla's linguistic theory and that is also related to the theological
crises of sixteenth-century Europe.[13]

[13]Richard Waswo, in his *Language and Meaning in the Renaissance*, does not
specifically discuss Rabelais in connection with his theory of the revolution
in linguistic understanding exemplified by the language theories of
Lorenzo Valla. His argument is basically that there was a shift, later
reversed, from a referential theory whereby words refer to a meaning that
is thought of as prior or external to language and thus fixed, to a relational
theory that understands meaning to be constructed in and posited by
discourse itself and is thus contingent. Like Thomas Kuhn in *The Structure
of Scientific Revolutions*, Waswo argues that a theoretical paradigm for this
shift was lacking, so that language continued to be thought of as referential
while being "relationally" practiced and described. I think that Rabelais's
linguistic practice as opposed to the pronouncements about language in the
text can be described in Waswo's terms, and I would link this linguistic
dilemma with theological developments in the sixteenth century. The conflict between (at least) two paradigms of truth, two radically opposed
interpretations of what is meant to be a unitary doctrine, became hege-
monic in the sixteenth century and was bound to destabilize the paradigmatic bases of theories of meaning and truth. One might argue that in
Thélème (see chap. 5) the dilemma is figured in terms of an economic and
political "paradigmatic shift" as well.

Chapters 8 and 9 reexamine the issue of signification and arrive at equally playful yet less optimistic conclusions about the ability to interpret signs correctly. These chapters question the grounds of signification and examine the status of the appeal to *auctoritas* to justify an interpretation. Parodies of misinterpretation that question the capacity of language to signify unambiguously do occur in *Pantagruel*, particularly in chapters 9 and 13. These passages, however, demonstrate rather than purport to analyze or question the slippage between sign and meaning. They unfold in a dramatic rather than an expository context, as a function of individual characters involved in specific situations. Chapters 8 and 9 of *Gargantua*, on the other hand, represent products of the (writing) narrator, Alcofrybas. As such, they constitute a pause in the narrative in favor of parodic exposition; Alcofrybas and his ilk come under scrutiny. But if Alcofrybas is the model of excessive or bad interpretation, no alternative or better interpretive models present themselves to resolve the dilemmas of interpretation posited in these chapters.[14] Modern readings of the arguments exposed in chapters 8 ("Des couleurs et livrée de Gargantua") and 9 ("De ce qu'est signifié par les coleurs blanc et bleu") themselves mime the difficulties of determining meaning that the chapters explore. What is striking in the survey of these readings is that they often produce interpretations that conform to the particular investment a critic has made in Rabelais. Camps divide into an "ancient" (realist) versus "moderns" (nominalist) debate, with a Rabelais confident of the inherent or natural connec-

---

[14]Defaux, in "Rabelais et son masque comique," 91, stresses the importance of the separation between the character Alcofrybas and the author Rabelais, which risks hypostatizing a narrative voice whose role as *personnage* remains very vague and rarely discernible. Walter Stephens concurs with this separation and brings much scholarship to bear to prove it. My argument is that there is a contamination effect; the pseudohistoriographer gets under Rabelais's skin. Others, such as Rigolot and Regosin, nuance the distinction between the author and the narrator, describing the relationship in primarily linguistic rather than overtly ideological terms.

tion between words and their meanings on the one hand and on the other a Saussurian writer conscious of the arbitrary link between signs and what they signify. The consequences of this choice are potentially far reaching, since they may support either a thoroughly orthodox Rabelais or an Ockhamistic (potentially Lutheran) Rabelais, one who would have radicalized the logician's sign theory to the point of severing all contact between discourse and the divine.[15]

William of Ockham, in a peculiarly "modern" way, radically problematized metaphysical discussions of signification primarily launched, in the context of Christian theology, by Augustine.[16] Against Augustinian Platonism (ever bordering, in spite of the rhetorician's efforts, on a dualistic vision of the world) whereby human discourse, because temporal, may approach eternal truth only asymptotically, and against the positivistic rationalism of Aquinas, whereby universal truth ("reality") may be said to coexist (though temporally prior) in things (and thus in words and concepts as well), Ockham plied his razor. Somewhat simply put, Ockham made possible the explicit questioning of linguistic referentiality. Whereas for Augustine eternal, divine truth (or God) constituted the ultimate referent, a silence for which "fallen" discourse nostalgically yearned, the mind itself, according to Ockham, could originate such abstract conceptualizations, for they were universal ideas.[17] And whereas Thomism placed the divine (or universal) idea, originating in God,

[15] See Steven Ozment on Ockham's thought, *The Age of Reform, 1250–1550: An Intellectual and Religious History of Late Medieval and Renaissance Europe*, chap. 2, "The Scholastic Traditions"; also Ernest A. Moody, *Truth and Consequences in Mediaeval Logic*. Jean Paris provides an interesting discussion of the implications of Ockhamism for Rabelais's thought, particularly with regard to *Gargantua*, chapter 9, in *Rabelais au futur*, 126–31.

[16] On Augustine's theory of signification see Margaret W. Ferguson, "Saint Augustine's Region of Unlikeness: The Crossing of Exile and Language"; also John Freccero, *Dante: The Poetics of Conversion*.

[17] Ferguson, "Saint Augustine's Region of Unlikeness," 844–45, and Ozment, *Age of Reform*, 58. See also Waswo's description of medieval and Renaissance linguistic theories in *Language and Meaning in the Renaissance*.

within the particulars of this world in order to account for knowledge, Ockhamism dispensed with the necessity for a presupposed mediating term and posited the mind as an independent means of apprehending reality. Thus, along positivistic lines (in the tradition of Aristotle and Aquinas) Ockham is said to have prepared the way for empirical science by positing "naturally universal" signs that can be understood by simple, intuitive knowledge. In a more Platonic and Augustinian vein, Ockhamism laid the foundations both for an assertion of the autonomy of language (its basis in convention rather than in nature or essence) and for the Lutheran claim that faith, not reason, is the only access man may have to the divine. The mind's capacity for "complex abstractive knowledge" enables it to create universal concepts, mental objects, with no previous extralinguistic references. This does not mean that the concepts (linguistic signs) cannot be universally understood, only that the basis for their apprehension does not lie in the realm of nature or of divine truth: "The other kind of universal is so by convention (*universale per voluntariam institutionem*). In this way an uttered word, which is really a single quality, is universal; for it is a conventional sign meant to signify many things (*signum voluntarie institutum ad significandum plura*). Therefore, just as the word is said to be common so it can be said to be universal. But it is not so by nature, only by convention (*non habet ex natura rei, sed ex placito instituentium tantum*)."[18] Thus, already in Ockham's time, the word relinquishes its analogical and essential connectedness to the world of things and to the divine in the "Great Chain of Being."[19]

Pantagruel, in the *Tiers Livre*, chapter 19, seems to present

---

[18]From *Ockham: The Philosophical Writings*, 34.

[19]I am referring here to E. M. W. Tillyard's book, *The Elizabethan World Picture*. Michel Foucault's claim, countered by Jean Paris in *Rabelais au futur* (see chap. 12, "Les signes de la rupture"), is that a connectedness between word and thing persisted through the Renaissance until the seventeenth century. See *The Order of Things: An Archaeology of the Human Sciences*, part 1, chap. 2, "The Prose of the World."

the position described above rather simply (Screech ed., 140). But here, in chapters 8 and 9 of *Gargantua*, where the question concerns symbolic signification in general, the argument is not so clearly stated. What occurs in these chapters, and perhaps generates such widely variant modern readings, is basically contradictory in a manner that, according to Richard Waswo, was characteristic of the Renaissance's "discovery" of relational semantics:

> The treatment of socio-historical usage as a determinant of meaning, the revival of the "probable" dialectics of Cicero and Quintilian, the insistence on a unified perspective from which to regard both the arts of discourse and the discourse they produce, and the pursuit of the cognitive consequences of these new forms of linguistic attention—all initiated by Valla—generated an implicitly revolutionary semantics that was embedded and transmitted therein. . . . The tension between language *treated* as creating meaning and conceived as but containing it begins to be felt as a result of the humanistic "rebirth" of classical letters in the Renaissance. ("The Reaction of Juan Luis Vives to Valla's Philosophy of Language," 603)

In these two chapters, then, Rabelais seems to worry about the very problem that is reiterated throughout the quest and that leaves the *Cinquième Livre*'s final revelation suspended in perpetual undecidability. Signs must mean *essentially*, if a universe informed by God's intentionality is to be assumed (however distant, unattainable, and otherworldly the meaning may remain), yet language continually escapes this leash, asserting its own discursive contingency.

Critics of the text, falling prey perhaps to the expository rather than the poetic style of the chapters, have rejected the undecidability in Rabelais's text as merely apparent, thus not granting even the less radical term "ambiguity," so easily accorded to the latter type of text. M. A. Screech, whose excavation of the intertextuality in chapters 8 and 9 initially

cleared the site for further investigation, states rather un-
selfconsciously, "The principal aim of chapter ten is to take
the interpretation out of the realm of personal opinion and
place it firmly within the *jus gentium*" ("Emblems and Colours: The Controversy over Gargantua's Colors and Devices," 75). Here Screech is restating a passage from chapter
9: "Et n'est poinct cette signifiance par imposition humaine
institué, mais repceue par consentement de tout le monde,
que les philosophes nomment *jus gentium*, droict universel,
valable par toutes contrées" (71) ("Nor is this significance
based on mere human interpretation. It is accepted by that
common consent which philosophers call *jus gentium*, universal law, valid in all countries" [59]). The distinction Screech
makes, based on this passage, between "the realm of personal
opinion" and "jus gentium" is by no means as clear-cut as he
presumes, constituting as it does the very humor of the argument developed in chapters 8 and 9. Gérard Defaux suggests
that the argument concerning the significance of the colors
blue and white may be in fact blatantly paradoxical, thus
ipso facto rendering comic the distinction between "personal" and "universal" interpretations: "Indeed, it seems that the
equations white = faith and blue = resolve had often been
accepted. The sophist Alcofrybas, far from wanting, as he
claims, to make *jus gentium* triumph, decides instead to wage
war against it" ("Rabelais et son masque comique," 120, n.
9). The argument concerning these colors was, at the very
least, a *querelle*, as Rabelais himself indicates, so that any
appeal to universal agreement could not be made without a
hint of irony.

Another ironic chuckle might be felt in the phrase "par
imposition humaine institué" in the passage cited above.
Chapter 8 opens with the quintessential authoritative "imposition" concerning the colors, the will of the father:

Les couleurs de Gargantua feurent blanc et bleu, comme cy
dessus avez peu lire; et par icelles vouloit son pere qu'on

entendist que ce luy estoit une joye celeste. Car le blanc luy signifioyt joye, plaisir, delices et resjouyssance, et le bleu, choses celestes. (64)

Gargantua's colours were white and blue, as you may have read above, by which his father meant it to be understood that he felt a heavenly joy. For white signified to him gladness, pleasure, delights, and rejoicing, and blue anything to do with Heaven. (57)

Grandgousier's gigantic "human imposition" suspends the question of universal agreement. Nothing more is needed in this context than his desire to effect a particular interpretation. This is true of the textual world in general, as the prologues themselves amply demonstrate. Nevertheless, even this solution to the dilemma of the debate about signs in these chapters is questionable. Although chapter 8 itself critiques the arbitrary imposition of meaning, thematically *Gargantua* will both approach and recoil from the sort of authority here exercised by Grandgousier. If such an exercise of will can exist in the linguistic realm, then it can also be applied in the political realm, where some guarantee continues to be sought to justify such an imposition.

Given the questionable nature of these chapters as "serious" argument, what can be said about the arguments themselves? What are the implications of the theory of interpretation developed in *Gargantua*, chapters 8 and 9? Thomas M. Greene underscores the text's self-contradiction by juxtaposing, in the following quotation, radically opposed notions of the grounding of signification, all of which appear in Rabelais's two chapters: "In rejecting the association of white with faith for its association with joy, he [Rabelais] is in effect rejecting an arbitrary system of medieval symbolism for an interpretation rooted in universal tradition (the "jus gentium"), in human physiology, and in the nature of things"

(*Rabelais: A Study in Comic Courage*, 38). Modern semiotic philosophies make rigid distinctions between the categories above, "jus gentium" (rhetorics), "human physiology" (linguistic naturalism), and "the nature of things" (philosophies of essence or ontologies) and require a choice that itself has ramifications. Lucien Febvre rightly cautions against ascribing modern specialized meanings to the terms employed by sixteenth-century theorists, although he too is a man of his era, conferring upon science the role of clarifying the obscure premodern discourse of philosophy.[20] Certainly there existed a greater degree of linguistic elasticity than in modern technical vocabularies, both because the vulgar tongue was still freely evolving (rather than institutionally determined) and because the humanistic disciplines were not as discretely categorized as they are today. But as Waswo has pointed out, the Renaissance grappled with a specific *décalage* between theory and practice in the area of linguistic philosophy, whereby a new metalanguage to describe an evolving practice had yet to be created, although existing theory had already become obsolete.[21]

In Rabelais's time, theoretical discussions about the nature

---

[20]Lucien Febvre argues: "The words that presented themselves to these men when they reasoned about the sciences in French—or simply when they reasoned—were not words made for reasoning, for explaining and demonstrating. They were not scientific words but words that belonged to the language of all, to the common, living language. They were accordion words, if I may say so. Their meaning expanded, contracted, altered, and evolved with a freedom that scientific words have ceased to exercise. The latter have the immobility of signposts" (*The Problem of Unbelief in the Sixteenth Century: The Religion of Rabelais*, 358). He goes on to conclude that "philosophy then was only opinions, a chaos of contradictory and wavering opinions. They wavered because they still lacked a steady, solid base, the firm base that would make them secure: science" (379). Recent work in philosophy has dismantled this base as well, exposing it as a product of its own desire to construct just such an unshakable foundation.

[21]See Richard Waswo, "The 'Ordinary Language Philosophy' of Lorenzo Valla," and his *Language and Meaning in the Renaissance*.

of signification and its relation to ontology had moved beyond the strictly philosophical and theological framework of the realist/nominalist debate and had extended to the "human sciences," to the realm of language in general. Philosophies of meaning had entered the nontechnical domain of the professional practitioners of language, the humanists. Thus, whereas Ockham was no doubt influential, his thought dominating theories of signification in the universities in the fourteenth and fifteenth centuries, it was not primarily from him that Rabelais received his descriptive manner of discussing the issue.[22] Ockham still belonged to the school of the Sophists that humanist learning eschewed. Rather, Rabelais's discourse seems to find its patron in the more rhetorically oriented arguments of Lorenzo Valla.

The narrator cites Valla's *Contra Bartoli libellum* to aid his demonstration that white is the color of light and therefore of joy:

> La clarté n'esjouist elle pas toute nature? Elle est blanche plus que chose que soyt. A quoy prouver je vous pourroys renvoyer au livre de Laurens Valle contre Bartole; mays le tesmoignage evangelicque vous contentera. (72)

> Does not light make all Nature glad? It is whiter than anything which exists. As proof of which I could refer you to the

[22]Jean Paris, in *Rabelais au futur*, 129–30, suggests that Ockham provides the philosophical context for Rabelais's discussion of signification. I think it is important, however, to stress the humanist mediation of Ockham's "purely philosophical" speculation, as provided by Lorenzo Valla (among others, such as Erasmus). Rabelais remains a humanist in his thoroughly rhetorical orientation to this philosophical question. It may be useful here to cite Charles Trinkhaus's statement on the relation between medieval and Renaissance approaches to philosophical issues: "It is well known by now that the Italian Humanists differed from their Scholastic rivals less in essential doctrines than in stylistic predilections, forms of presentation, and classical mentors" (in Ernst Cassirer, Paul O. Kristeller, and John H. Randall, Jr., eds., *The Renaissance Philosophy of Man*, 148).

book of Laurentius Valla against Bartolus. But evidence from
the Gospels will satisfy you. (60)

The passage refers to an error in the Vulgate edition of Mat-
thew 17 that read "vestimenta eius facta sunt alba sicut nix"
("and his rainment was white as the snow"). Valla, in con-
demning Bartolus for designating gold as the color of light,
also points out that, in the Greek, the sentence above has the
word "light" rather than "snow," so that the Gospel itself
designates white as the color of light. Screech indicates the
importance of this quotation and the ensuing association of
white and light for the argument Rabelais is trying to make
by pointing out that it enables Rabelais to include the example of Tobias and the angel ("Emblems and Colours," 77).
The Tobias example, in turn, derives its importance from the
association (albeit rather indirect) of light with joy: "Et
Thobie (*cap. v*) quant il eut perdu la veue, lors que Raphael le
salua, respondit il pas: 'Quelle joye pourray jeavoir, moy qui
poinct ne voy la lumiere du ciel?'" (73–74) ("And Tobit—in
chapter v—when he had lost his sight said in answer to
Raphael's salutation: 'What joy can I have who see not the
light of Heaven?'" [60]). Valla was not alone in pointing out
the textual error that, when corrected, produced the "lumi-
nous whiteness" so useful in chapter 9's proof. Yet whether
or not Valla's *Contra Bartoli* is incidental to the discourse (as
are most of the authorities cited in this chapter), the mention
of the humanist's name in the context of this discussion suggests a broader subtextual influence.

Valla himself was greatly influenced by Ockham, whom
Jean Paris sees as informing the Rabelaisian discussion. He
spent time at Pavia, which was Ockhamist in orientation, and
owes a great deal to the logician in terms of method and
philosophical orientation.[23] Ockham, as I mentioned earlier,

[23]See Giovanni di Napoli, *Lorenzo Valla: Filosofia e religione nell'umanesimo
italiano*, 213.

made possible the philosophical separation between language (or categories of thought) and being (categories of reality) and concentrated on the former as the only knowable object of man's inquiry.[24] Valla, approaching these problems from a grammatical and rhetorical, rather than a metaphysical, point of view, translated the category "thought" or "knowledge" into an almost exclusively linguistic category. Thus dialectic, which for Scholastics had been an instrument for exploring Truth or Reality, took on its linguistic function, as a science of language whose object is the discursive process.[25]

In the realm of signification, then, language begins to be thought of as relational rather than referential. Ockham distinguished between intuitive knowledge (a direct knowledge of the particulars of the world), abstractive knowledge (the natural generation in the mind of abstract concepts, or universals, deriving from the particulars), and their translation into language, the "arbitrary" or conventional signs that de-

[24]Ernest Moody comments, "The primary significance of what is called the 'nominalism' of William of Ockham is its rejection of the confusion of logic with metaphysics, and its vigorous defense of the older conception of logic as a *scientia sermocinalis* whose function is to analyze the formal structure of language rather than to hypostatize this structure into a science of reality or of Mind" (*Truth and Consequences*, 5–6).

[25]An unpublished paper by Shane Gasbarra, "The *Dialecticae Disputationes* of Lorenzo Valla: Book One" (Yale University) has helped me formulate my thinking on Valla along these lines. He writes (p. 6): "Thus Aristotle establishes a sort of 'logical decorum' among the object of inquiry, the discursive mode, and the premises on which the given type of syllogism is based. Far from being the science of sciences and the privileged method of philosophy, dialectic treats of probability and opinions and never the nature of things. It is not identical with scientific demonstration and therefore cannot achieve logical certainty. This conception of dialectic as strictly a *scientia sermocinalis*, i.e., a 'science' of language whose categories are never supposed to correspond to those of an objective reality, is the very notion which animates Valla's *Dialecticae Disputationes* and upon which it is implicitly based."

signate the natural signs occurring in the mind. Valla's work, focusing on the primacy of linguistic expression, draws this Ockhamist contradiction to the surface in his discourse. These contradictions become clear in the very difficulty of Valla's formulation:

> The human voice is indeed natural, but its meaning descends from instruction; for men devised words which they might adjust to things known. Of whom Adam was the first, with God the creator, as they taught words with their meanings to posterity. As sounds are indeed from nature but words and meanings from a contriver, so the sounds lay hold of the ears, the meanings of the mind, the words of both. Afterwards letters are discovered as mute words or images of words, just as words themselves are as images of meanings which are now properly called names. Hence this is whatever we say; yet it is also the substance, quality, action itself, and in fact the thing itself. . . . Consequently, it makes no difference whether we say, what *is* wood, what is stone, what iron, what man, or what *does* "wood," "stone," "iron," "man," *signify*—about the matter of which objects nothing can be said: what the thing is and what "thing" signifies, being the same "what," is dissolved in that thing. But if I ask, what *word* is "thing," you will respond rightly: it is a word signifying the meaning or sense of all other words, but which now signifies whatever belongs to it. (*Opera omnia, Dialecticae*, 1, 14: 676–77)[26]

In this passage Valla establishes the conventionality of language: "Vox humana naturalis illa quidem est, sed eius significatio ab institutione descendit," then he goes on to equate the word as sign with name, meaning (signified), and with the thing itself: "Voces sunt quasi imagines significationum quae iam proprie dicuntur vocabula. Atque hoc est quicquid loquimur: etiam ipsum substantia, qualitas, actio: atque adeo

---

[26]This passage is cited and translated by Waswo, "'Ordinary Language Philosophy,'" 265.

ipsum res." Thus he collocates both signifier and signified in
the realm of language, alluding to referentiality (in the real or
external world) only by saying that nothing can be said of
that (external reality) to which a word refers: "Quapropter
nihil interest utrum dicamus, quid est lignum, quid est lapis,
quid ferrum, quid homo, an quid significat lignum, lapis,
ferrum, homo, quorum nihil de res dici potest."[27] Meaning,
it seems, is to be constituted not by external reality reference, but by contextual linguistic usage. Yet Valla persists in
theorizing a distinction between a linguistic object and an
object of reference in reality that his discourse cannot express, while his own linguistic usage undoes the possibility of
such a distinction.[28]

Valla's linguistic philosophy is in many ways exemplified
in the discourse of Rabelais, to the point of persisting in the

[27]Waswo, "'Ordinary Language Philosophy,'" 268: "What the thing is is
what the word means. This equation is Valla's most profound critique of
all the assumptions about the relation of word/object/meaning contained
in the traditional process of signification or representation. It wholly de-
nies both the correspondence theory of truth and the referential theory of
meaning: neither truth nor meaning is to be sought in preextant, a priori
'objects,' about which 'nothing can be said,' since those objects are coextensive with, being created by, the words that name them. Language does not
'represent' a reality but constitutes one."

[28]Referring to a phrase in the argument where Valla writes "itaque res
significat rem: hoc significatur, illud huius est signum: illud non vox, hoc
vox est," Waswo notes: "The old process of signification which located the
meaning of words in the objects, whether perceivable by the senses or laid
up in a Platonic or Christian heaven, that they were said to 'represent,' has
been modified almost out of existence by being reduced to tautology.
Almost—but not quite, for Valla continued to use the vocabulary of the
old process ('What is signified by x,' 'x signifies all things') in ways not
incompatible with the presupposition that meaning was an object of reference instead of a function of use. . . . By examining the 'common usage' of
words, therefore, Valla has indeed arrived at the limits of language—the
vertiginous point at which the perceptual and conceptual categories imposed by that usage must themselves be called into question" ("'Ordinary
Language Philosophy,'" 269).

contradiction that, while meaning is effectively constituted by language and within discourse, some other, external (or "natural," to use Rabelais's term) signifying process must exist that language persistently attempts and fails to express or demonstrate. Unlike Augustinianism, which accepts this failure, this discourse vacillates between a celebration of its own autonomy (philosophically and rhetorically demonstrated by Valla) and an attempt, through language, to arrive at and incorporate an otherness of referentiality. Whereas at first in chapter 9 the conventional nature of linguistic signs is extended to a more general semiotic theory, whereby jus gentium, the rhetorical measure of human truth, determines meaning, a little later a different mode of signifying, resembling Ockham's intuitive and abstractive knowledge, is brought to bear upon the argument:

> Lequel consentement universel n'est faict que nature n'en donne quelque argument et raison, laquelle un chascun peut soubdain par soy comprendre sans aultrement estre instruict de persone—laquelle nous appellons droict naturel.
> Par le blanc, à mesmes induction de nature, tout le monde a entendu joye, liesse, soulas, plaisir et delectation. (72)

> Now this universal agreement would not obtain if Nature did not give some argument and reason for it, which everyone at once can understand for himself without further instruction from anybody—and this we call the Law of Nature. By white, according to this same natural induction, therefore, all the world has understood joy, gladness, solace, pleasure, and delight. (59–60)

The claim for an immediacy of the signified contradicts the rhetorical strategies employed in this chapter to convince the reader of the meaning of the color white. That the case of black precedes that of white already suggests such an awareness, as though its meaning were somehow more obvious than the meaning of white. The passage is framed by a "logi-

cal rule" and by historical and biblical arguments that repeatedly attempt to persuade ("Does not light make all Nature
glad?" [72; 60]; "Read the ancient histories" [74; 60]; "If you
ask why Nature intends the colour white to stand for joy and
gladness, I reply . . . " [76; 61]). The repetition of proofs and
formulas of persuasion undermines the claim for a nature-
induced enlightenment "which everyone can at once understand for himself without further instruction from anybody."
The necessity for rhetorical argument renders moot the point
about natural signification. Were the symbolic meaning of
white evident, no such *querelle* would exist.

Screech has noted the enthymemic (or falsely syllogistic)
structure of the Aristotelian proof presented at the beginning
of chapter 9, which argues that (1) black and white are contraries; (2) joy and sorrow are contraries as well; (3) therefore,
since black signifies sorrow, white must signify joy. Here
Screech accuses Rabelais of having made a "gaffe": "Sadness
and joy are indeed contraries, but are they contrary *in species*?
If he [Rabelais] had read his Thomas he would have known
they are not" ("Emblems and Colours", 79). Gérard Defaux
has suggested in turn that the "gaffe" belongs to Screech and
considers this faulty "proof" one more detail in Rabelais's
portrait of a Sophist (Alcofrybas Nasier) ("Rabelais et son
masque comique," 109–10). Alcofrybas, as Sophist, merely
exemplifies the vacuity of a certain type of syllogistic reasoning: "In fact, everything becomes clear if we remember the
definition of a sophist: he who possesses apparent, but not
real, knowledge" (Defaux, 110, n. 63). Neither necessarily
clarifies this passage. Screech's supposition that Rabelais had
not been reading masks the critic's own oversight: the qualifi-
cation that opposites must be of like "species" (*espece*) appears
four times after the mention of the Aristotelian argument.
"Virtue and vice" and "good and evil" represent the explicit
examples of contraries in species, whereas "joy and sadness"
and "white and black" justifiably correspond, "for these are
physical opposites" (71; 59). Physical opposition need not

necessarily translate a contrary "by species" state but may reflect a rhetorically (rather than logically or dialectically) based opposition having to do with effects only. Enthymemic reasoning need not be confined to its negative definition as faulty logic but may be conceived in positive terms as what "conviegne raisonnablement" (70) ("is reasonably suited") to common opinion.

The strangeness of the proof, played out by the rest of chapter 9, lies primarily in the first premise (Jean Paris, *Rabelais au futur*, 124). It is questionable, whether willfully flawed as a misrepresentation of the Aquinian argument (as Defaux claims) or rhetorically persuasive as an appeal to common opinion, for the petitio principi exposes itself as it were, revealing rather than masking the suppressed assumption that black = sorrow or mourning. The text goes on to declare ("as you well know" [71; 59]) that black means mourning to all people, but it undermines this "well-known fact" by mentioning the exception: "Je excepte les antiques Syracousans et quelques Argives qui avoient l'ame de travers" (71) ("I except the ancient Syracusans and some Argives who had perverse natures" [59]). The exception brings the passage back to the realm of opinion in which white = joy already found itself. This second argument, which claims that black naturally means mourning, then becomes the basis for a corresponding association of white and joy: "By white, according to this same natural induction, therefore, all the world has understood joy, gladness, solace, pleasure, and light" (72; 60).[29]

These arguments, then, do not address logic or provide a formal demonstration of proof. They constitute a series of rhetorical gestures, persuasive strategies that, paradoxically, lay bare the nonlogical foundations of their premises even as they argue a particular point. Aquinian logic is being par-

[29]Rigolot discusses Alcofrybas's arguments in these chapters in "Cratylisme et Pantagruélisme."

odied, but not perforce in the person of the narrator. Instead, rhetoric performs a subtler action on logic—it reveals the latter's own conventional or arbitrary grounding in common opinion (as, for example, the statement that almost all nations associate black with sorrow). Proof in this chapter becomes persuasion, whose tactics are exposed as rhetorical rather than being masked as truth.

The rhetorical posturing of the discourse leads Gérard Defaux to suggest that all of *Gargantua* consists of a series of such antithetical poses, as though the relationship between Scholasticism and humanism were being played out in the text ("Rabelais et son masque comique," 33). In simplifying the text to a series of binary oppositions, however, Defaux excludes the differences that remain beyond these equivalencies—equivalencies that in effect reduce a text to univocality. In his schema, it seems, the only "difference" between the poles of the antitheses is one of the author's hypothesized partisanship, which positively valorizes only one term, yet defines it *in terms of* its other. If indeed the game is Sophistic, how can Defaux claim there is partisanship for one position over the other? *Gargantua*'s debate about language and signification cannot be explained solely in terms of antithetical relationships. The contradiction between "common opinion" and "natural law" is one difference among many that escapes the either/or of positive and negative terms.

Common opinion mediates between a complete arbitrariness, the tyrannical arrogance of him "[who has presumed that] without other proofs and valid arguments the world would regulate its practice by his foolish impostures" (65; 58) and the laws of nature, which "everyone can at once understand for himself without further instruction from anybody" (72; 60). Yet in this comic context, where the commonly agreed-upon meaning is precisely what is in dispute, no final theoretical solution can be arrived at. The fiction asserts a contingent link between sign and meaning (Grandgousier's will) while it argues—with analytical, exegetical, historical, etymological, and medical evidence—for a signification established by universal agreement and aided by nature. The final sentence of the chapter demonstrates this paradox once again: "[I] will briefly say that of course blue signifies heaven and heavenly things, by the same symbolism ["par mesmes symboles"] that makes white stand for joy and pleasure" (78; 62). The joke points both to the obvious "natural" connection between blue and the sky and to the absolutely inimitable chain of interpretations generated by this particular text to produce the symbolic equivalence white = joy. "By the same symbolism" either cannot establish this link (because it establishes a different one) or can generate a chain of signifieds that will arbitrarily produce blue = heavenly things as white = joy. The discourse cannot ground itself in "natural" understanding because it cannot reproduce the gesture by which "everyone can at once understand for himself without further instruction from anybody." It must signify in language, that is, discursively or rhetorically. Unmediated understanding, if possible at all, leaves (as do the "Fanfreluches") an unreadable trace.

These chapters allegorize the possibility of immediate understanding in terms of an ideal origin:

> Bien aultrement faisoient en temps jadys les saiges de Egypte, quant ilz escripvoient par letres qu'ilz appelloyent hieroglyphicques, lesquelles nul n'entendoyt qui n'entendist et un chascun entendoyt qui entendist la vertus, proprieté et nature des choses par ycelles figurées. (67)

> The sages of Egypt followed a very different course, when they wrote in letters that they called hieroglyphs—which none understood who did not understand, and which everyone understood who did understand, the virtue, property, and nature of the things thereby described. (58)

Hieroglyphs here become figures for a transparent symbolism, a system of signs that resists the facile (usually phonetic and punning) confusion of surface (sensible representation) and depth (meaning). They constitute a sign system that clearly includes and excludes, not susceptible to the centrifugality of interpretations that mislead or lead away from meaning, because hieroglyphs are nonlinguistic and do not require interpretation, like the "Pythagorean symbols" of the Prologue. They make up the language of an informed elite, controllable and contained by a community of initiates. The passage expresses nostalgia for a symbolic origin, a pre-Babel state of unity between signifier and signified.[30]

Although nonmediate understanding constitutes a lost and longed for origin, it also menaces, pointing to that absent place where writing and the text no longer exist:

> Si demendez comment par couleur blanche nature nous induict entendre joye et liesse, je vous responds que l'analogie et conformité est telle. Car—comme le blanc exteriorement disgrege et espart la veue, dissolvent manifestement les esperitz visifz . . . —tout ainsi le cueur par joye excellente est interiorement espart et patist manifeste resolution des esperitz vitaulx; laquelle tant peut estre acreue que le cueur demoureroit spolié de son entretien, et par consequent seroit la vie estaincte. (76)

> If you ask why Nature intends the colour white to stand for joy, I reply that the analogy and conformity is like this: As externally white distracts and dazzles the sight, manifestly dissolving the visual spirits, . . . —so internally the heart is dazzled by exceeding joy and suffers a manifest dissolution of the vital spirits, which can be so heightened that it is deprived of its nourishment, and consequently life is extinguished by this excess of joy. (61)

---

[30]The nostalgia for Egypt as a lost origin can almost be called a topos. It is frequently evoked in Plato's *Dialogues*, and Erasmus also addresses the theme. For the importance of hieroglyphs in the Renaissance, see Liselotte Dieckmann, *Hieroglyphics: The History of a Literary Symbol*.

The unmediated natural experience of white and joy is threatening in its excess, and joy may kill one who experiences its direct effect. Without the descent of signs into language, without the necessary prodigality of signification, the text would cease to exist.[31] This death, which Augustine (for whom fallen texts were in a sense already dead) desired as the Second Coming, cannot but threaten this playful yet aggressive rival fiction's life. Unlike the Bible, which derives its authoritative guarantee of referentiality from God, this text, like *Le blason des couleurs* (64), runs the risk of illegitimacy, for it

> a ausé prescrire de son autorité privée quelles choses seroient denotées par les couleurs, ce que est l'usance des tirans qui voulent leur arbitre tenir lieu de raison, non des saiges et sçavens qui par raisons manifestes contentent les lecteurs. (65)

> [has dared] to prescribe by [its] private authority what things shall be denoted by what colours; which is the custom of tyrants who would have their will take the place of reason, not of the wise and learned, who satisfy their readers with display of evidence. (57–58)

Signification, arbitrarily imposed, becomes tyranny, the inauthentic abuse of power. In this nonsacred text, nature provides that guarantee of transcendent truth (or authentic reference) that separates *jus gentium* from human imposition. But whereas the Bible justifies its existence in terms of a nec-

---

[31]Terence Cave explores this aspect of textuality, particularly as it applies to interpretation. See *The Cornucopian Text: Problems of Writing in the French Renaissance*, 111: "Indeed, the perpetual deferment of sense encourages—even constitutes— *copia*, defined as the ability of language to generate detours and deflections. Textual abundance (the extension of the surface) opens up in its turn an indefinite plurality of possible senses. The intention (will, *sententia*) which was supposed to inform the origin of a text and to guarantee the ultimate resolution of its *sensus* remains forever suspended, or submerged, in the flow of words."

essary mediation between man and God, requiring interpretation, nonsacred signs—if everyone can immediately
understand them—require no mediation, and fiction, the
elaboration of linguistic signs, has no reason to exist. The
chapter ends with the threat of death from a plenitude of
immediately comprehended meaning. Literalized clarity
may be blinding ("and you will find the same by experience
when you cross snow-covered mountains, and complain that
you cannot [see well]" [76; 61]). Between the nostalgia for a
silent origin in hieroglyphs (where no text would ever have
been necessary) and the impossibility of that final silence
where sign and signified are one (the death of writing), the
text errs among signifiers, asserting but never "proving" their
sense, persuading but always deferring ("So here I will pull
down my sails, consigning the rest to the book which is to be
entirely devoted to it" [78; 62]).

The narrative's digression into the grounds of signification
constitutes another moment in the struggle between autonomy and legitimate inheritance at work in Rabelais's text. Figured in its very modus operandi are the impossibility of self-
evident signification and the textual desire for an autonomous
world of signifiers. Yet the anxiety remains; a guarantee of
referentiality is needed to limit arbitrariness, the tyranny of
will over reason, to endow the chain of signifiers with a *telos*, a
revelation at the end of the quest for meaning. What Waswo
declares to be "the dilemma of the age—the search for absolute knowledge by means increasingly recognized as contingent" (*Language and Meaning*, 293) plays itself out in the
course of *Gargantua* linguistically as well as thematically. The
overall structure of the Rabelaisian novel enacts the dilemma
as well in its quest narrative, while its continuator "resolves"
the question of linguistic meaning's contingency by supplying
a revelation at the end of the quest.

The concluding chapters of *Gargantua* bring together the
thematic and structural aspects of the narrative's preoccupa-

tion with genealogy as filiation, inheritance, authority, while further exploring the impasses of the quest for transcendent meaning or closure. In these chapters the political also appears, explicitly related to these concerns, as suggested by the Prologue's promise to speak of matters "que concerne nostre religion que aussi l'estat politicq et vie oeconomic-que"(14) ("concerning not only our religion, but also our public and private life" [38]).

The prose-verse alternation in the structure of the Thélème episode links it to the beginning of *Gargantua*, where a similar enigmatic discovery in verse is unearthed and transcribed for the reader. This framing of the book lends an apparent order, one that is reinforced by the thematics of "disinterment and construction" that constitute the Renaissance genealogical enterprise (Thomas M. Greene, "Resurrecting Rome: The Double task of the Humanist Imagination," 48). Thélème seems to provide *Gargantua* with symmetry of form and closure.

The kind of closure performed upon *Gargantua* differs considerably from the ending of *Pantagruel* while returning to a similar theme. The penultimate chapter of *Pantagruel*, like Thélème, discloses another world, set apart from existing society by virtue of being contained within Pantagruel's body. The description abounds in detail, but here its specificity produces a microcosmic mirror image of the world outside:

> Le premier que y trouvay, ce fut ung bon homme qui plantoit des choulx. Dont, tout esbahy, luy demanday: "Mon amy, que fays-tu icy?" "Je plante," dist-il, "des choulx." "Et à quoy ny comment?" dys je. "Hà, monsieur, dist il; nous ne pouvons pas estre tous riches." (*Pantagruel*, chap. 22, 171)

> The first man I met was a good fellow planting cabbages, and in my amazement I asked him: "What are you doing here, my friend?" "I'm planting cabbages," he said. "But how and what

for?" I asked. "Ah, sir," said he: " [. . . ] we can't all be rich."
(273)

Economic disparity, lawlessness, plague—Pantagruel's body is by no means a perfect (or perfectly ordered) world. And although Pantagruel's activities determine to some extent the state of affairs in this other world (as with the plague, which "was a rank breath which had been coming from Pantagruel's stomach, since he ate so much garlic sauce" [172; 274]), the young prince claims no sovereignty over the realm. The world inside the giant's mouth is subject to the organic conditions of the body and not, as in Thélème, to the verbal will of a creator.[32]

The microcosms that temporarily effect closure on Rabelais's first two books emblematize the relation of organicity to structuredness that metaphorically governs the transition from *Pantagruel* to *Gargantua*. The first book reaches completion by revealing, through the organic conceit of the body, that "Pantagruel," as body and as book, contains an entire universe. *Gargantua*, in turn, culminates in the explicit, artificial construction of an alternative verbal world.

Neither "book," however, ends the Rabelaisian text. The alternative worlds in *Pantagruel* and *Gargantua* do not achieve perfection but require further purgation. Both contain mysterious elements at their core that trouble them and impede their completion. The need to resolve these puzzling and "fundamental" obscurities—the "stinking and infectious exhalation, which had recently been rising from the abyss" (172; 274), and the "enigme qui feut trouvé au fondemens de l'abbaye" (*Gargantua*, chap. 55, 305) ("riddle which was found in digging the foundations of the abbey" [160])— provides the narrative deferral that is constitutive of romance. *Pantagruel* stages a scene of restoration: the body is

[32]Thus Pantagruel must ask Alcofrybas about his activities rather than overseeing them, as Gargantua does by decree at Thélème.

purged of its disease, while an appended passage promises the continuation of the chronicle. In *Gargantua* the situation is more complex. On the one hand, Thélème seems a resolution in itself, all the more so because utopia represents the culmination of any vision of social perfectibility. At the end of *Gargantua*, the perfect world has been constructed. The "enigme en prophétie," however, reopens the closure of Thélème and literally deconstructs it, for it forces a return to the foundations of the structure and places them in question. At the same time this poem, which turns on Thélème and unravels it, elegantly resolves *Gargantua*, for it completes the frame. By recalling the "Fanfreluches" of chapter 2, the "enigma" provides *Gargantua* with a paradoxical closure of form. Uncertainty, finally, triumphs over the work, whether in the form of a threatening *non-sens* or in the undecidability of interpretation that is the subject of its last chapter.

The negativity that frames the body of the text places the status of the abbey in question. Critics have not ceased to argue the "two sides" of Thélème: static parody or Renaissance ideal. On the one hand, scholars such as Fernand Desonay assert that "Thélème is nothing but a farce" ("En relisant 'L'Abbaye de Thélème'" [102]), while the other side sees in Thélème the Renaissance belief in human perfectibility on earth: "The abbey of Thélème, built for Frère Jean as a reward for his military service, represents the culmination of that evolutionary process, both individual and social, which this volume is at pains to trace. It stands clearly as an answer to the violence and the stupidity of Picrocholine aggression, but more than that, it represents a hypothetical form in which human experience on earth might flower into delight" (Greene, *Rabelais*, 48). The paradoxical nature of Thélème gives rise to certain speculations. Was Thélème, as M. A. Screech suggests, written early on in the composition of *Gargantua*, then juxtaposed with the "enigme en prophétie" after the persecutions of October 1534 and January 1535 (*Rabelais*, 200)? In this case Thélème would, in fact, represent a utopian moment (and perhaps a will to closure) in the progress of the narrative. Revisions made of comic passages, rendering them more explicit, lend support to the hypothesis of an early "serious" version of these episodes. That Thélème acquired more humorous characteristics might indicate a growing skepticism with regard to the possibility of practicing a liberal Erasmian Christianity in an atmosphere of inquisitorial censorship.

A brief comparison of these descriptive details and their revisions demonstrates the heightened absurdity of Thélème's physical layout in the definitive edition. The first such detail occurs in chapter 51 (Abel Lefranc ed., 53):

| | |
|---|---|
| Ledict bastiment estoit cent foys plus magnificque que n'est Bonivet; car en icelluy estoient neuf cens trente et deux chambres. . . . (Calder, Screech, and Saulnier ed., 286) | Ledict bastiment estoit cent foys plus magnificque que n'est Bonivet, ne Chambourg, ne Chantilly; car en ycelluy estoient neuf mille troys cens, trente et deux chambres. . . (*Gargantua* 2:406) |

The said building was a hundred times more magnificent than Bonnivet [or Chambord or Chantilly]. For it contained [nine hundred thirty-two] nine thousand, three hundred and thirty-two apartments. (152)

Enumerative comparison and hyperbole collaborate in the 1542 edition to signal the text's exaggeration. A similar addition of detail in chapter 53 (Abel Lefranc ed., chap. 55) renders the galleries of the "manor" patently absurd:

Le dedans du logis sus ladicte basse court estoit sus gros pilliers de cassidoine et porphyre, à beaux ars d'antique, au dedans des quelz estoient belles gualeries, longues et amples, aornées de painctures, de cornes de cerfz et aultres choses spectables. (Calder, Screech, and Saulnier ed., 294)

Le dedans du logis sus ladicte basse court estoit sus gros pilliers de cassidoine et porphyre, à beaux ars d'antique, au dedans desquelz estoient belles gualeries, longues et amples, aornées de pinctures et cornes de cerfz, licornes, rhinoceros, hippopotames, dens de elephans at aultres choses spectables. (*Gargantua* 2:418)

The rooms of the building above this first court stood upon stout pillars of chalcedony and porphyry, with magnificent old-fashioned arches between; and inside were fine, long, spacious galleries, decorated with paintings, with horns of stags, [unicorns, rhinoceroses, and hippopotami, with elephants' tusks] and with other remarkable objects. (155)

These additions render apparent the failure of Thélème as social ideal, through the ironic distance established between reader and text by means of the absurd detail. Laughter disrupts the seriousness of the abbey and forces these chapters to be read in a different light.

# 4

# Thélème: Temporality,
# Utopia, Supplement

Thélème is a monument to failed desire, with humor serving to situate and accentuate the author's ironic stance. Several approaches may be taken to elucidate this failure. On the one hand, the theme of filiation, which allegorizes the genealogical problematic at work structurally in the text, produces Thélème as a reaction to the father-son relationship developed in the course of the Picrocholine battles. If the Thélème chapters are to be understood in any sense as evolving out of the rest of *Gargantua*, then the Picrocholine episode must be read in connection with Thélème. Most critics have, however, accepted the desire for separation, an effect of the text that defines Thélème as a utopian construction within the text itself, and have read these chapters apart from the rest of the narrative. M. A. Screech writes, for example: "Thelema is in fact rather crudely attached to the general course of the story. Theoretically designed for the Friar to order in his own terms as recompense for his bravery in battle, it in fact develops under Gargantua's dictation, with the monk playing a very minor rôle indeed. It bears the mark of having been written separately and then loosely attached" ("The Sense of Rabelais's 'Énigme en

Prophétie' [*Gargantua* LVIII]," 393). It is unclear (for he does not develop this point) where Screech locates the telltale mark that separates Thélème, but I suggest that it is Thélème as genre, that is, utopia, that produces the effect of detachment from the narrative line. "Utopian thought is incarnated in a regime of writing and representation, specific and unassimilable to other forms of literary writing or scientific deduction. . . . The utopian city is laid out in a single closed space where everything is exposed simultaneously and offered to the viewer, who therefore contemplates a veritable map" (Jean-Jacques Wunenburger, *L'Utopie, ou La Crise de l'imaginaire*, 144). The mapping out of Thélème, and its detachment from a narrative continuum is, as Wunenburger suggests, a constitutive part of the utopian machinery. Nevertheless, contrary to Screech's opinion, a thematic or allegorical relationship can, I think, be seen between Thélème and the chapters preceding it.

Like *Pantagruel*, *Gargantua* culminates in a war waged upon Gargantua's territory, forcing the son to return to his homeland to fight. In *Pantagruel*, the father has already been lost (chap. 15, 125–26), and his absence, as the absence of the law (and of the proper name), is figured by the king whose name, a common noun, means disorder: Anarche. The enemy represents another shadowy doubling, for like Pantagruel's family, it is a race of giants. In the midst of this inverted world, an oedipal battle takes place (see chap. 3). Loupgarou challenges Pantagruel to one-on-one combat. His club functions as semiotic indicator of the phallic nature of their conflict:

> Alors Loupgarou s'adressa à Pantagruel avecques une masse toute d'acier, pesante neuf mille sept cens quintaulx, d'acier de Calibbes, au bout de laquelle y avoit treze poinctes de dyamens, dont la moindre estoit aussi grosse comme la plus grande cloche de Nostre-Dame de Paris—il s'en falloit par avanture l'espesseur d'ung ongle, ou au plus (que je ne mente)

d'ung doz de ces cousteaulx qu'on appelle *couppe-oreille*: mais pour ung petit, ne avant ne arrière. Et estoit phéée, en manière que jamais ne povoit rompre, mais au contraire, tout ce qu'il en touchoit rompoit incontinent. (*Pantagruel*, chap. 19, 152–53)

Werewolf then faced up to Pantagruel with a club of solid steel weighing nine hundred and seventy tons, one hundred-weight. It was of Chalybean steel, and at the tip were thirteen diamond studs, the smallest of which was as big as the largest bell in Notre-Dame at Paris—or smaller, perhaps, by the thickness of a nail, or at most, to be quite truthful, by the blunt edge of one of those knives they call ear-cutters, but not a bit more than that either at front or back—and it was so enchanted that it would never break. On the contrary, everything that he touched with it shattered immediately. (261)

This overdetermined description supplies the phallic connections: Loupgarou's club is implicitly larger than Pantagruel's, for the latter's weapon receives no description at all. The repetition of "steel" underscores its weight and durability; it is decorated with gigantic jewels, which the mock debate about size and thickness links to other anatomical parts: "nail" ("ongle"), "back," and "ear." The phrase "ung doz de ces cousteaulx qu'on appelle *couppe-oreille*," though referring to the blunt edge of a knife, nevertheless seems to place curiously appropriate emphasis on weaponry's castrating function. Finally, the club is described as possessed of magical potency, the kind that turns out to be nearly sufficient to destroy Pantagruel and in any case renders his club impotent:

Ce que voyant, Pantagruel, qui s'amusoit à tirer sadicte masse, qui tenoit en terre entre le roc, luy court sus, et luy vouloit avaller la teste tout net: mais son mast, de male fortune, toucha ung peu au fust de la masse de Loupgarou, qui estoit

phéé (comme avons dit devant). Par ce moyen, son mast luy rompit à troys doigts de la poignée. (155)[1]

Seeing Werewolf engaged in pulling out his same club, which was stuck in the ground, deep in the cleft of the rock, Pantagruel ran at him, intending to strike his head right off. But, by ill-luck, his mast brushed against the handle of Werewolf's club, which was—as we have already said—enchanted; and as a result the mast broke off, three fingers' breadth from the shaft. (263)

The "son," however, emerges victorious; the decisive moment comes when Pantagruel, having killed Loupgarou, uses his body as a weapon to club the other giants to death. Phallic identification takes place; by a series of synecdochic equations, Pantagruel is able to claim possession of the superior potency of the (evil) father's phallus. The other father figure, the king Anarche, receives humiliating punishment at the hands of Panurge. His fate reveals his castration, for he is emasculated by a woman: "But I have been told since that his wife pounds him like plaster; and the poor fool dares not defend himself, he is so simple" (chap. 22, 169; 272).

There are many parallels between this episode and the events that transpire in *Gargantua*. In both cases an initiatory battle takes place in which the son must prove himself through a displaced battle with the father. In *Pantagruel* the son replaces the father in all the latter's functions (the famous letter of chap. 8 prefigures this). *Gargantua*, however, represses the moment of explicit filial succession, for Grandgousier remains present until the episode of Thélème. This time there is only one father substitute, Picrochole, who like

[1]In the passage just preceding, another oedipal detail of the conflict is made literal. For the war itself is being waged over the territory of the mother, Utopie, and Loupgarou at this point violently thrusts his club deep into the ground, splitting a rock that then spews forth fire (155).

Anarche incarnates the symbolic aspect of the father as king. The more threatening sexual struggle with Loupgarou is here rendered unnecessary (or censored) by the father's presence.

Grandgousier himself, with his emphasis on the strong kinship ties between himself and his adversary and by his reluctance to fight in *Gargantua*, makes the comparisons that identify Picrochole as a father figure:

> "Holos! holos! (dist Grandgousier), qu'est cecy, bonnes gens? Songé je, ou si vray est ce qu'on me dict? Picrochole, mon amy ancien de tout temps, de toute race et alliance, me vient il assaillir? Qui le meut? Qui le poinct? Qui le conduict? Qui l'a ainsi conseillé?" (*Gargantua*, chap. 26, 177)

> "Alas, alas!" cried Grandgousier. "What is this, good people? Am I dreaming, or is what they tell me true? Picrochole, my old and perpetual friend, united to me by blood and by alliance, has he come to attack me? Who is inciting him? Who is urging him on? Who is leading him? Who has advised him to do this?" (102)

When Ulrich Gallet is sent to plead with Picrochole, he reminds the king of the intimate ties uniting the two leaders (chap. 29, 184–85; 104–5). The strange irrationality of Picrochole's breach of alliance suggests the substitutive function of this figure: one way or another, the king must be replaced, for as Grandgousier himself suggests, he has become too old and weak to rule:

> "Las! ma viellesse ne requeroyt dorenavant que repous, et toute ma vye n'ay rien tant procuré que paix. Mais il fault, je le voy bien, que maintenant de harnoys je charge mes pauvres espaules lasses et foibles, et en ma main tremblante je preigne la lance et la masse pour secourir et guarantir mes pauvres subjectz." (chap. 26, 178)

"Alas, all that my old age called for was repose. All my life I have sought peace above all things. But now I plainly see that I shall have to load my weak, tired shoulders with armour, and take the lance and the mace in my trembling hand, to help and protect my poor subjects." (102)

Yet for reasons that will be discussed later on, open aggression against the father is censored, and it is his double, Picrochole, from whose hands power must be wrested. The danger Picrochrole represents, according to the text, is unbridled imperialism, the will to power over all, as chapter 31 demonstrates. This is true from the perspective of the son, whose name the text bears.[2]

The key figure in this episode who performs a doubling or substitutive function for Gargantua, as Panurge does for Pantagruel, is Frère Jean. Unlike Panurge, this friend receives paternal sanction, for it is Grandgousier who inspires in his son the desire to know Frère Jean:

Grandgouzier commencea raconter la source et la cause de la guerre meue entre luy et Picrochole, et vint au poinct de narrer comment Frère Jean des Entommeures avoit triomphé à la defence du clous de l'abbaye, et le loua au dessus des prouesses de Camille, Scipion, Pompée, Cesar et Themistocles. Adoncques requist Gargantua que sus l'heure feust en-

[2]This is implicitly true of the symbolic father, but all the potentially threatening attributes of the father have been displaced onto Picrochole. Thus Grandgousier appears to incarnate the very opposite of imperialist aspiration. If the son in this text seems more hostile than Pantagruel, it is because *Gargantua* is textually a son (the book comes after *Pantagruel*) whose desire (and destiny) is to become the father. Further evidence that Gargantua is here conceived as a son and later becomes the father is provided by chapter 52 of the *Tiers Livre*, where it says that "*Pantagruel* ordered all the doors, gates, windows, gutters, weather-moulding, and facings of Thélème to be made of it [larix]" (my emphasis) (353; 432).

voyé querir, affin qu'avecques luy on consultast de ce qu'estoit à faire. (chap. 37, 221)

Grandgousier began to recount the origins and cause of the war being waged between him and Picrochole; and when he came to the point of narrating how Friar John of the Hashes had triumphed at the defence of the abbey-close, he commended his prowess as above that of Camillus, Scipio, Pompey, Caesar, and Themistocles. Then Gargantua desired that the friar should be sent for at once, so that he might be consulted on what was next to be done. (123)

Frère Jean, like Panurge, is a trickster figure, the shadow of the hero, one who transgresses in language as well as in action.[3] He, for example, performs the most bloodthirsty killings, in sharp contrast to Grandgousier's repeated reluctance to shed blood. In the letter to Gargantua, Grandgousier declares, "Our measures will be carried out with the least possible bloodshed" (chap. 27, 181; 103), thus de facto constraining his son's violence. The monk, however, is under no such constraints. In one scene he does not even hesitate to kill a soldier who has demanded mercy:

"Monsieur le Priour, mon bon petit Seigneur le Priour, je me rends à vous!—Et je te rends (dis le Moyne) à tous les diables." Lors d'un coup luy transchit la teste, luy coupant le test sus les os petreux, et enlevant les deux os bregmatis et la commissure sagittale avecques grande partie de l'os coronal, ce que faisant luy tranchit les deux meminges et ouvrit profondement les deux posterieures ventricules du cerveau; et demoura le craine pendant sus les espaules à la peau du per-

[3]For a branch of the genealogical tree to which the trickster figure (and so Panurge and Frère Jean) belongs, see the article by Henry Louis Gates, Jr., "The 'Blackness of Blackness': A Critique of the Sign and the Signifying Monkey." The signifying monkey is a trickster figure; its many talents include verbal play, punning, and rhetorical fluency, linking it even more closely with these Rabelaisian figures.

icrane par darriere, en forme d'un bonnet doctoral, noir par
dessus, rouge par dedans. Ainsi tomba roidde mort en terre.
(chap. 42, 248)[4]

"Oh, oh, hey, no, my lord Prior, my dear kind lord, my noble
Prior, I surrender to you!" "And I surrender you to all the
devils," said the monk. Then at one blow he sliced his head,
cutting his skull over the temple-bone and taking off the two
parietal bones and the sagittal suture, together with a great
part of the frontal bone; and in doing this he cut through the
two membranes and made a deep opening in the posterior
lobes of his brain. So his cranium remained hanging on his
shoulders by the skin of his pericranium, falling backwards
like a doctor's cap, black outside and red within. And he fell to
the ground stark dead. (134)

Thus Frère Jean, on one level, serves as substitute for
Gargantua. The friendship between them seems to arise as
instantaneously as that between Panurge and Pantagruel,
each of the two mourning and rejoicing when the other is lost
and then found.[5] Finally, during the decisive battles in each
book, Panurge and Frère Jean intervene to tip the scales.
These double figures replace the projected superior strength
of the father, particularly of his name, to provide the addi-
tional assistance the hero needs—in *Pantagruel* the hero calls
out to Panurge, who does not directly participate ("'Ho, Panurge, where are you?'" [*Pantagruel*, 156; 263]), while in *Gar-*

[4]Note how the verbal pleasure of recounting this in anatomical detail
reinforces the notion that Frère Jean delights in his massacre.

[5]For their meeting, see *Gargantua* chap. 37, 221. In chapter 42, when
Frère Jean cannot immediately help Gargantua against the enemy, his
reaction is sorrow: "Seeing them thus depart in disorder, the monk guessed
that they were going to charge on Gargantua and his men; and he was
strangely sad that he could not come to their assistance" (247; 133). Later,
during a feast, Gargantua mourns the absence of Frère Jean: "But [Gargan-
tua] was so upset that the monk had not turned up that he would neither
drink nor eat" (251; 135–36).

*gantua*, Gargantua's pronouncement of the monk's name signals Picrochole's defeat:

> Mais Picrochole pensoit que le secours luy venoit de la ville, et par oultrecuydance se hazarda plus que devant, jusques à ce que Gargantua s'escrya: "Frere Jean, mon amy, Frere Jean, en bon heur soyez venu." Adoncques, congnoissent Picrochole et ses gens que tout estoit desesperé, prindrent la fuyte en tous endroictz. (chap. 46, 268–69)

> But Picrochole thought that this was help coming to him from the town, and foolhardily took greater risks than ever, until the moment when Gargantua shouted: "Friar John, my friend, Friar John, welcome! You've come at a good moment!" Upon this Picrochole and his men recognized that all was lost, and took to flight on every side. (144)

When the war ends Picrochole flees and, in a characteristic reversal of status, is humiliated by becoming a porter. Grandgousier holds a feast for Gargantua and his companions, doling out rewards to them for their service in battle. At this point he is still the supreme authority. Chapter 50 then opens with the following: "There only remained the monk to be provided for, and Gargantua wanted to make him abbot of Seuilly, but he refused the post" (280; 149). In one brief sentence, a transfer of power occurs and Gargantua assumes the role of king and legislator for this "new world."

Unable to claim possession of the father's domain or to engulf the world (the microcosm in Pantagruel's mouth being a kind of biological literalization of imperialism), Gargantua creates his own, apart from the rest of the text, mapping out or spatializing his desire in a concrete wish fulfillment. Claude-Gilbert Dubois discusses the logic of paternal identification that structures utopia in his *Problèmes de l'utopie*. He stresses, however, the point I am trying to make that utopia marks a failure to appropriate the father's identity (what belongs to the father), producing the schizoid and autistic effect of a separation of worlds so often remarked by critics of this text. "In fact, utopia results from a failed attempt to identify, and one that proceeds by fraudulent means: the utopian writer, unable to arrive at the paternal image, adapts it, tames it, molds it to his size, recreating a science or a society according to his own desires. In this way the utopian writer expresses an inclination toward adaptation, but also a failure to adapt that leads him to make the world conform to his desires rather than adapt to the world" (*Problèmes de l'utopie*, 6). Frère Jean, as Gargantua's double and paternal emissary of sorts, becomes the agent for the creation of this world, which both rivals the father's kingdom (indirectly, since it is Frère Jean who serves as mouthpiece to Gargantua's desire) and unfolds under his sanction (since Frère Jean, who has Grandgousier's blessing, must also be provided for).

The opening passages of chapter 50 ("Comment Gargantua feist bastir pour le Moyne l'abbaye de Theleme") illustrate Gargantua's "takeover" of the abbey of Thélème. As many have pointed out, this takes place through a pronominal effacement of Frère Jean as the subject of the desire to found Thélème. After the monk makes his request to "'found an abbey after my own devices'" (280; 150), the text continues:

> La demende pleut à Gargantua, et offrit tout son pays de Theleme, jouste la riviere de Loyre, à deux lieues de la grande forest du Port Huault. Et requist à Gargantua qu'il instituast sa religion au contraire de toutes aultres. (281)

> This request pleased Gargantua, and he offered him all his land of Thélème, beside the River Loire, to within six miles of the great forest of Port-Huault. The monk then requested Gargantua to institute his religious order in an exactly contrary way to all others. (150)

As Jean-Yves Pouilloux has noted of this passage, "a certain interference is at work that produces uncertainty about the identity of the speaking subject," which in effect shifts the focus from Frère Jean (who disappears in the ensuing chapters) to Gargantua as founder and legislator of the abbey ("Notes sur l'abbaye de Thélème," 201). Another change takes place in the transition from the monk's wish to Gargantua's command. The creation of the abbey, initially presented as a positive project—"to found an abbey after my own devices"—becomes instead a negative enterprise, undertaken in opposition to what exists: "The monk then requested Gargantua to institute his religious order in an exactly contrary way to all others."

The construction of an antisystem in opposition to established order is a familiar theme of filial rebellion (which should not be confused with subversion). What lends Thélème its specificity, its finality, its self-sufficiency and its closure is the way filiation in these chapters narrates allegorically the fable of the book itself. *Pantagruel*, written first and bearing an original name in the sense that the story of Pantagruel had not been written before, claims textual primacy in the genealogical line that includes both tradition and the Rabelaisian sequence. Defined as a story of the son, *Pantagruel* has no need to assume the burden of primacy, for it is the second book in the Rabelaisian system, the book of the son. It must equal and supersede the first, but it does not need to occupy the origin of the work. *Gargantua*, on the other hand, must work with greater anxiety against its own belatedness. The name itself signals a repetition; the chronicles preceding it render problematic any will to priority. Furthermore, while being the story of the father it nevertheless comes after *Pantagruel*. The secondariness of *Gargantua* comes to be effaced in two ways: first, by the reference in the Prologue to the "certain books of our invention, such as *Gargantua, Pantagruel*" (11; 37), and in chapter 1: "For knowledge of the Gargantua's genealogy and of the antiquity of his descent, I refer you to the great Pantagrueline Chronicle, from which you will learn at greater length how the giants were born into this world, and how from them by a direct line issued Gargantua" (19; 41), whereby Rabelais eliminates outside tradition and cites himself as precedent for the book. The second effacement occurs in the reordering of the first two books so that *Gargantua* appears to come before *Pantagruel*.[6]

The narrative problem of *Gargantua*'s (non) priority is symptomatic of a larger narrative, historical, and philosophical paradox of origins that Jacques Derrida has written of as "originary delay."[7] Vincent Descombes provides a condensed summary of the event:

> If *from the origin onwards* (each time there is origin), from the "first time" onwards, there were no *différance*, then the first time would not be the "first time," for it would not be followed by a "second time"; and if the "first time" were the "only time," it would not be at the origin of anything at all. In a way which is perhaps a little dialectical, but not at all improper, it must be said that the first is not the first if there is not a second to follow it. Consequently, the second is not that which merely arrives, like a latecomer, *after* the first, but that which permits the first to be the first. (*Modern French Philosophy*, 145)

[6]"Alcofribas's text of the son Pantagruel originates before that of the father Gargantua; when the book of the father follows, it frees the son from his legendary origins in the Grandes Chronicques and inserts him in a fictional filiation which is guaranteed by the order in which the two books are meant to be read, from father to son. . . . No longer can the question be posed in terms of either-or; the origin of the book cannot be considered to emerge entirely from historical or biographical factors, nor wholly from within the writing itself, determined by its own form and structure." See Richard Regosin, "The Ins(ides) and Outs(ides) of Reading: Plural Discourse and the Question of Interpretation in Rabelais," 67.

[7]For discussions of this concept see Jacques Derrida, "Freud and the Scene of Writing," in *Writing and Difference*; also *Of Grammatology*, esp. 269–316.

This principle implies (and this is particularly clear in Derrida's reading of Freud's theory of the return of the repressed) the repetition of the nonoriginariness of the origin that persists as trace from the origin on.[8]

The narrative construction of Rabelais's first two books makes literal this principle of nonprinciples. For *Gargantua* to attain priority, it must be followed by and must imply *Pantagruel*. There is no father without a son (*sic*)—for the son constitutes fatherhood as origin. The origin is necessary, of course, insofar as the books propose a narrative of the history of the giants in general and of Pantagruel, as hero figure, in particular.[9] *Pantagruel* and *Gargantua* repeatedly rehearse the scene of the origin in a repressed, or allegorical, mode. *Pantagruel*'s double move is to repress its nonorigin in the father work and to reenact, in fragmentary form, the scene of killing off the father. Pantagruel and *Pantagruel* replace a nonexistent father and reestablish the priority of the son. *Gargantua* cannot function this way. The son cannot replace the father, for Gargantua must somehow constitute an absolute origin for Pantagruel (which he does, as the figure of authority and as law, in *Pantagruel* and in the *Tiers Livre*).

*Gargantua* cannot, in the economy of the text, overcome its belatedness except within another system, just as Gargantua

8"The trace is the erasure of selfhood, of one's own presence, and is constituted by the threat or anguish of its irremediable disappearance, the disappearance of its disappearance. . . . This erasure of the trace . . . is the very structure which makes possible . . . something which can be called repression in general, the original synthesis of original repression and secondary repression, repression 'itself.'" See "Freud and the Scene of Writing," in *Writing and Difference*, 230. See also Descombes, *Modern French Philosophy*, 148.

9See my previous chapters on the genealogy of the giant and of the book. Patricia Tobin makes the point as follows: "Science, philosophy, history all become possible once a beginning or origin can be sanctioned in such a way that all future stages in the process that follows can be referred back to that initial authority." See *Time and the Novel: The Genealogical Imperative*, 19.

cannot be originary (within *Gargantua*) except by creating another origin. *Fiat* Thélème. The textual belatedness of Thélème is overcome by its closure, its finality, its quality as a world to end all worlds, a utopia. *Gargantua*'s answer to the textual world of romance (including *Pantagruel*), to the priority-without-origin of the anonymous chronicle of Gargantua, is the positing of a new, specifically Renaissance world. In this way Thélème "supplements" the Gargantuan text. Critics complain of its excess, its appended quality, just as the supplement "is all too rapidly likened to a surplus, a supernumerary appendixed to the integral whole. As if, in other words, there were one already complete whole and, *outside* of it, the supplement" (Descombes, *Modern French Philosophy*, 147–48).

In fact Thélème, though affixed to the end of the book and constituting a system outside that of *Gargantua*'s world, functions according to the logic of the supplement, supplying *Gargantua* with something that never was, thereby testifying to its defect.[10] Thélème thus marks the absence of Gargantua as origin, as originator, so necessary to the logic of the narrative that follows. What the metaphysical genealogy of the

---

[10]"If the supplement is something rather than nothing, it must expose the *defect* of the whole, for any whole that is able to accommodate the addition of a supplement testifies thereby to the lack of something *within* itself. The supplement outside stands for the missing part of the whole. It is because the whole does not succeed in *being everything* that a supplement from without must be added, in order to compensate for its defective totality" (Descombes, *Modern French Philosophy*, 148). See also Jacques Derrida, *Of Grammatology*, 144–45: "For the concept of the supplement . . . harbors within itself two significations whose cohabitation is as strange as it is necessary. The supplement adds itself, it is a surplus, a plenitude enriching another plenitude, the *fullest measure* of presence. It cumulates and accumulates presence. . . . But the supplement supplements. It adds only to replace. It intervenes or insinuates itself *in-the-place-of*; if it fills, it is as if one fills a void. If it represents and makes an image, it is by the anterior default of a presence." Also cited in Josué Harari, ed., *Textual Strategies: Perspectives in Post-Structuralist Criticism*, 33–34.

text erases, the absence of Gargantua (and *Gargantua*) "at the origin," persists in Thélème as trace. And as if to punctuate the place of usurpation or replacement constituted by Thélème, the chapters begin by reenacting Gargantua's inaugural usurpation, for he takes the place of Frère Jean in the founding of the abbey. Yet this transgression or replacement itself becomes law. The narrative voice is impersonal; not only does Gargantua occupy the place of the law in his self-substitution for the father, he becomes the law.[11]

Critics have argued whether Thélème can properly be called a utopia. Michel Beaujour insists on the difference between this "idealistic feudal system," motivated by a sovereign will (Gargantua's) and partaking of fairyland, and utopia proper (*Le Jeu de Rabelais*, 105). As he notes, the word "utopia" itself is never used in connection with the abbey. Utopie, in Rabelais, is a proper name, the homeland of Badebec, Pantagruel's mother, which passes into Gargantua's possession in *Gargantua*. Utopie is barely described; its unspecified location, susceptibility to invasion, and magical, wombish qualities link it more closely with the arcadian or "faerie" regions of medieval romance than with the austere social organization created by Thomas More.

Thélème, on the other hand, resembles utopian constructions in several ways, both rhetorically and structurally. First of all, it seems to stand apart from the rest of the book structurally, descriptively, and thematically, much as More's island occupies a separate book in the treatise entitled *Utopia*. Raoul Morçay publishes Thélème as a separate work; Beaujour describes it as an "appendix."[12] Pierre Jourda also notes

---

[11]"Utopia posits transgression as a norm: it gives a sense of absoluteness to the transgression of an institution. Subversion appears in utopia as the figurative representation of the law, as the norm. In other words, in utopia transgression is not relative to a law, it has become law" (Louis Marin, *Utopiques: Jeux d'espaces*, 110).

[12]See *L'Abbaye de Thélème*, ed. Raoul Morçay, and Michel Beaujour, *Le Jeu de Rabelais*, 89.

the discontinuity, while M. A. Screech supplies reasons for his sense of the episode as a *non sequitur*:

> The prose chapters are carefully written, though not without minor blemishes, nor without the odd construction suggestive of an early date of composition. The original conception of the abbey may date from the period of the 1533 *Pantagruel*, where Rabelais first revealed his concern with *liberté totalle*. There certainly are aesthetic tensions which give rise to the hypothesis (which may seem cogent) that the prose chapters of Thelema were written without any idea of persecutions being in Rabelais's mind. (*Rabelais*, 199)

Other factors, internal to the text, isolate these chapters from the rest of *Gargantua*. Thélème has delineated boundaries. Although Gargantua declares there will be no walls (chap. 50), the description of the construction necessitates their projection onto the arrangement of towers: "Le bastiment feut en figure exagone, en telle faczon que à chascun angle estoyt bastie une grosse tour ronde à la capacité de soixante pas en diametre, et estoient toutes pareilles en grosseur et protraict" (chap. 51, 285–86) ("The building was hexagonal in shape and so planned that at each angle was built a large circular tower, sixty yards in diameter; and all were alike in size and architecture" [151]). Thus, geographically, the hexagon of Thélème separates inside from outside, sets apart a utopian space. Narration moves into description, and unlike the rest of the book, where humor erupts, exploding passages of sustained seriousness, these chapters intermingle straightforward description with subtle irony or comic paradox. There are moments when the discourse undermines the verisimilitude it constructs by means of detailed description, as does More's text, particularly in the letter to Giles: "According to my own recollection, Hythlodaeus declared that the bridge which spans the river Anydrus at Amaurotum is five hundred paces in length. But my

John says that two hundred must be taken off, for the river there is not more than three hundred paces in breadth. Please recall the matter to mind. If you agree with him, I shall adopt the same view and think myself mistaken" (*Utopia*, Surtz ed., 5). Or again, concerning the location of Utopia: "We forgot to ask, and he forgot to say, in what part of the new world Utopia lies. I am sorry this point was omitted, and I would be willing to pay a considerable sum to purchase that information" (*Utopia*, 6). Rabelais's mensurational humor remains unmarked, not escaping, of course, the Scholastic diligence of his editors, who point out the impossibility of constructing 9,332 habitable rooms within the given dimensions of the abbey.[13]

More farcical elements of Thélème are embedded in the description so that a very different comic effect is produced than in the previous chapters, one that is more ironic: "Au milieu de la basse court estoyt une fontaine magnificque de bel alabastre; au dessus les troys Graces, avecques cornes d'abondance, et gettoient l'eau par les mamelles, bouche, aureilles, oieulx, et aultres ouvertures du corps" (chap. 53, 294) ("In the middle of the first court was a magnificent fountain of fine alabaster, on the top of which were the three Graces with horns of abundance, spouting water from their breasts, mouths, ears, eyes, and other physical orifices" [155]). While for the most part the fountain conforms to those grotesque Mannerist fantasies found in the Tivoli gardens and at Fontainebleau, the final act of inclusion, "and other physical orifices," descends to the crude with a (barely) euphemistic formulation. Finally, as in *Utopia*, the text employs another device to undermine the description. Just as More's

[13]The editors of the Abel Lefranc 1542 edition include the following note: "Fantasy is not absent from this architectural description. The 9332 rooms or rather 'apartments' of Thélème would not have been even a meter each in width, in spite of the vast dimensions of the edifice as a whole" (*Gargantua*, 2:406, n. 38). The revised edition is in fact more marked than the first; the description uses hyperbole to enhance its *invraisemblance*.

language abounds in negatives, so the language of Thélème uses another kind of enumeration to produce an ironic effect. "Beau" and "tout" are constantly reiterated throughout chapter 53. Leaving aside for the moment the interpretive consequences of these comic effects, it seems that Thélème operates in a different comic register from the rest of *Gargantua*, more subtle and perhaps concealed, one that resembles the strategies of humor deployed in *Utopia*.

The thematic concerns of the Thélème chapters are analogous to those of utopian literature: the abbey is founded in specific opposition to existing social institutions in order to criticize them and, as their opposite, remains structurally similar to monasteries. The same structural features are compared and found opposite in content. Here too Thélème resembles *Utopia*, for critics have found allusions to England in the description of the island, while in Amaurotum there hides an epithet for foggy London, the "darkling city" (*Utopia*, 59, 61). Hypermathematization, whereby description is minutely and numerically detailed, constitutes another distinguishing feature of utopic constructions, producing effects of the real or of rationality (Dubois, *Problèmes de l'utopie*, 6).

Thélème is a fictive, projective entity, a place set apart from reality in a relatively timeless framework. Beaujour shows how the frequent use of the narrative imperfect conveys this sense of ahistoricity and immutability: "The building, completely furnished, is already there—as if by magic. A simple modulation of verb tenses situates the construction of the abbey in a vague and hazy past. Furthermore, the use of the imperfect suggests a 'fairy' climate: an unsituated voice recounts the discovery of a marvellous edifice that already existed at its [the voice's] arrival" (*Jeu de Rabelais*, 91). Although the unreality of Thélème may seem to link it with other imaginary lands in the faerie tradition or with the "pays de Cocagne," a final aspect of the abbey brings it closer to the utopian tradition than some of its more fantastic ancestors. This thematic element (which could be included in the

category of verisimilitude, another factor distancing Thélème from its fairyland counterparts) is a preoccupation with
social organization. Thélème poses an alternative to existing
society that, by its minutely specified detail, demands consideration (however much in bad faith its author might seem).
Social, political, and economic factors are taken into account—
there is an attempt to leave no ground uncovered in this
microcosmic world.

The opening chapter of the Thélème episode makes explicit its polemic stance as a discourse having its referent in
society, in the "certain monasteries in [of] this world," which
the text itself constructs in order to oppose. It is this aspect of
Thélème, as a political figure rather than merely an ideal
representation, to which I now turn, basing my analysis on
the groundwork provided by Louis Marin's *Utopiques: Jeux
d'espaces*. Marin's aphoristic statement that "Utopia is an ideological critique of ideology" (*Utopiques*, 249) can elucidate the
contradictoriness of Thélème, its undecidabilty, as a function
of rhetorical procedures that are necessary and inevitable in
the construction of a utopia. An analysis of the conflict of
ideological registers, of the strategy of utopia, may better
clarify the "outcome" of Thélème in terms of the novel itself,
in relation to both the prophetic riddle and the subsequent
Rabelaisian books.

The abbey of Thélème combines a humanist critique of
religious institutions with a glorification of feudal values, the
latter being developed less explicitly but perhaps more consi-
stently. The initial chapter of the episode, the founding narrative of the abbey and the declaration of its laws, constructs
the primary referent for Thélème. The construction of such
a referent and its identification with the "real," followed by
the subsequent negation or neutralization of that real, constitute the political force and the specificity of utopia, the
way it operates as a critique and sets itself apart from other

genres.[14] This occurs not only in the repeated construction/ cancellation or negation procedure that operates throughout chapter 50, but also in the text's continual allusions to France, in the form of place-names or comparisons. Thus Frère Jean is first offered the directorship of two "existing" abbeys: "He next proposed to give him the abbey of Bourgueil or of Saint-Florant" (280; 149). The place of Thélème is then located, and Thélème, though nonexistent, bears some relation to an actual site. Just as, in fact, the description of the building begins to lead away from such references to existing locations, a comparison between Thélème and "Bonivet," "Chambourg" and "Chantilly" (*Gargantua*, Lefranc ed., 2:406) reestablishes the link, which is then immediately neutralized with an "absurd" detail (the 9,332 rooms).

Chapter 50 sets up the initial oppositions at work in Thélème by constructing the reference that Thélème is supposed, term by term, to negate. This subtext, generated as such by the text itself, provides the entire foundation for the ideology of Thélème.[15] Unlike other kinds of imaginary worlds, including the textual world to which Thélème is in a general way some kind of response, Thélème is constituted as the negative of existing institutional laws, characteristic of the "certain monasteries in [of] this world," which the dis-

---

[14]"In the case of the Utopian narrative, the place of the Real—of that which must first be constituted within the work before it can be dissolved or 'neutralized' by the work as process—may be identified by the obsessive references to actuality which seem part of the conventions of such texts, the perpetual play of topical allusion throughout the narrative which, intersecting the more properly diegetic interest, is constantly on the point of fragmenting the text into an anecdotal and discontinuous series of vertical indicators" (Fredric Jameson, "Of Islands and Trenches: Neutralization and the Production of Utopian Discourse," 7).

[15]"Now the Utopian text is not figuratively established across its referential sub-text, but rather literally founded and edified on the latter's historical emplacement" (Jameson, "Of Islands and Trenches," 9).

course itself creates as reference ("Utopian law is not another law but the 'other' of the law and, in its most rigorous organization, the law's inverse, its negation" [*Utopiques*, 113]).

Thélème is not another world, another kind of organization; rather, chapter 50 creates a binary relation, the monastery and *its* opposite, so that the process at work becomes one of neutralizing a given ideology rather than the independent, positive ideological construction of an ideal world. This can be demonstrated easily at two points in the text where the rigorous negation of conventional laws results in equally restrictive "absurd" and ideological formulations that contradict the ideal Thélémite philosophy described in later chapters. In the first instance, not only is it revealed that the Thélémites are constrained to perform certain tasks (thus calling into question the implications of "Do what you will"), but that the task itself, according to chapter 54, which defines the Thélémites as "monks and nuns," is problematic, not to say impossible:

> Davantaige, veu que en certains convents de ce monde est en usance que, si femme aulcune y entre (j'entends des preudes et pudicques), on nettoye la place par laquelle elles ont passé, feut ordonné que, si religieux ou religieuse y entroyt par cas fortuit, on nettoiroyt curieusement tous les lieux par lesquelz auroient passé. (281)

> Moreover, seeing that in certain monasteries in this world it is the custom that if any woman enters—I speak of chaste and honest women—they wash the place where she trod, it was ordained that if any monk or nun happened to enter there, the spot where he or she had stood should be scrupulously washed likewise. (150)

A further instance of the way Thélème operates as process rather than place occurs in a passage where once again what is narrated contradicts a later description of the Thélémites' segregated sleeping quarters:

Item, par ce que es conventz des femmes ne entroient les hommes si non à l'emblée et clandestinement, feut decerné que jà ne seroient là les femmes au cas que n'y feussent les hommes, ny les hommes au cas que n'y feussent les femmes. (283)

Item, because men never entered nunneries except secretly and by stealth, it was decreed that here there should be no women when there were no men, and no men when there were no women. (150)

The problem that emerges in chapter 50 relative to the subsequent mapping out of the abbey is analogous to the conflictual discourses of narration and description, as developed by Marin, although the contradictions that arise in the text do not always fall neatly into these categorical divisions.[16] What is important, for both Thomas More's work and Théléme, is that the noncoincidences of the narrational passages with the descriptions of the place itself symptomatically signal other ideological contradictions at work in the very construction of the utopian ideal. As Fredric Jameson remarks of More's *Utopia*:

These [the most important findings of *Utopiques*] bear on the non-congruence of text and geography in the three fundamental areas of Utopian social structure, political organization, and economic activity respectively, the point being that in no one of the three can Hythloday's account be perfectly matched, in a one-to-one correspondence, against the "ideal map" projected by the data he supplies. But this is something more than mere sloppiness or imaginative failure: rather, the

[16]See Jameson, "Of Islands and Trenches," 16: "Thus there emerges a tension, profoundly characteristic of all Utopian discourse, between description and narrative, between the effort of the text to establish the coordinates of a stable geographic entity, and its other vocation as sheer movement and restless displacement, as itinerary and exploration and, ultimately, as event."

inconsistencies thereby revealed are systematic, and the structural discrepancies are not random but determinate ones, their
absences and lacunae now readable as symptoms of some
deeper contradiction within the text. ("Of Islands and
Trenches," 17)

Before turning specifically to the three areas mentioned in
the passage above, I need to mention one simple yet fundamental noncongruence between narration and description.
This is the often-cited contradiction between Gargantua's
edict—"'First of all, then,' said Gargantua, 'you musn't
build walls round it. For all other abbeys have lofty walls'"
(281;150)—and the description of the abbey, which implicitly requires the establishment of boundaries.[17] The most
familiar of all utopian mechanisms, placing the ideal city
outside time, history, and process in some imaginary space to
create a self-enclosed system, works counter to the Thélémite philosophy. Yet not only do the fortifications seem to
require a wall, but the inscription on Thélème's gate also
reinforces such a boundary effect by establishing a principle
of exclusion and inclusion.

The inscription of chapter 52 functions like a verbal wall,
constructing an outside and an inside for the abbey.[18] The
combination of an open society without walls where "both
men and women, once accepted, could depart from there
whenever they pleased, without let or hindrance" (283; 151)
and an elect group, "people who are free, well-born, well-
bred" (302; 159), requires the structural displacement of
walls to the inscription, where Gargantua's command be-

[17]François Rigolot comments: "The space in between the towers is in
fact full: in describing the three hundred and twelve steps between
them . . . Rabelais invites us to connect the towers to each other with
walls" (*Les Langages de Rabelais*, 83).

[18]"Its function is to develop the system of oppositions ('enter not
here/enter here') established in Gargantua's edict by rigidifying them (rendering them 'lapidary')" (Beaujour, *Jeu de Rabelais*, 91).

comes fully impersonalized, thus paradoxically more authoritative and less dictatorial, in a community where, apparently, no *one* rules, and where free will constitutes the only
"law" ("All their life was regulated not by laws, statutes, or
rules, but according to their free-will and pleasure" [301;
159]).[19] The narrative presents the inscription as a discovery—"Above this gate was written in large Gothic letters
the following inscription" (288; 152)—only the title of the
next chapter betraying the agency of a will at work: "Inscription mise sus la grande porte de Theleme" (289) ("Inscription
placed above the great gate of Thélème"). To include the
subject of this utopian product (Gargantua) would be to link
it to its context, the narrative *Gargantua*. The impersonal,
inscriptive procedure separates—and reinforces the separation between—Thélème and the history that produces it.
This is further stressed by the exclusion of a part of *Gargantua*'s readership, the "very esteemed and poxy friends" to
whom Rabelais's writings are dedicated (Prologue, 9).[20] This
emphasis on the disjunction of worlds serves both to create a
space for Gargantua's replacement of Grandgousier (to become his own world) and to exclude from Thélème the elements of disorder and the imperialism that occupy the rest of
the text.

Mikhail Bakhtin discusses the structural organization of
this *cri*:

[19]Jean-Yves Pouilloux also comments on this displacement, suggesting,
however, that it occurs to express forbidden themes: "These 'fluctuations'
in the *récit* authorize a description of a state for which no one is, in effect,
responsible; in other words, they authorize the use of forbidden ideological
themes without incurring risks—for example the description of a humanity before [the existence of] original sin." See "Notes sur l'abbaye de
Thélème," 202. The problem, as I am defining it, consists in having
somehow to reconcile ideological conflicts internal to the structure of
Thélème itself.

[20]In chapter 52, 291, those who are "gnawed to the bone by pox" (154)
are excluded from the abbey. Jean-Yves Pouilloux also makes this point in
"Notes sur l'abbaye de Thélème," 203.

The inscription can be divided into two parts: the words that expel and those that invite. The first part has a purely abusive character; the second part contains words of pure praise. The abusive character of the first part is strictly observed. In the first stanza, for instance, Rabelais abuses hypocrites with fifteen different epithets, among them *hypocrites, bygotz, vieux matagotz, marmiteux*. Nearly all the words of this stanza have an abusive nuance (*abus meschant, meschanceté, faulseté, troublez*). In the stanzas that proffer an invitation (starting with the fifth), all the words, on the contrary, have a positive connotation and are chosen to express praise and friendliness (*gentilz, joyeux, plaisans, mignons, serains, subtilz*). Thus the two strictly organized groups of praise and abuse are opposed to each other. (*Rabelais*, 431)

He rightly indicates the enumerative excess of the expulsive passages of the *cri*, pointing to no fewer than fifteen abusive terms in the first stanza alone. Yet by claiming for the inscription a symmetry between abuse and praise, Bakhtin overlooks its more specific function of expelling violence by enumerating abusive words and placing them outside Thélème. The inclusive section of the inscription, by contrast, lacks such endless lists of analogous terms and adheres to a more declarative mode. The relation between the two parts is symptomatically asymmetrical; the first half expels with invectives, the second half merely defines the inclusion. Nor is the violence thus evoked conjured up from the void of "the unreality of myth," as Rigolot claims.[21] Its threat can be located within the text, in the chapters leading up to Thélème, to which Thélème is an attempted utopian alternative.

The inscription reveals, in the second half of the *cri*, another referent Thélème is built upon, one that includes "noble

[21]"The subject-matter having prevented him from creating movement inside Thélème, he compensates by creating a 'court of miracles' at the gates of the sanctuary. Life returns at the threshold of the void. The unreality of the myth has given rise to the reality of an anti-Thélème" (Rigolot, *Langages de Rabelais*, 86).

gentlemen" and "ladies of high lineage." The configuration suggests (and this is in effect the main thesis of Beaujour's discussion of Thélème) a courtly setting. Beaujour notes that "the invitation to medieval courtly values opposes the exclusion of the abuses of the age of the Goths."[22] Another indication of the courtly aspect of Thélème occurs immediately afterward, in chapter 53, where the title transforms the abbey into a castle: "Comment estoit le manoir des Thelemites" ("Concerning the Establishment of the Thélèmites' [Manor]" [155]). Even the general architecture of the abbey, according to the editors of the Abel Lefranc edition, "reminds us more of a feudal castle than of a Renaissance palace" (*Gargantua*, 2:404). Here lies a source of many of the contradictions generated by this utopian figure, for the conflicting ideologies of monastic and courtly institutions are juxtaposed and neutralized, but not reconciled or synthesized into a harmonious discourse. As Marin points out, the utopian discourse situates itself between poles, creating a neutral space that belongs to neither ideological system and can be reappropriated (as critics have done with Thélème) only at the cost of ignoring contradictions.[23]

The feudal or courtly model seems at first an attempt to resolve the problems inherent in the monastic institution as it is represented in chapter 50, providing an image or figure for

[22]See also Beaujour, *Jeu de Rabelais*, 105: "Surreptitiously, Thélème has been transformed from an abbey into a castle, and from a convent into a court. It is the ideal court of the good sovereign Gargantua whose just will always evokes the assent of those whom his generosity transforms into people under obligation [to him]."

[23]Marin, *Utopiques*, 20–21: "Is not a space set up, not on this or that side of affirmation and negation, but *between them*, a distance that prevents them from exhausting the possibilities of truth? Neither yes nor no, neither true nor false, neither one nor the other: the neutral . . . the neutral as the gap between contradictories, as contradiction itself maintained between true and false, opening a space in the discourse that the discourse itself cannot accomodate; a third term, but *supplementary*, and not synthesizing."

the antiabbey of Thélème. Corresponding to the monastic vows, then, are attributes more appropriate for the court:

> Item, par ce que ordinairement les religieux faisoient troys veuz, sçavoir est de chasteté, pauvreté et obedience, fut constitué que là honorablement on peult estre marié, que chascun feut riche et vesquist en liberté. (283–284)

> Item, because ordinarily monks and nuns made three vows, that is of chastity, poverty, and obedience, it was decreed that there anyone could be regularly married, [that each one was] rich, and [lived] at liberty. (151)

A discrepancy emerges here, however, between narrative and description in one of the important areas of utopian society outlined by Jameson—its social organization. The demands of the two ideological systems, religious (though evangelical and humanist) and courtly, conflict in the area of social-sexual practices. For though the courtly model permits the social integration of men and women, through marriage and through women's prominent role in determining pastimes and fashion ("for everything was done according to the will of the ladies" [299; 159]), the description enacts the segregation of the sexes necessitated by the Christian ethos, however liberal it might narratively seem. Beaujour humorously points to a premonition of this fact in the arrangement of stanzas in chapter 52, noting that "it is not by chance that the stanza inviting the preachers comes between the stanza that invokes the knights and the one that invokes the ladies" (101). The description of the living quarters in chapter 53 assumes the separation between men and women: "The ladies' lodging stretched from the Arctic tower to the Mesembrine gate, the men occupying the rest" (294; 155–56). The last chapter describing Thélème also reveals that marriage is effectively excluded from the abbey:

> Par ceste raison, quand le temps venu estoit que aulcun d'icelle abbaye, ou à la requeste de ses parens, ou pour aultres

causes, voulust issir hors, avecques soy il emmenoyt une des
dames, celle laquelle l'auroit prins pour son devot, et estoient
ensemble mariez. (chap. 55, 304)

For that reason, when the time came that anyone in that
abbey, either at his parents' request or for any other reason,
wished to leave it, he took with him one of the ladies, the one
who had accepted him as her admirer, and they were married
to one another. (159–60)

The confusion of social institutions in Thélème extends to
the very names for the Thélémites: they are alternately
"knights" or "gentlemen" and "ladies" or "monks" and
"nuns." This confusion applies to their essential makeup as
well, where the ethics of aristocratic *courtoisie* and the Christian doctrine of original sin (and nature versus grace) seem to
clash:

En leur reigle n'estoit que ceste clause, *Faictz ce que vouldras*,
par ce que gents liberes, bien nez et bien instruictz, conver-
sans en compaignies honestes, ont par nature un instinct et
aguillon, qui tousjours les pousse à faictz vertueux et retire de
vice, lequel ilz nommoient honneur. (chap. 55, 302)

In their rules there was only one clause: DO WHAT YOU WILL
because people who are free, well-born, well-bred, and easy
in honest company have a natural spur and instinct which
drives them to virtuous deeds and deflects them from vice;
and this they called honour. (159)

Rigolot, Beaujour, Pouilloux, and others have found this passage, in its claim for natural good, problematic in terms of
Christian doctrine, which requires the intervention of God's
grace to transform man's blighted nature into a will to virtue.
M. A. Screech, however, synthesizes the passage into a fully
coherent Christian message:

It is here that Rabelais is perhaps the most difficult to follow;
behind the word *honneur*—an appropriate one for ladies and

gentlemen to be guided by—hides the more complex theological concept of "synderesis." Synderesis is that aspect of moral
judgment and persuasion in the soul which, although weakened at the Fall, was not obliterated. . . . This force in man is
both an *instinctus bonus* and an *instinctus naturae*. To make the
then semi-technical word *instinct* clear, Rabelais uses it with
its French doublet, *aguillon* (goad). It is amusing to think that
some have seen in this part of Thelema a denial of original sin!
The interpretation of synderesis as a good natural instinct,
encouraging good conduct and discouraging evil, is totally at
home in Christian philosophy. (*Rabelais*, 191)

Although Screech's exposition may indeed serve as a corrective to imprecisions in interpreting Rabelais's vocabulary, the
critic "translates" *honneur* as synderesis, thus reducing the
polysemous capacity of the entire phrase, which retains both
theological and aristocratic connotations. The critics' debate
simply reinforces the notion of a confusion of systems and
discourses at work in Thélème. Both the Christian humanist
and the chivalric ethos inhabit the text.

Although the juxtaposition of courtly and monastic institutions seems an attempt to square the circle of social relations in Thélème, both models suppress a third term in the
area of political organization. The previously outlined non-
congruences, between the absence of law and Gargantua's
total control through the "impersonalization" of commands,
between the Thélémites' supposed liberty and the description of their restrictions, between the declared geographic
openness of the abbey and the rigorous exclusion enacted by
the inscription, symptomatically suggest a deeper conflict in
the political organization of Thélème.

The chapters leading up to Thélème deal explicitly with
the proper use of political authority. In these chapters benign
and malignant forms of authority are pitted against each other and against the will of the son in his struggle for autonomy. It has been suggested that the Picrocholine war alludes

to the wars between Francis I and the emperor Charles, and it might be said that Thélème as utopia attempts to address the concerns of a France engaged in a costly and ultimately fruitless struggle for European hegemony. Chapter 31, with its references to "two columns, grander than the columns of Hercules" (194; 110), the emblem of Charles V, sketches a portrait of imperialism resembling the emperor's declared aspirations.[24] Picrochole's advisers, the duke of Menuail, Count Spadassin, and Captain Merdaille, seem to mirror the role played by Charles's advisers, the grand chancellor Gattinara in particular, in the formulation of his imperialistic and Dantesque dream of *monarchia*.[25] Picrochole's expansionist policy includes, as did that of Charles, not only all of Europe, but Africa and the "pagan" East as well.

From the point of view of the narrative, these practices are condemned, and Ulrich Gallet's statement—

"ainsi ont toutes choses leur fin et periode. Et, quand elles sont venues à leur poinct supellatif, elles sont en bas ruinées, car elles ne peuvent long temps en tel estat demourer. C'est la fin de ceulx qui leurs fortunes et prosperitez ne peuvent par raison et temperance moderer" (chap. 29, 186)

"for all things have their term and period, and when they have reached their highest point they are in a trice tumbled down, since they cannot long remain at such an eminence. Such is

[24]For the allusions to contemporary politics in chapter 31, see the notes to pages 193–201 in the Calder, Screech, and Saulnier edition of *Gargantua*. François Rigolot discusses the connections between Charles VIII, André de La Vigne, and Rabelais in *Le Texte de la Renaissance: Des rhétoriqueurs à Montaigne*, 113ff.

[25]H. G. Koenigsberger and G. Mosse, *Europe in the Sixteenth Century*, 176–77. Cortés, writing to Charles about his New World conquests, remarks: "'If I do this, there would be nothing more left for Your Excellency to do in order to become ruler of the world'" (175). Koenigsberger and Mosse also quote Gattinara's statement to Charles: "'God has set you on the path towards world monarchy'" (176).

the end of those who cannot by reason and temperance mod-
erate their fortunes and prosperity" (105)

—summarizes the stance on imperialism taken in these chapters. Grandgousier, however, with his desire for peace at
almost any cost, offers restitution and more to the Picrocholine contingent rather than face a military confrontation
(chap. 30, 189). Grandgousier does not provide a satisfactory
alternative to Picrochole's threat (Rabelais's allusion, perhaps, to Francis I's lack of success in his dealings with
Charles).[26] Gargantua, who does not hesitate to go to war in
self-defense yet, having conquered, displays moderation and
magnanimity toward the enemy, wins the day. The discourse
poses the question of the proper measure of authority, of
which Gargantua becomes the prime example. Thélème,
presumably his kingdom, seems an attempt to hypothesize
about the effects of this proper measure, yet the very founding constitutes a usurpation (since the abbey was supposed to
be for Frère Jean). The text alternates between a discourse of
absolute authority ("it was ordained" [281; 151]) and a rhetoric of absolute liberty ("Nobody woke them; nobody compelled them either to eat or to drink, or to do anything else
whatever" [302; 159]). The problem of authority, as it is presented both by the Picrocholine episode (secular, political
authority) and by the portrait of religious institutions sketch-
ed at the beginning of Thélème (chap. 50, the temporal aspect of religious authority) is neutralized by the juxtaposition, in Thélème, of polar contradictions: hierarchy versus
equality, collectivity versus individual freedom, and so on.
Furthermore, in both the political and religious domains, the

[26]During the first war between Charles and Francis, when Francis was
taken prisoner, the king signed the Treaty of Madrid, conceding a great
deal of territory to the emperor. See G. Dujarric, *Précis chronologique de
l'histoire de France*, 84–86. The affinities between Grandgousier and
Picrochrole suggest the likeness between Francis and Charles, both kings
having presented their candidacy for emperor in 1519.

explicitly marked person and place of authority are absent: there is no prince or court, nor is there a priest or church.[27] The absence of the locus of authority in Thélème is not an answer to the problem of power raised by *Gargantua*'s last chapters; rather it marks, by a gap, the place where a theoretical formulation may later be elaborated; as Marin remarks, "The discourse of utopia accompanies ideological discourse as its inverse and designates, by its absence, the place of a scientific theory of society" (*Utopiques*, 255). In France the theory will be monarchical, but for the moment Rabelais's Thélème hovers tensely between an archaic, feudal mode of existence, framed by the will of an absolute ruler, and a progressive religious institution governed by the free will of its inhabitants.[28]

One place where the two modes clash, symptomatically marked by a later addition, is in chapter 54, "Comment estoient vestuz les religieux et religieuses de Theleme" ("How the monks and nuns at Thélème were dressed"). The opening passage contains both the free religious institution and the sovereign will that governs it and introduces an element of historical process that disturbs the atemporal perfection or self-enclosure of Thélème: "Les dames, au commencement de la fondation, se habilloient à leur plaisir et arbitre. Depuis, feurent reforméez en la faczon que s'ensuyt" (297)

[27]Beaujour remarks (*Jeu de Rabelais*, 104): "The Rabelaisian text conceives liberty—and authority—in the mode of monarchic sovereignty; but its ruse—or its candor—is to make the sovereign's presence in its court disappear." For the absence of a church, see Dennis Costa, *Irenic Apocalypse: Some Uses of Apocalyptic in Dante, Petrarch and Rabelais*, 119–23, where he discusses Thélème as a *typus ecclesiae*, the text being interwoven with allusions to Revelation and lacking a temple, like the New Jerusalem.

[28]Apropos of Thélème's feudalistic organization, Claude-Gilbert Dubois has this to say: "The sentimental ideal is a historical product with a relationship to specific economic conditions; now, when these conditions are about to disappear, utopia takes on the quality of perpetuating a superseded stage of development, as pure reactionary nostalgia" (*Problèmes de l'utopie*, 9).

("The ladies, at the foundation of this order, dressed according to their own taste and pleasure. Afterwards, [. . . ] they [were reformed] in the following fashion" [157]). This passage contradicts two fundamental tenets of Thélème, presented farther on in the text: that being by nature "people who are free, well-born, well-bred," the women of Thélème should need no outside reformation, and that in any case the Thélémites may do what they please. Later versions of this passage mitigate the contradiction by the addition of "par leur franc vouloir" ("of their own free will") after "feurent reforméez," but the passage, with its inclusion of authoritative intervention in the customs of the Thélémites, nevertheless introduces change, the effect of historical process, which should not be necessary within the perimeter of Thélème. The gap created by the conflictual models Thélème is built on opens the way for the entry of history into Thélème's verbal fortress.

The moment when the historical process breaks into discourse—that is, when history, by its very suppression, invades Thélème from within—occurs in the passage of chapter 54 where the narrator alludes to the modes of production at Thélème:

En ces vestemens tant propres et acoustremens tant riches ne pensez que eulx ny elles perdissent temps aulcun, car les maistres des garderobbes avoient toute la vesture tant preste par chascun matin, et les dames de chambre tant bien estoient aprinses, que en un moment elles estoient prestez et habilléez de pied en cap. Et, pour iceulx acoustremens avoir en meilleur oportunité, au tour du boys de Theleme estoit un grand corps de maison long de dimye lieue, bien clair et assortye, en laquelle demouroient les orfevres, lapidaires, brodeurs, tailleurs, tyreurs d'or, veloutiers, tapissiers, et aultelissiers, et là oeuvroient chascun de son mestier, et le tout pour les susdictz religieux et religieuses. Iceulx estoient fourniz de matiere et estoffe par les mains du seigneur Nausiclete, lequel par chascun an leurs rendoyt sept navires des Isles de Perlas et

Canibales, chargées de lingotz d'or, de soye crue, de perles et pierreries. (299–300)

Do not suppose, however, that any time was wasted by either men or women over these handsome clothes and rich accoutrements. For the masters of the wardrobe had all the clothing so neatly laid out each morning, and the chambermaids were so skilful, that in a minute they were all ready and dressed from head to foot. And in order that they might have these accoutrements close at hand, around the Thélème wood was a great block of houses, a mile and a half long, very smart and well-arranged, in which lived the goldsmiths, jewellers, embroiderers, tailors, wire-workers, velvet-weavers, tapestry-makers, and upholsterers; and there each man worked at his trade, and all of them for the aforesaid monks and nuns.

They were provided with supplies and material by the lord Nausiclete, who brought seven ships to them each year from the Perlas and Cannibal Islands, loaded with gold ingots, raw silk, pearls, and precious stones. (158)

Here emerges the final conflict between narrative and description, in the area of economic activity, mentioned by Jameson as characteristically contradictory in the utopian text. No mention has been made of the "great block of houses, a mile and a half long," which is situated, not insignificantly, outside the actual castle, separated from it, perhaps, by the "Thélème wood."[29]

Suddenly a much larger population occupies Thélème than was at first stipulated: other classes besides the nobility reside there and practice their crafts for the Thélémites. Although this would not necessarily seem strange in the context of a feudal manor, it is interesting that the other classes normally found there—peasants in particular—and other necessary life-supporting functions (agriculture, cooking) are

[29]It is unclear whether the phrase "au tour du boys de Theleme" ("around the Thélème wood") means that the forest is situated between the abbey and the group of houses or whether it surrounds them both.

absent from Thélème.[30] The sudden presence of the petit bourgeois and of the bourgeois or merchant-class representative, "seigneur Nausiclete," opens Thélème up to a more global socioeconomic landscape. Thélème can no longer remain self-sufficient and self-enclosed: the raw materials required necessitate its dependence on an extensive capitalist economy that includes the newly exploited markets of the West Indies.[31] Imperialism, which the archaic manor of Thélème sought to exclude, returns to its place within the economy of the abbey. The "nonsaid" of Thélème, what it can point to only because it suppresses history (and what it points to in this way only because it does suppress history), resides in this juxtaposition of the idealized, self-contained monastery-court (the inside) and a vast economic network, the outside, that supports it. The outside inhabits Thélème from within; it is the context that Thélème depends on and cannot do without. In the context of the work as a whole, Thélème marks a turning point where the notion of genealogical progress, or perfectability, reaches an impasse. The *Tiers Livre* will confront, through the person of Pantagruel and in more contradictory terms, the archaism of the humanist endeavor that Defaux has so interestingly intuited in *Pantagruel et les sophistes*. It is all the more ironic then, and symptomatic, that twentieth-century Western "humanists" have seen in Thélème the reflection of their own social ideals.

Thélème, as utopian figure, functions as a supplement in the economy of *Gargantua*. Its appearance immediately following Gargantua's speech to the vanquished and the doling out of rewards—two chapters that underscore the humanis-

[30]Certain other personnel are mentioned, such as the "masters of the wardrobe" and the "chambermaids," both appearing on the scene shortly before the cited passage (299), but it is not explained where they live.
[31]Beaujour recognizes this aspect of Thélème as well. He writes: "The blossoming of the Thélémites is possible only at the cost of a global enslavement" (*Jeu de Rabelais*, 102).

tic (humanitarian, rational, and liberal) optimism of the humanist's political philosophy—becomes a sign of what Jameson calls "that radical insufficiency in it [the humanist rhetoric] which seems to demand the generation of a Utopian anecdote for its own completion": "An overemphasis on the power of rationality in general and a basic and constitutive over-estimation of the functional role of rhetoric and persuasion in particular in the historical process whereby an imperfect world may be transformed into a more satisfactory one" ("Of Islands and Trenches," 19). In a sense, then, the impossibility of the idealized outcome of the Picrocholine war generates Thélème, a nondiscursive figure for the ideal society. Thélème is the figural sign of a perceived failure in the rhetoric of the preceding chapters.[32]

The Thélémite utopia is itself a failure, however, as I have suggested. A supplement, it is itself subject to the logic of the supplement. The other—imperialism and its accompanying violence—that Thélème sought to exclude reappears within the confines of the abbey. This supplement receives explicit figuration in the text, just as Thélème figured an absence in the final chapters of *Gargantua*. Alcofrybas adds, at the end of chapter 55, "I must not forget to write down for you a riddle which was found in [. . .] the foundations of the abbey, engraved on a great bronze plate" (305;160). An enigma appears, belatedly, almost forgotten, as an addition or appendix to the text.[33] Yet its temporal place in the structure is

[32]Jameson continues, commenting on More's work: "*Utopia* would then be generated, not so much by an overestimation of the powers of reason, as rather by an unformulated consciousness of its failure, and by Hythloday's experience (in Book One) of the impotence of discursive argument and disputation in the making or at least the transformation of history" ("Of Islands and Trenches," 19).

[33]M. A. Screech suggests that the enigma's belatedness might have been, in fact, literal: "The Enigma is introduced, not by Gargantua or Frère Jean, but by a narrator (*Je*), with a laconic phrase bearing all the signs of an afterthought" (*Rabelais*, 200).

"in/at the foundations"—it was always already there, at the origin of Thélème's founding, preceding the abbey's construction without itself originating from any particular founding moment. It is also a structural feature of the abbey; it occupies a place in the foundations of the construction, it is a negativity the structure is built on. The enigma literally undermines the abbey; it constitutes a reversal of the process of exhumation and reconstruction outlined by Thomas Greene (*The Light in Troy*, 237). Just as *Gargantua* seems to participate in such a movement, so the enigma seems to call into question not only the utopian completeness of Thélème, but also the entire constructive process of *Gargantua*.

The enigma opens up the text to history. Its message and the message of the ensuing preface to the *Tiers Livre* change the focus of the work, moving it into closer correspondence with the times, with the present of the text's historical reality. Thélème's most pressing political message, then, parallels that outlined by Jameson: "Utopia's deepest subject, and the source of all that is most vibrantly political about it, is precisely our inability to conceive it, our incapacity to produce it as a vision, our failure to project the other of what is, a failure that, as with fireworks dissolving back into the night sky, must once again leave us alone with *this* history" ("Of Islands and Trenches," 21).

At the end of the *Tiers Livre*, in the second chapter on the plant Pantagruelion (chap. 52, 348), "Comment certaine espece de Pantagruelion ne peut estre par feu consommée," Rabelais himself suggests that Thélème fails as a utopia, for it cannot resist the forces of history:

> Congneut Caesar l'admirable nature de ce boys [larix], lequel de soy ne faict feu, flambe ne charbon, et seroit digne en ceste qualité d'estre on degré mis de vray Pantagruelion, et d'autant plus que Pantagruel d'icelluy voulut estre faictz tous les huys, portes, fenestres, goustieres, larmiers et l'ambrun de Theleme . . . ne feust que larix, en grande fournaise de feu prove-

nent d'aultres especes de boys, est en fin corrumpu et dissipé comme sont les pierres en fourneau de chaulx; Pantagruelion Asbeste plus tost y est renouvelé et nettoyé que corrompu ou alteré. (Screech ed., *Tiers Livre*, chap. 52, 353)

Caesar learned the marvellous nature of that wood [larix], which of itself produces neither fire, flame, nor charcoal. In this respect it would deserve to be ranked with the true Pantagruelion—the more so because Pantagruel ordered all the doors, gates, windows, gutters, weather-moulding, and facings of Thélème to be made of it, . . . —were it not for the fact that larix in a great fiery furnace consuming other kinds of wood, is finally consumed and destroyed in the same way as the stones in a limekiln. Whereas the asbestine Pantagruelion is renewed and cleansed by this treatment rather than consumed and changed. (432)

Fire is the ironically appropriate figure for these forces, since it combines an apocalyptic notion of destruction ("in a great fiery furnace") and a concretely historical reference to the burning of heretics, a practice that accelerated about the time Rabelais was completing *Gargantua*.[34] The enigma also refers to destruction by fire, in a context that suggests both the apocalypse and the religious persecutions of 1534:

> Et toutesfoys, devant le partement,
> On pourra veoir en l'air appertement
> L'aspre chaleur d'une grand flame esprise
> Pour mettre à fin les eaux et l'enterprise.
> (*Gargantua*, chap. 56, 311)

> Nevertheless, before this parting comes
> There shall be seen most clearly in the air

[34]For the historical events occurring at the time of *Gargantua*'s publication, see Screech, *Rabelais*, 201–6: "Sedition, persecution, and the 'affaire des placards.'"

> The rigorous heat of a great flame, intent
> On quelling both the flood and enterprise.
>
> (162)

Immediately following these lines are the ten lines Rabelais is said to have composed himself (311); both versions refer to a persecuted religious elect. Thélème cannot guard its inhabitants against such persecution, nor can it stop time and effect closure on the processes that willed it into being: "Utopia is a refusal of incoherence, even if the refusal results in unreality. The utopian writer, creator of paradise, takes up, in his turn, the design of the Great Architect. . . . But he is not the Great Architect: his world only has an ideal form, and the incarnation of that idea does not seem able to escape the dialectic of the Fall" (Dubois, *Problèmes de l'utopie*, 54).

The enigma opposes the abbey in that it moves rapidly through time to the apocalypse and the eschaton, while Thélème remains serenely, perhaps complacently, fixed in time. It is not clear, from the enigma alone, whether the prophecy speaks to the present of the abbey's existence or whether, the poem having been written at some unspecified point in the past, Thélème is supposed somehow to represent that culmination in joy alluded to by the last ten lines.[35] Gargantua's comment suggests that the enigma does refer to the past and that he and his companions find themselves at present in a situation similar to the one that inspired the enigma's gloomy predictions: "'This is not the first time that men called to the Gospel faith are persecuted'" (312; 163). Although Dennis Costa (*Irenic Apocalypse*) and David Quint (*Origin and Originality*) see in this text and in Gargantua's response Rabelais's aesthetic of irenic apocalypse, it seems there is no position within the text from which the "hopeful message" may be definitively privileged. If in fact Thélème

[35]Emile Telle discusses the problem of time in the enigma. See "Thélème et le paulisme matrimonial erasmien: Le Sens de l'enigme en prophétie," 110.

itself testifies optimistically to the enigma's exhortation to persevere (the abbey being the fruit of such perseverance), then Gargantua's response must be seen as undermining its status as culmination. His comment suggests that the present (of the reading of the inscription) is a time of persecution. Once this is the case the abbey becomes either a vision in the past that has since been destroyed or a present that is contrary to fact, since Gargantua places in doubt the peaceful existence of its inhabitants.

The enigma, in the context of Thélème's construction and Gargantua's response, describes a repetition without finality. The process of persecution, perseverance, and salvation prophesied by the enigma enacts a telos, but one that is subjected to parody by the text itself.[36] The first time of the enigma (the persecution of the elect) corresponds to the present of Gargantua's statement, which repeats the prophetic pattern but is then returned to the present by Frère Jean's opposing interpretation.

This chapter presents action and time as problems of writing and of interpretation. On the one hand, the text frames the paradigm of Christian history as the unfolding of divine meaning in time within a context of nonteleological repetition, so that the paradigm itself is called into question. The futurity of the supplementary enigma is absolute and unknowable, yet it determines the "present" of Gargantua's utterance, which thus becomes a present that is absent to itself. This present that is absent to itself is wholly consonant with Augustinian theology, in that Presence cannot truly occur except at the end of history, when the Logos returns. Thus prophecy cannot exist except by virtue of this absence, and such prophecy may even be said to defer the final pres-

[36]See, on the one hand, Dennis Costa's discussion of the enigma and its "irenic apocalypse" aesthetic in *Irenic Apocalypse*, 122–23, and on the other, Terence Cave's contention that "the text parodies a fictional and philosophical *telos* while enacting it" in *The Cornucopian Text: Problems of Writing in the French Renaissance*, 120, n. 60.

ence by perpetuating interpretation and commentary. The enigma opens Thélème, and the text, to history because it in effect promises deferment rather than fulfillment. The consequence of such deferment then becomes Frère Jean's interpretation, a game of interpretation conducted upon a text that turns out to be about a game of tennis, an allegorization like those referred to in the Prologue. The tennis game itself foregrounds the problematic at work, for Montaigne will later use it as a figure for reading.[37]

The effort to interpret the enigma results in a gloss that returns prophecy to fallen discourse. Frère Jean effects a closure upon this discourse, but it has the status of an interruption, a departure from the text not to a plenitude of meaning but to a this-worldly activity outside the text: "'La fin est que apres avoir bien travaillé, ilz s'en vont repaistre; et grand chiere!'" (314) ("'The ending is that after having worked hard, they go refresh themselves; and here's good cheer!'").[38] Frère Jean's reading both mystifies the enigma and demystifies Gargantua's response. Furthermore, his response brings *Gargantua* to a close. Its position at the end of the book lends it weight and suggests the ultimate undecidability of

[37]Costa remarks of the tennis game that it is "a powerful image of the problem of action in time: humanity's problem, the abbey's problem, the reader's problem" (*Irenic Apocalypse*, 123). Cathleen Bauschatz discusses Montaigne's metaphor of the tennis game in "Montaigne's Conception of Reading in the Context of Renaissance Poetics and Modern Criticism." She also argues that "Rabelais may also be using the tennis game as an analogy for the reading process in this passage, and . . . the analogy finally manages to turn the adversarial relationship between reader and writer into a playful and productive one" ("'Une Description du Jeu de Paulme Soubz Obscures Parolles': The Portrayal of Reading in *Pantagruel*, and *Gargantua*" 74).

[38]One might also read, in Frère Jean's conclusion, the Gargantuan joke at the reader's expense of a very Rabelaisian Rabelais; that is, the enjoinder to feast joyfully after the difficult labor of interpreting his text. Michel Jeanneret has written on Rabelais's use of feasting in *Des mets et des mots: Banquets et propos de table à la Renaissance*.

chapter 56's interpretive dilemma. Through the juxtaposition of these two readings, Gargantua's and Frère Jean's, the community of Thélème dissolves, the common will of the inhabitants disseminating into irreconcilable interpretive possibilities.

The problems posed by the enigma and the interpretive responses it elicits within the fiction extend to the presence of the document itself in Rabelais's text. All but the last ten lines make up Mellin de Saint-Gelais's poem, "Enigmes en façon de prophétie" and, according to the marginal commentary of the author, describe "a game of tennis veiled in apocalyptic language" (*Gargantua* 306, n. 5). On one level the poem parodies the Christian telos by inscribing repetition, as the tennis game, within a description of the apocalypse. This is so, however, only if the author's marginalia are privileged; otherwise, as Thomas Sebillet notes in *Art poétique françoys* (176), the description adapts itself to more than one meaning, both presumably assuming equal importance as the signified of the allegory. Rabelais's intervention (the addition of lines), may be seen as an attempt to resolve the indeterminacy of the enigma—an attempt that fails, as Frère Jean's interpretation, returning to the tennis game, demonstrates. Nor is Frère Jean's allegorizing reading necessarily definitive, though his interpretation echoes the intention of the enigma's author. The closure in resolution that Rabelais imposes on the enigma becomes all the more ironic in that it is not Gargantua, but Frère Jean, who echoes that "falsely cheerful" closure.

Thélème and its enigma bring to an end of sorts the genealogical or historical books of Rabelais's work. This history of the giants is itself a meditation on history in narrative, on the impossibility of fixing an origin as well as enacting closure. *Gargantua*, the belated origin, depends upon the son that preceded it, *Pantagruel*, for its status as origin of Rabelais's oeuvre. Nor, on the other hand, can *Pantagruel* claim a place at the origin, for as Rabelais himself notes in the Prologue, it too comes from elsewhere. There is no present origin, either in *Gargantua* (a "copy" of *Pantagruel*) or in *Pantagruel* (described as "another book of the same stamp" [*Pantagruel*, 6; 168]), for both books constitute a repetition whose origin cannot be found.

This schematic articulation of *différance* more closely resembles the problems of (re)writing (to distort Cave's phrase) for Rabelais than does the nineteenth century's ideologized term "renaissance," which posits a new, gigantic birth from the privileged origin of antiquity. Although *Pantagruel* and *Gargantua* thematize birth, it is a birth that "kills" the mother and privileges the father as origin. It is perhaps not too far-fetched to suggest that the sixteenth-century French humanist project involved just such a denial of the mother (tongue, tradition) in order to privilege a patriarchal origin in Greece and Rome.[39] Origination from the father is a metaphor; this figural relation structures the very books of father and son, books that reveal in their texts the absence of an origin and of a birth. Structurally a rebirth cannot take place, as the writing of *Pantagruel* and *Gargantua* shows.

What has no beginning has no end. Just as the genealogical quest is parodied, so too is closure, that tending toward a telos that will complete the work. What Rabelais presents as a problem of interpretive closure at the end of both *Pantagruel* and *Gargantua* is also the problem of writing the books. The narrator's return in *Pantagruel* and Frère Jean's conclusion in *Gargantua* halt the narrative, not as completion, but as interruption.

The struggle in the first two books to posit an origin and realize an ideal whose location "wants to" but cannot be the present (Thélème) may indeed bear out Mikhail Bakhtin's analysis of the transition from epic to novel as from a narra-

---

[39]Margaret Ferguson discusses the ambivalence toward the immediate or historical past in Du Bellay's Defence and other Renaissance texts; see her *Trials of Desire: Renaissance Defenses of Poetry*.

tive of an absolute, completed, and sacrosanct past to contemporaneity, the "'low' present," with the corresponding parody of the "high genres and of all lofty models embodied in national myth" (*The Dialogic Imagination: Four Essays*, "Epic and Novel," 16–21). Walter Stephens has shown how epic distance posed a dilemma for those seeking to construct a national myth for France and agrees with Richard Berrong that *Gargantua* displays a greater reliance on "high culture" than on popular tradition—what I have described as its metaphor of construction for the textual world, corresponding to an absence of ideological tension and a relative endorsement of established authority and its nationalist myths (*Giants in Those Days*, 290–91).[40] Symptomatically, the second book also "returns" to the father.

The disjunction between past and present and the confrontation between absolute past and present undecidability, between a desire or nostalgia for closure and the realization of its impossibilty, find increasing thematic, linguistic, and structural expression over the course of the two books. But whereas in *Pantagruel* the celebration of the present, the story of the son, receives direct thematic figuration in a continuing, if failed, confrontation between authority and its subversion, in *Gargantua* there is an attempt to resolve the dilemma, thematically evaded, by fixing historical process in an eternalized, idealized present that demonstrates itself to be ultimately untenable, subject itself to the historical processes it seeks to exclude. Could the humanists of early modern France have confronted European imperialism in any other way?[41]

[40]Berrong argues that the change in Rabelais has to do in part with being in Cardinal Du Bellay's retinue: *Rabelais and Bakhtin: Popular Culture in "Gargantua and Pantagruel,"* part 2, chap. 2. See also Walter Stephens, *Giants in Those Days: Folklore, Ancient History, and Nationalism*, 314.

[41]At least one Renaissance author did. Montaigne, in "Des cannibales" (in *Essais*), uses the tropes of utopia to conduct a scathing critique of Eurocentrism.

# 5

# The Quest

Whereas the first two books contend in genealogical form with the problem of origin, familial and textual, the third book constitutes a turning point. It is the first book to which Rabelais attaches his name and in which he claims ownership of the other two.[1] The Prologue to the *Tiers Livre* situates its author in contemporary France, not in the fabulous, magical, or archaic realm of Alcofrybas and the giants. It is also the book that announces the beginning of a quest.

In the Prologue, this first Rabelaisian book assumes a demystified stance toward writing as that which is nonoriginary. The figure of iterability is Diogenes rolling his tub, to whom the author compares himself in the act of writing.[2]

---

[1] "For the benefit of the warriors I am about to rebroach my cask, the contents of which you would have sufficiently appreciated from my two earlier volumes if they had not been adulterated and spoiled by dishonest printers. I am about to draw for them, out of the product of our after-dinner entertainments, a gallant third draught—and later a jovial fourth—of Pantagrueline Sentences" (*Tiers Livre*, Prologue, 16; 284–85).

[2] I am using iterability here as a designation for the repetition of a figure rather than an isolated sign. See Jacques Derrida, "Signature Event Con-

The cynic Diogenes replaces the genealogist as the figure for the writer (Screech ed., 11–12). Repetition of an action accompanies the agent's loss of control over that action; like Sisyphus, Diogenes cannot control the downward path of the tub. The enumerative list of verbs describing Diogenes' action upon the tub itself enacts this process, whereby the words threaten, with their generative capacity, to overrun the governing description. Rabelais compares the Diogenic tub to his own act of writing, allowing the "tonneau Diogenic" to take on many heterogeneous meanings in the course of the Prologue. The passage emphasizes repetition and, with its stress on the first person pronoun, authorial control:

> Prins ce choys et election, ay pensé ne faire exercise inutile et importun si je remuois mon tonneau Diogenic, qui seul m'est resté du naufrage faict par le passé on far de Mal'encontre. A ce triballement de tonneau que feray je en vostre advis? Par la vierge qui se rebrasse, je ne scay encores. Attendez un peu que je hume quelque traict de ceste bouteille: c'est mon vray et seul Helicon, c'est ma fontaine Caballine, c'est mon unicque Enthusiasme. Icy beuvant je delibere, je discours, je resoulz et concluds. Après l'epilogue je riz, j'escripz, je compose, je boy. (14)

> Having made my choice, having made up my mind, I decided that I should perform no useless or tiresome role if I were to tumble my Diogenic tub, which is all that is left me from the shipwreck of my past in the Straits of Misfortune. Now, how do you advise me to set about my tub-rumbling? By the Virgin who ups her skirts, I do not yet know. Wait a little, till I've swallowed a draught from this bottle. It is my true and only Helicon, my one Pegasus spring, my sole enthusiasm. As I

---

text," 180–82. See also Thomas Greene's discussion of the concept in *The Light in Troy: Imitation and Discovery in Renaissance Poetry*, 11 ff., where he proposes an alteration of the term to account for Renaissance imitation.

drink I here deliberate, discourse, resolve, and conclude. After the epilogue I laugh, write, compose, and drink again. (284)

Writing is seen as an endless activity that begins "after the epilogue," an activity for which the author relinquishes responsibility, in the sense that he does not know its outcome. Later on in the Prologue he reclaims control over his books, and in the conclusion he forcibly attempts, but in vain, to exclude the "Caphards" or hypocrites who would misappropriate his work ("What, are you still there?" [21; 287]). Nevertheless the cynic eventually gives way to the quester for meaning and truth. As he says of his bottle, "As in Pandora's jug, good hope lies at the bottom, not despair, as in the Danaïd's tub" (19–20; 286).

From such vacillation emerges the quest that will structure the last three books of Rabelais. The paradox of this quest is that it is both parody, the cynical tub rolling of Diogenes—

Ce voyant quelqu'un de ses amis, luy demanda quelle cause le mouvoit à son corps, son esprit, son tonneau ainsi tormenter. Auquel respondit le philosophe qu'à aultre office n'estant pour la republicque employé, il en ceste façon son tonneau tempestoit pour, entre ce peuple tant fervent et occupé, n'estre veu seul cessateur et ocieux. (12)

At the sight of this activity one of his friends asked him what moved him thus to torment his body, his spirit, and his tub. To which the philosopher replied that, not being entrusted with any other duties by the State, he was giving his tub a thrashing in order not to seem the one lazy idler among a people so feverishly busy (283).

—and the "good hope" of a quest for meaning, the narrative extension of the utopian figure, Thélème.

Unlike the previous books, which enjoin the reader to laugh and read, the *Tiers Livre* opens with a mock plea from the author: "The aforesaid author beseeches his kindly readers to reserve their laughter till the Seventy-eighth Book," signaling the self-conscious comic seriousness of these last books and introducing the theme of deferral, sine qua non of the quest. Deferral is already at work in the first two books, where Pantagruel's story is delayed in favor of a recapitulation that moves further back into the past to narrate the life of the hero's father. It is as though Panurge's fear of the future, which is also a fear of the disruption to lineage represented by cuckoldry, is the text's own, so that it must go back to fix its roots securely in the past. So as not to confront the radical contingency of history and meaning, as Rabelais's text so often does, the book must secure its origins, must find a ground that will lend cohesiveness and continuity to its development.

The thematic enactment of this grounding and the narrator's attempt to establish an authoritative literary origin from which *Pantagruel* and *Gargantua* can be born find their counterpart in the author's explicit claim to ownership that arrives, belatedly, in the *Tiers Livre*.[3] The king replaces the thematic father and with his *privilège* lends authority to the work. The king, as father, frees the author to claim paternity, in his own name, for the third book and the others that preceded it.[4] On the one hand, such legitimation (taking place five years after Rabelais legitimized his children) constituted a necessary protection; as I discussed earlier (chap. 4), "bastard" versions of *Gargantua* and *Pantagruel* were still causing problems with the Sorbonne.[5] On the other hand,

[3]Michel Charles writes, apropos of the revised editions of the first two books and their title changes: "Through the play of titles, Rabelais effaces the origin of his novel; first he gives a son to the legendary Gargantua; then to the son he gives a father, his own Gargantua" (*Rhétorique de la lecture*, 40).

[4]Rabelais mentions the other two books in the *Tiers Livre*, Prologue, 16, as his "two earlier volumes."

[5]M. A. Screech, *Rabelais*, 207–11. See also Michel Foucault's "What Is an Author?" "In our culture (and doubtless in many others), discourse was not originally a product, a thing, a kind of goods; it was essentially an

the legal sanction of the father frees the *Tiers Livre* from the constraints of textual inheritance, authority, and authorization. The book seems less thematically obsessed with genealogy, as though the king's intervention rendered less compelling the search for a grounding in literary tradition or a narrative filiation that guaranteed the outcome of the quest. Critical comments on the *Tiers Livre* often reflect this difference by underscoring its autonomous quality as a genre. Floyd Gray remarks: "The fictional structure of the *Tiers Livre*, however, was quite unlike anything the world had ever seen. It is not constructed around the life of a hero, does not include a progressive revelation of character, follows neither an ascending nor descending line of development, conforms, in short, to no known fictional pattern" ("Structure and Meaning," 61).[6] The *Tiers Livre* founds its lineage upon the word of the king, which confers, along with its secular authority, a measure of divine right.[7]

But the sovereign as father also takes away. Nowhere has the writer as writer appeared more vulnerable. The sovereign's "privilege" is both to confer it and to exercise it; it is a law that enables as well as speaks an interdiction. Censorship, political repression, and the king's weighty sanction converge on this text to deflect it into that most highly politically coded of discourses, the *querelle des femmes*. Marriage, as

---

act—an act placed in the bipolar field of the sacred and the profane, the licit and the illicit, the religious and the blasphemous. Historically, it was a gesture fraught with risks before becoming goods caught up in a circuit of ownership" (148).

[6]Although I would take issue with some of the specific remarks Gray makes concerning this book, the question of character development in particular, this statement nevertheless reflects the impression of "originality" conveyed by the *Tiers Livre*.

[7]Thus it might be said that the king's *privilège* also allays some of the anxieties involved in the project of rewriting or displacing the biblical "father text." The king's approval can in this respect be seen as divine sanction of Rabelais's fallen text.

the theme of the *Tiers Livre*, is both the sign of a displacement of the political and a symptom of paternal interdiction.[8] It is perhaps no coincidence that the author describes himself as having been deemed impotent by his bellicose compatriots.

The confidence in lineage enabled by the king's *privilège* seems to find its culmination at the end of the book, in chapter 51, where the Olympian gods express the concern that Pantagruel's children might one day succeed in reaching their abode:

> Les Dieux Olympicques ont en pareil effroy dict: "Pantagruel nous a mis en pensement nouveau et tedieux, plus que oncques ne feirent les Aloïdes, par l'usaige et vertus de son herbe. Il sera de brief marié, de sa femme aura enfans. A ceste destinée ne povons nous contrevenir, car elle est passée par les mains et fuseaulx des soeurs fatales, filles de Necessité. Par ses enfans (peut estre) sera inventée herbe de semblable energie, moyenant laquelle pourront les humains . . . s'asseoir à table avecques nous, et nos déesses prendre à femmes, qui sont les seulx moyens d'estre deifiez." (346–47)

> In a similar fright the gods of Olympus cried: "By the power and uses of this herb of his, Pantagruel has given us something new to think about, which is costing us a worse headache than ever the Aloides did. He will shortly be married. His wife will bear him children. This is fated and we cannot prevent it. It has passed through the hands and over the spindles of the fatal sisters, the daughters of necessity. Perhaps his children will discover a plant of equal power, by whose aid mortals will

[8]Leon Battista Alberti's *Della famiglia* and Baldassare Castiglione's *Cortegiano*, like Rabelais's *Tiers Livre*, deal with the "question of woman" in the third book of their dialogic treatises. I think it can be argued that in each the discourse on woman is politically coded: all three are constrained in their writing by an interdiction on the level of the political. In Castiglione's work, of course, the comparison is explicit: the discussion of the relation between a courtier and his prince becomes instead a discussion about the court lady.

be able to . . . sit down with us at table there and marry our goddesses: which is their one means of rising to be gods." (428–29)

Genealogy is projected into the future, with Pantagruel posited as origin. The writer has indeed become the author, while the movement of inheritance becomes a progressive one, each generation improving upon its ancestors until it achieves semidivinity. The form the threat to the gods takes is also telling: Pantagruel's desire and the gods' fear is that his descendants will marry "their" goddesses, which in turn will confer divinity or sovereignty. The desire for a telos is nowhere more evident, though this vision too is finally qualified, not only by the parenthetical "perhaps" but more threateningly (and definitively, if we remember Homer, Plato, and Virgil) by the final sentence of chapter 51: "In the end they decided to deliberate on a means of preventing this, and called a council" (347; 429).

The reminder, at the end of the chapter, that the Olympian gods have many times struck down arrogant giants who aspire to the divine throne and the inscription of this literary topos into the text point to another component, both structural and thematic, of the *Tiers Livre*: repetition. In the Prologue, the figure of repetition marks the author's self-consciousness about the problem of genealogical succession in all its textual forms and the problematic alternation of *copia* or plenitude and emptiness, so well charted in Rabelais by Cave. Diogenes performs a series of more or less synonymous actions upon his tub and repeats this performance endlessly and futilely. The enumeration itself mimes the description, with words engendering one another not as progressive succession but as an emptying out of signification, such that they themselves, not what is being described, become the focus of the passage. A third dimension of repetition can be seen on the intertextual level: the very fact of using Diogenes's tub rolling as a figure for writing, for its relative uselessness, repeats the gestures of Lucian and Budé in their own texts.[9]

Rabelais's *prise de conscience* as author produces this cynical redefinition of writing as a circular activity that threatens, by its very generativity, to empty out meaning—"ce rien, mon tout, qui me restoit" (14) ("that nothing, which is all I have left, my all" [284])—or as Cave puts it, the tendency of writing "to enact the cornucopian movement as an emptying out rather than a filling up" (189). Thus the references to Diogenes' silence ("without uttering a word"), the emptiness of his barrel, and the way the words of the descriptions take over what is being described.[10] At the same time, this emptying out performs a subtle critique on the wartime preparations being described by creating both a contrast and an analogy between Diogenes and the Corinthians. Diogenes' (and the writer's) contribution to the war effort is either as "useless" as the effort itself or is a form of protest whereby the hyberbolic repetitive activity undermines the seriousness of the other, goal-directed preparations.

Whereas Berrong, among others, reads this Prologue as a

[9]Lucian uses the Diogenes anecdote in his treatise *The Way to Write History*, while Budé compares himself to the philosopher in his *Annotationes in Pandectas*. See Floyd Gray, "Structure and Meaning in the Prologue to the *Tiers Livre*," 58, and Thomas M. Greene, *Rabelais: A Study in Comic Courage*, 62. Gray says of the authors: "They transfer the intense activity of the Corinthians to the literary scene of their own times, and Diogenes's tub is made to represent their own efforts which they term insignificant compared to the more laborious undertakings of their contemporaries" (59). Rabelais reinstates the context of war and uses the figure for satirical purposes. In this respect I agree with Walter Kaiser's interpretation of the Prologue as antiwar satire; see *Praisers of Folly: Erasmus, Rabelais, Shakespeare*.

[10]Alice Fiola Berry has an interesting discussion of Diogenes' "rhetoric of silence" in "Apollo versus Bacchus: The Dynamics of Inspiration (Rabelais's Prologues to *Gargantua* and to the *Tiers Livre*)," 91. She also discusses the opposition "en vin/en vain," fullness and emptiness, that structures the Prologue to the *Tiers Livre*.

sign of Rabelais's endorsement of war, of authority and order, Greene at least recognizes the Diogenes anecdote as ironic, while claiming that Rabelais criticizes Erasmus's position in "Dulce bellum inexpertis" in the passage referring to "certain botchers of old Latin tags" (12–13; 283) on the subject of the etymology of the term for war.[11] "Nothing in this passage authorizes us to read its [war's] praise ironically," Greene writes ("Unity of the *Tiers Livre*," 295). Yet this discourse culminates in a focus on the writer's position in relation to national mobilization; the irony is primarily self-directed, and as such its status as critique remains necessarily ambiguous.[12]

The writer has been judged "too weak and impotent" (13; 283) to participate in the offensive; he contrasts himself with the "valorous, eloquent, and warlike persons who are performing their noble interlude and tragi-comedy before the watching eyes of all Europe" (13–14; 284), using theatrical language bordering on satire. His promise to become epic chronicler of the deeds and exploits of France's warriors— "they shall have me as their faithful steward, . . . and as the eulogist, the indefatigable eulogist, of their brave and glorious feats of arms" (16; 285)—is never borne out, for unlike the other books, the *Tiers Livre* contains no great epic gestes. Whether as a response to the failure of irenic and anti-imperialist representations of France (Thélème) in the context of ongoing wars and political repression or as a result of an authorial autonomy severed, through printing as the agent of transmission, from a known and reliably sympathetic community of readers, the writer retreats from the position

[11]Richard Berrong, *Every Man for Himself: Social Order and Its Dissolution in Rabelais*, 40–41; Thomas Greene, "The Unity of the Tiers Livre."

[12]As Berrong, Stephens, and others have noted, Rabelais's position in the service of Cardinal Du Bellay, as well as his *privilège* from the king, perforce constrains him to be critical in the (safely subtle) mode of irony. See also the notes in the Guy Demerson edition, *Oeuvres complètes*, 363–64, n. 25, and the Screech edition, *Le Tiers Livre, Edition critique*, 9, n. 46.

of national chronicler, however playfully parodic that endeavor might have been. Instead he engages in the less intelligible activity of "tub rolling," whereby writing becomes a privatized pursuit, and turns to a markedly domestic theme, marriage.

The effacement of the writer's importance conflicts with another discourse in the Prologue. This latter discourse evolves through the metamorphosis of the empty tub into a barrel of wine. Writing is metaphorized as wine in order to evoke plenitude ("In this way the cask will remain inexhaustible, endowed with a living spring and a perpetual flow" [19; 286]). Cynicism gives way before an affirmation of abundance and an expression of good faith: "C'est un vray Cornucopie de joyeuseté et raillerie. Si quelque foys vous semble estre expuysé jusques à la lie, non pourtant sera il à sec. Bon espoir y gist au fond" (19) ("It is a true cornucopia of ridicule and fun; and if at times it seems to you to be emptied to the lees, still it will not be dry. As in Pandora's jug, good hope lies at the bottom" [286]).

In the final movement of the Prologue, the author draws back from this plenitude and seeks, this time, to restrict participation in his cornucopian text. In this respect Rabelais acts out his new function as author, to restrict or impose certain limits on the proliferation of his fiction and the way it is to be read. "The author does not precede the works, he is a certain functional principle by which, in our culture, one limits, excludes, and chooses; in short, by which one impedes the free circulation, the free manipulation, the free composition, decomposition, and recomposition of fiction . . . The author is therefore the ideological figure by which one marks the manner in which we fear the proliferation of meaning" (Foucault, "What Is an Author?" 159). Author and author function converge in Rabelais's Prologue. The accession of the printed book to a marketplace economy, a relatively new development for sixteenth-century authors, as well as for Rabelais as best-selling novelist, produces the symptomatically juridical response of the author, to limit or curb (to control) the threatening dissemination of his work.[13]

Although Foucault's statement suggests that such a limiting of meaning comes to discourse from the outside—that, for example, literary historians designate works as "authored" texts—here a certain autodesignation is at work. What Foucault does point to that is so strikingly evident in this text is the way the material conditions of book production are intimately linked to the thematic concerns of the fiction. Rabelais's attempt to exclude a certain readership ("[Why?] Because they are not of good, but of evil" [20–21; 286]), his efforts to guide readers toward an *in bono* interpretation of his text, find a more philosophical counterpart in the quest for a certain stability of meaning in the last three books.

Countertendencies are continually at work: on the one hand, signs proliferate; signification operates independent of authorial control, subject also to the historical contingencies of context and readerly reception. On the other hand, these signs are constantly being brought under the ideological control imposed by the quest and its "resolution." The confrontation with contingency and the multiplicity of interpretations brings with it the fear of empty repetition (Diogenes' tub) or of an abundance that will be construed as monstrous (*uber/tuber*), like the black Bactrian camel or the bicolored slave.[14] Rabelais's progeny, however temporarily secure in

[13]By incorporating Foucault into this discussion, I hope to continue to explore the ways the material aspects of text production and dissemination are written into and intimately shape discourse and meaning in a fictional text.

[14]Terence Cave, expanding Alfred Glauser's discussion of the opposition/relation *uber/tuber* in *Rabelais créateur*, writes about the threatening aspects of fictional productivity in Rabelais, the way the "very celebration of fertility, plenitude, presence, reveals an inverse movement toward emptiness or absence." See *The Cornucopian Text: Problems of Writing in the French Renaissance*, 187. See also Cathleen Bauschatz, "'Une Description du

their legal grounding, nevertheless are subject to genealogical uncertainty—the benevolent giants may indeed transform themselves into their monstrous counterparts, the evil giants of literary tradition.[15]

Against this threat Rabelais asserts his status as author, his ability to legitimize his offspring with his name and the king's and thus to regulate the way his fictions will be read. The danger is both external and internal. Rabelais's readers may misinterpret the signs of the text, while printers ("l'imposture des imprimeurs" [16]) ("if they had not been adulterated and spoiled by dishonest printers" [284]) may produce unauthorized (and unexpurgated) editions. At the same time, those signs cannot be brought entirely under the author's control. There is no longer, in the *Tiers Livre*, any "natural" connection between signs and their meanings to guide signification along the designated path of the quest and guarantee a communal response to the text.

Nor can such coincidence of meaning and truth be guaranteed (and this becomes increasingly clear in the last three books) by the transcendental guidance of God. In chapter 19 Pantagruel argues, "'Les languaiges sont par institutions arbitraires et convenences des peuples; les voix (comme disent les Dialecticiens) ne signifient naturellement, mais à plaisir" (140) ("Languages arise from arbitrary conventions and the needs of peoples. Words, as the dialectitians say, have meanings not by nature, but at choice" [339]). Human convention determines meaning, for the most part—and herein lies Rabelais's concern for his readers—yet the phrase "les voix . . . ne

---

Jeu de Paulme Soubz Obscures Parolles': The Portrayal of Reading in *Pantruel* and *Gargantua*," and Alice Fiola Berry, "The Mix, the Mask and the Medical Farce: A Study of the Prologues to Rabelais's *Quart Livre*," for discussions of Rabelais's attitudes toward his readers. See also Floyd Gray, "Rabelais's First Readers," a study of the Prologues to the first two books.

[15]This is perhaps why, from the *Tiers Livre* on, the reader is made less aware of the gigantism of Rabelais's protagonist.

signifient naturellement, mais à plaisir" points not only to the author's own arbitrary imposition of meaning, but also to the sign's capacity to generate signification "of its own accord," as it were.[16] Words love each other and multiply. This proliferation is both joyful and menacing, threatening meaninglessness and hiding the agency of "quelque beau diable." Fallen discourse errs, leading away from truth and into the underworld of the *Quart Livre*, Rabelais's "season in hell" (Alice Fiola Berry, "Les Mithologies Pantagruelicques: Introduction to a Study of Rabelais's *Quart Livre*," 471).

The last three books differ considerably from the first two. Although the *Quart Livre* will return, in a sense, to the recounting of deeds and exploits promised by the conclusion to *Pantagruel*, it will do so in an entirely different mode, with a satirical edge missing from the other books and without a central hero.[17] The enterprise of national mythmaking and its parody, both of which Stephens sees as germane to Rabelais's "gigantology," no longer play a central role in the narrative. Indeed, the national myth that Rabelais is said to have helped constitute through his works derives from the two books that bear the giants' names, not from the other three. The gigantic dimensions all but disappear, while the

[16]As Charles Méla points out, referring to the proverb cited in the Prologue of Chrétien de Troyes's *Perceval*, "qui peu sème, peu récolte" ("who little sows, reaps little"), in language that enacts the fertile prodigality he is describing: "Beneath the Gospel of the Grail appears the Gospel of literature, whose commandment would formulate itself in the famous terms of the prologue to *Perceval*: that words love each other, that the charity of the letter happily sows the sense [ *sens*] that suddenly animates it, evoking the soul of Life [ *l'âme de vie*]. But what is at play here? That wicked complicity of words covers some fine devil (for whom laughter is fitting, as everyone knows, since Merlin's *facéties*). To speak truly, understanding [ *le sens*] illuminates nothing that is not simultaneously subtracted from it" ("La Reine et le graal," 302).

[17]For a detailed study of the *Quart Livre*, see Paul J. Smith, *Voyage et écriture: Etude sur le "Quart Livre" de Rabelais*.

declared structuring principle is the "medievalizing" quest with its privatized individual quester rather than the nationalistic epic with its public warrior-hero.

The confrontation between semiotic contingency, the uncontrolled or self-generating tendencies of language, and authorial control of meaning that characterizes the Prologue prepares the way for the quest that will emerge as the structure and theme of the last two books. The dominant generic model within which the quest unfolds is romance, or rather that hybrid form of epic and romance that evolves in the course of the later Middle Ages.[18] Errance, in both thematic and semiotic terms, is constitutive of the genre. "'Romance' is characterized primarily as a form which simultaneously quests for and postpones a particular end, objective, or object. . . . When the 'end' is defined typologically, as a Promised Land or Apocalypse, 'romance' is that mode or tendency which remains on the threshold before the promised end, still in the wilderness of wandering, 'error,' or 'trial.'" (Patricia Parker, *Inescapable Romance: Studies in the Poetics of a Mode*, 4).[19]

---

[18]Neither genre can be strictly defined by the sixteenth century in France. For the development of these generic categories in the Middle Ages, see W. P. Ker, *Epic and Romance: Essays in Medieval Literature*; Eugène Vinaver, *The Rise of Romance*; Northrop Frye, *The Secular Scripture: A Study of the Structure of Romance*; and Daniel Poirion, ed., *Précis de littérature française du Moyen Age*, 83–128. For Rabelais's use of romance see especially Nemours H. Clement, "The Influence of the Arthurian Romances on the Five Books of Rabelais," and Edward Morris, "Rabelais, Romances, Reading, Righting Names."

[19]See also Parker's first chapter, "Ariosto and the 'Errors' of Romance," in *Inescapable Romance*. Roger Dragonetti, in his *La Vie de la lettre au Moyen Age*, explores the errance of signs as a constitutive feature of the medieval *roman*. See also Kevin Brownlee and Marina Brownlee, eds., *Romance: Generic Transformation from Chrétien de Troyes to Cervantes*. Nemours H. Clement has exhaustively cataloged the references to medieval romances in Rabelais and has also shown that the themes and structure of the first two books correspond to those of the Arthurian corpus: "The chief *matière* of

The strangely submerged path that Arthurian romance follows in Rabelais's text is glimpsed in one of *Pantagruel*'s intertexts, the *Grandes et inestimables chronicques du grant et enorme geant Gargantua*. The *Grandes Chroniques* open with Merlin offering to help King Arthur fight the many enemies he will shortly be encountering. To this end Merlin travels to the highest mountain of the Orient, taking with him some of Lancelot's blood and Guinevere's fingernail parings. There he creates Gargantua's parents, Grant-Gosier and Galemelle, who in turn beget Gargantua and set off toward Great Britain. Gargantua's parents die en route, and Merlin reappears to conduct the young giant to Arthur's court. There Gargantua goes into battle, defeating "Gos et Magos" and a third giant, thus restoring peace to the realm until his death:

> Et ainsi vesquit Gargantua au service du Roy Artus l'espace de deux cens ans troys moys et iiii jours justement; puis fut porté en faierie par Gain la Phée, et Melusine, avecques plusieurs aultres, lesquelz y sont de présent. ( Huntington Brown ed., 126)

> And so Gargantua lived in the service of King Arthur for the space of two hundred years three months and four days, exactly; then he was transported to fairyland by Morgan le Fey, and Melusine, along with several others who are there now.

The literary genealogy of the *Grandes Chroniques*, like the genealogy of the character Gargantua, constructs itself from the relics of Arthurian romance ("a phial of Lancelot's blood that he had collected from his wounds," "fingernail parings

---

the books of the first part is the *matière* of such Arthurian Romances as the *Lancelot* and, in minor measure, of the Gest Romances: the *enfances* of the hero and his exploits in war and in peace hold the chief place in them" ("Influence of the Arthurian Romances," 161). The last books, he notes, are loosely modeled on the Grail-quest romances, as the symbolic configuration represented by the Holy Bottle seems to suggest.

of the beautiful Guinevere, wife of King Arthur" [106]) and of precisely that adulterous union that further delays the quest.[20] The secret ingredients that assist in Merlin's monstrous and gigantic creation, those relics of adultery, mark Gargantua with a kind of original sin that is also the mark of post-Babel discourse, the "errance" of the secular narrative that is a theme of romance. Rabelais's novel inherits this sin while self-consciously parodying its own attempts to adhere to a "correct" path of narrative progression.

Rabelais translates this remnant of adultery at the origin of *Gargantua*'s lineage into a concern with genealogy, a concern that endangers the parody of genealogy by its very obsessiveness. The obsession continues in the quest, but submerged or displaced, as a concern with future lineage, onto the character Panurge, who, precisely, has neither parents nor home (*Pantagruel* chap. 12, 99). This comic displacement of what in *Perceval* is "an attempt to relocate and thus to restore the integrity of a lineage that is from the beginning unrecognizably fragmented" (Bloch, *Etymologies and Genealogies*, 207) effects a generic scrambling: "The relationship of the opposing generic terms of comedy and romance is thus to be seen as a functional one of substitution or repression in which one mode is used to defuse the other, for an explicitly ideological purpose" (Fredric Jameson, "Magical Narratives: Romance as Genre," 154). In Jameson's passage it is unclear which of the genres substitutes, represses, or defuses (although in context he seems to be taking the Bakhtinian position that comedy constitutes the disruptive force, which must then be glossed over or disguised by romance). Rabelais's text is similarly ambiguous; whereas in the first two books one might say that romance generally serves to defuse the social antago-

---

[20]Howard Bloch, in *Etymologies and Genealogies: A Literary Anthropology of the French Middle Ages*, examines the relation between adulterous or illicit desire and the disruption of narrative and genealogical continuity in medieval romance.

nism that emerges through the comic mode, particularly in the Prologues, in the last books there is a reversal whereby comedy, as generated principally by Panurge and Frère Jean, disguises or masks the disturbing problematics of romance narration. The one obvious exception is *Pantagruel*, chapters 14–15, where Panurge's comic degradation first of the Parisian noblewoman and then of another lady's letter speedily represses the "question of woman" in the heroic tale.

Predictably, then, the romance motif that emerges as problematic in the last three books, and that is also fundamentally connected to the problems of narration and signification addressed through the quest theme, is marriage.[21] Although it is clear that the sixteenth-century *querelle des femmes* shaped in large part the debates of the *Tiers Livre* and that, as M. A. Screech has so well documented in *The Rabelaisian Marriage*, Rabelais was engaged in marriage propaganda specific to his times, the question of marriage in these books testifies to a more general problematics of medieval romance, one that turns out to be an allegory of father and son.[22] "The *roman* is, de facto, the privileged locus of the discourse of love, but to define it as love hides the true question, one that persists even in the guise of a refusal, the question of marriage. All

[21]Patricia Parker studies the connections between representations of women and rhetoric, property, and literary genre in *Literary Fat Ladies: Rhetoric, Gender, Property*.

[22]Rabelais dedicates the *Tiers Livre* to Marguerite de Navarre, sister of Francis I. More work needs to be done to uncover the relation between the question of woman addressed in this book and Marguerite's own problematizing of gender relations. Marriage was very much on Marguerite's mind in the period between 1546 and 1552. The marriage of her daughter, Jeanne D'Albret, had just been annulled for political reasons in 1545. Francis died two years later, and in 1548 Jeanne was married to the duke of Vendôme, out of which union would be born Henry IV; see my entry on Marguerite de Navarre in Denis Hollier, ed., *A New History of French Literature*.

romance is nuptial romance where to take a wife means (and
this is the secret motor [*ressort*] of the crisis) to succeed the
father. That a hero should become, in his turn, king, this is
what constitutes the true *roman* of love" (Charles Méla, "Romans et merveilles," 218). Méla goes on to point out that the
medieval oedipal motif per se comes to an end with Chrétien
de Troyes's focus on the Grail in *Perceval le Gallois, ou Le Conte
du Graal*, but that the problematic persists in another guise:
"Chance may offer the mother or her shadow in marriage to
the son, following profound desire, but this is not what is
essential, for the mother is less the object of his secret desire
than the place where the secret of his desire is kept, that is to
say, that which she herself desires" (220).[23]

What is in fact at work in the question of the hero's marriage is a certain relation to paternity. In *Perceval* this relation
is one of absence, the absence of the father and a name (the
name-of-the-father, in Lacan's terms). This absence poses the
problem of the hero's identity, which is revealed to him
through the quest as a filiation with him who is "other" than
the father, the transcendent paternal figure.[24] The Other
may be either diabolical or divine, the devil or God; he must
in any case be greater or more powerful than the father in

[23]Jacques Lacan's formulation is that "man's desire is the desire of the
Other," so that what is desired is so by virtue of being desired by the
Other. Not only does the son desire the mother, but the desire is for what
she in fact desires (which is always "other" than the father). See *Ecrits: A
Selection*, esp. 269, 288. René Girard's notion of triangulated desire, formulated as a critique of the oedipal complex in Freud, focuses on the relation
of mimetic desire that must exist between father and son in order for the
son to desire what the father desires (the mother); see *Violence and the
Sacred*.

[24]Charles Méla notes that "it always turns out that an Other than the
father haunts the dream or the desire of the mother and that the hero must
go all the way back to him in order to be, in his turn, stricken, before
being, at last, reborn" ("Romans et merveilles," 229).

order to confer meaning upon the son's quest, since the father proves radically insufficient to the quester's desire for an idealized, and lost, origin.[25] Thus genealogy is also linked to theology through the quest. The quest for divine presence is a semiotic quest, linked as well to the search for meaning and for narrative closure. Questing, in its Christian version at least, posits meaning, as Richard Waswo notes of referential theories in general, "not just as a substance, but as an eternal one" (*Language and Meaning in the Renaissance*, 80).[26]

*Le Conte du Graal* remains radically unfinished, Perceval's failure to arrive at and comprehend the Grail paralleling the author's own failure to bring his narrative to a close. Thus already in the twelfth century the impossibility of narrative "rectitude," of a completeness of meaning beyond words, the failure of the quest, is enacted in what might be called the purposeful nonclosure of Chrétien de Troyes's romance.

This preliminary digression on the narrative strategies of Chrétien's *Conte du Graal* may begin to lay the ground for a genealogy, both structural and thematic, of Rabelais's problematization of marriage and its relation to the father and the quest.[27] The *Tiers Livre* brings with it a "return of the re-

[25] For the relation between woman's desire and the divine, see Jacques Lacan, "Dieu et la jouissance de la femme," in *Le Séminaire de Jacques Lacan: Livre XX encore*.

[26] "The attempt to return to the Grail Castle becomes, then, an attempt to relocate and thus to restore the integrity of a lineage that is from the beginning unrecognizably fragmented—and, at the same time, to restore a lost plenitude of meaning situated beyond signs. In the quest for union with the lost father lies the wish to unite the signifier with its signified. . . . Here again, *Le Conte du Graal* falls within the romance mode of a simultaneous problematization of paternity and of narration" (Bloch, *Etymologies and Genealogies*, 206).

[27] "Genealogy" is being used here in the sense given the term in Friedrich Nietzsche's "On the Genealogy of Morals" (in *Basic Writings of Nietzsche*) and Michel Foucault's "Nietzsche, Genealogy, History," with the pertinence to source criticism given it by Paolo Valesio: "The intertextuality of this narration is located in the vertical dimension and in depth—

pressed," once again in the form of reference to an absent lady whose mention carries with it a relation of desire between son and absent father, for in *Pantagruel* her message was the message of the son to the absent and quintessentially idealized father: God. In that chapter (*Pantagruel*, chap. 15) the connection to writing was made as well; the "Pythagorean symbols" of the lady's letter were indecipherable, requiring decoding by one who practices "that art by which letters can be read that are not apparent" (*Gargantua*, 23; 42). Each encounter with "woman," and more specifically with marriage, repeats the accession to Lacan's Symbolic order (the order of language), the intervention of the (law of the) father, Freud's "primal father" whose death instantiates the incest taboo.[28]

Problems of signification, paternity, and marriage all converge in chapter 35 of the *Tiers Livre*. The context is a dinnertime conversation at the palace, with Panurge seeking further advice on marriage.[29] The debate with Trouillogan provides the occasion for Gargantua's resurrection and his reappearance on the scene. Trouillogan's name (translated by

---

not in the horizontal dimension. The vertical dimension, or rather, source criticism, hopefully expanded and somewhat refined in its conception, is nevertheless assumed without any embarassment. . . . Source criticism is the materialistic and systematic side of literary history. . . . To expand the traditional practice of source criticism means to speak not only of literary derivations, but of psychological origins as well. Source criticism, therefore, inevitably becomes genealogy. . . . What is genealogy? It is (I will suggest here) the unartistic and so often (except for its tenaciousness) disappointing art of groping for a beginning" ("Genealogy of a Staged Scene [ *Orlando Furioso* V]," 7–8).

[28]Sigmund Freud, *Totem and Taboo*, trans. James Strachey, 132–46. On Lacan's Symbolic in relation to Rabelais and the father, see my "The 'Instance' of the Letter: Woman in the Text of Rabelais."

[29]*La Queste del Saint-Graal* begins in this manner, with a conversation at the round table in King Arthur's palace. There the place is the locus of community or society from which the knights will set forth on their individual quests.

Cohen as "Wordspinner") is generally thought to derive from *trouil*, meaning a reel for winding or unwinding thread. Abel Lefranc speculates that Ockham is the philosopher behind Trouillogan, both because of the "ogan" (Okan) ending and because of Trouillogan's association with skepticism ("'So the most learned and cautious philosophers have all joined the thinking establishment of the Pyrrhonians, Aporrhetics, Sceptics, and Ephectics, have they?'" [253; 389]).[30] Gargantua's entrance into the room at the point when the sceptical philosopher speaks, he who undermines the certainty of meaning (and, as I discussed in chap. 4, severs language from reference), is hardly fortuitous.

His appearance is marked by a solemnity that disturbs the comic tenor of the chapter: "'Our king is not far away. Let us stand up.' And no sooner had he spoken than Gargantua entered the banqueting hall. Everyone then arose to make him a bow" (243; 385). In response to Panurge's frustration with Trouillogan's answers—"Panurge protests against these [repugnant] and contradictory replies, and objects that he can't understand a word of them" (244; 385)—Gargantua works to resolve the contradictions and fashion a meaningful answer from the philosopher's equivocal phrases:

"Je l'entends (dist Gargantua) en mon advis. La response est semblable à ce que dist un ancien philosophe, interrogé s'il avoit quelque femme qu'on luy nommoit: 'Je l'ay (dist il)

[30]*Tiers Livre, édition critique*, ed. M. A. Screech, lxxxvi: "What is hidden in this word: *ogan*? We hardly hesitate to respond: the name of a famous medieval philosopher, Ockham, which was pronounced Okan, barely modified and easily recognizable. Trouillogan would then represent "Ockham's reel." And this connection seems even more likely in that Trouillogan's scepticism, as the dialogue reveals it, very much resembles that of the new Ockhamism that develops in France, especially in the University, at the end of the fifteenth century and during the first quarter of the century following." Bloch has an interesting discussion of the connections between medieval skepticism, the speculative grammarians, and theory of narrative in *Etymologies and Genealogies*, chap. 4.

[amie], mais elle ne me a mie; je la possede, d'elle ne suys
possedé.'" (244)

"I believe that I understand, though," said Gargantua. "This
answer is like the one given by an ancient philosopher, when
asked whether he had a certain woman, whose name they
gave him as his wife. 'I have her,' he answered, 'but she hasn't
got me. I possess her, but I'm not possessed by her.'" (385)

When Abel Lefranc declares that "there is no doubt that
Rabelais always professed a declared antipathy toward these
theories" (lxxxvi), he does not take this passage into account.
It is Panurge who becomes frustrated with the philosopher's
responses, not Pantagruel or Gargantua. Although in chapter
36, Gargantua will be the one to reject Trouillogan's discourse, the grounds for his rejection do not necessarily reflect on the philosopher's speech itself. At this point in the
debate, he does not question the good sense of the philosopher's double-talk.

Chapter 36 stages a stychomythic exchange between Panurge and Trouillogan. Panurge seeks a firm resolution to
Trouillogan's argument—"'Let's come to some conclusion'"
(251; 388)—whereas the latter constantly eludes him. Panurge's distress becomes quite visceral (251), and as Screech
has noted, although the passage is undoubtedly comic, it is
also clear that Panurge is in dire straits (*Rabelais*, 260).[31] Finally, he gives up:

"Or ça, de par Dieu, j'aymeroys, par le fardeau de sainct
Christofle, autant entrependre tirer un pet d'un asne mort que

[31]It is strange that M. A. Screech should consider Trouillogan of minor
importance, given that his discourse occasions the reappearance of
Gargantua. He writes: "Two figures stand out from the third in the consultations proper: the theologian Hippothadeus and the doctor Rondibilis
(*Rabelasian Marriage: Aspects of Rabelais' Religion, Ethics and Comic Philosophy*,
66).

de vous une resolution. . . . Par la chair, je renie; [par le sang, je renague; par le corps,] je renonce. Il m'eschappe." (252)

"Come now, in Heaven's name! By the burden of Saint Christopher, I'd as soon undertake to get a fart out of a dead donkey as an answer out of you. . . . God's flesh, I give it up! God's blood, I throw in my hand! God's body, I abjure! He's slipping out of my grasp." (389)

At this point Gargantua intervenes. His speech is worth quoting entire, for it marks, in spite of its humorous moments, another solemn interruption in the comic flow of the debate.

A ces motz, Gargantua se leva et dist: "Loué soit le bon Dieu en toutes choses. A ce que je voy, le monde est devenu beau filz depuys ma congnoissance premiere. En sommes nous là? Doncques sont huy les plus doctes et prudens philosophes entrez on phrontistere et escholle des Pyrrhoniens, Aporrheticques, Scepticques et Ephectiques? Loué soit le bon Dieu. Vrayement, on pourra dorenavant prendre les lions par les jubes, [les chevaulx par les crains,] les boeufz par les cornes, les bufles par le museau, les loups par la queue, les chevres par la barbe, les oiseaux par les piedz; mais jà ne seront telz Philosophes par leur parolles pris. Adieu, mes bons amys." (253)

At these words Gargantua got up and said: "Good God be praised in all things! So far as I can see, the world's got into a fine old mess since first I began to watch it. Now we've come to this, have we? So the most learned and cautious philosophers have all joined the thinking establishment of the Pyrrhonians, Aporrhetics, Sceptics, and Ephectics, have they? Good God be praised! Truly, from now on it will be easier to seize lions by the mane, horses by the hair, oxen by the horns, wild oxen by the muzzle, wolves by the tail, goats by the beard, and birds by the claws, than to catch philosophers of this kind by the words they speak. Farewell, my dear friends!" (389)

Gargantua's declaration, which has often been understood as Rabelais's condemnation of Sophism and of skeptical philosophy in general, ambiguously reflects (given its context) both upon the philosopher's obscurity and upon Gargantua's own relation to the world he has returned to.

Up to this point, the conversation between Panurge and Trouillogan has been about the desire for certainty or resolution and the impossibility (expressed by the skeptic philosopher), on one hand, of satisfying that desire (Panurge is never satisfied with any of the answers he receives) and, on the other, of there being any guarantee of certainty or resolution. Gargantua comments first on the world, specifically on the world as progeny—"Le monde est devenu beau filz depuys ma congnoissance premiere"—then on the fact that philosophers cannot be pinned down to one meaning ("par leur parolles pris"). He expresses regret that the philosophers may have become skeptics, but this is not to deny that skepticism may be the only appropriate philosophical response to the world as it is now. His statement is more a reflection of the gap between his world and the present one of the *Tiers Livre* than a condemnation of skeptical philosophy as such.

The strange poignancy of the company's response to Gargantua's departure provides a glimpse into that gap between *Gargantua* and its "beau filz," the *Tiers Livre* of the 1540s: "After pronouncing this speech he withdrew from the company, and Pantagruel and the others wished to follow him. But he would not allow them to" (253; 389). The nostalgia for a return to a less confusing, clearer past, when philosophers presumably could be "taken at their word," is nowhere more apparent, and joined to this nostalgia is also the nostalgia for a union with the father who comes from that past. There is also the awareness, however, that such a return is impossible. The impossible return figured by the *Conte du Graal* is here made explicit through the "impossible return" (to life) of Gargantua, as the repressed desire of sons to reunite with fathers. Here too the Petrarchan sense of having

been forgotten by the ancients emerges as a rejection by the
father of the son's desire to return. Whereas the earlier works
alternated between an (albeit ambivalent) celebration of the
elasticity and contingency of meaning, the *Tiers Livre* longs
for a final resting place. Waswo calls this "the tyranny of
reference, the ineradicable dream that language has got to
represent something, if only itself," which "produces a pre-
dictable sadness at the heart of all the revelling even in those
who know it to be a dream" (*Language and Meaning*, 304).

Gargantua's retreat from the farce signals the necessity for
the quest, although it has not yet been proposed. His with-
drawal carries a certain finality (though he will reappear to
give his son consent), as the final confrontation with the
inability of the son, of the tale, of signification, to return to a
holistic origin. The quest, then, arises from the necessity to
seek an alternative to return, to find (or become) a new father, so to speak. It is interesting, then, in this context that
the rejection of the past must be projected as the father's
rejection of the present, so much so that Gargantua is resurrected for that purpose. The quest takes place not in spite of,
but because of the father. In this most autonomous of
Rabelais's books, a corresponding "anxiety of originality" is
at work, figured as the necessity, rather than the desire, to
find an alternative path in a semiotically obscured forest.
Gargantua, as epic hero, becomes the absolute, simpler, and
more serene past to which the present protagonists cannot
return.[32]

[32]Jameson writes, in "Magical Narratives": "Romance as a form thus
expresses a transitional moment, but one of a very special type: its contemporaries must feel their society torn between past and future in such a way
that the alternatives are grasped as hostile but somehow unrelated worlds"
(158). This statement, which may be said to describe a whole Renaissance
ethos, suggests a context for the conflict between past and future at work
in Rabelais. See also Paul de Man, "Literary History and Literary Modernity," in *Blindness and Insight: Essays in the Rhetoric of Contemporary Criticism*,
and Mikhail Bakhtin, *The Dialogic Imagination: Four Essays*, "Epic and
Novel."

In chapter 47, after numerous consultations, Panurge proposes an arbitrary means to end the endless repetition of questions and answers that have brought the narrative to a standstill: "'So I renew my former vow, and swear by the Styx and Acheron in your presence to wear spectacles on my cap and no codpiece on my breeches until I have the Holy Bottle's answer to my question'" (313; 416). What in fact marks the quest as parodic, from its outset, is the arbitrariness of its function in the plot; Panurge has received the answer many times over, and there is no reason to suppose that the word of the Holy Bottle will put his questioning to rest. The quest takes on the appearance of a formal necessity in the text, a way for it to arrive at a "dramatic unity and formal closure within the confines of an increasingly fragmented textual tradition" (Bloch, *Etymologies and Genealogies*, 207). At the same time, unlike the quest narratives Bloch's comment refers to, the effect of the quest motif in Rabelais is to reassemble a completely fragmented textual tradition, several traditions, and thus to invent a new generic category, which incorporates a quest because in fact it cannot do otherwise.[33]

The desire for narrative continuation effects a comic displacement of the question of marriage from Pantagruel to Panurge. The question of marriage should focus on the hero, whereas in the *Tiers Livre* the question centers on Panurge. Chapter 48, in which Pantagruel asks his father's permission to go on the quest, presents an elaborate dismissal of the issue insofar as it concerns Pantagruel. Gargantua, expressing the wish that his son marry, launches into a diatribe

[33]Rabelais's quest combines the medieval grail-quest narrative with the genre of fantastic voyages—such as Lucian's *True History*, the *Navigatio Sancti Brendani* (a subgenre of overseas voyages or *imrama*), which itself influenced the Grail romances, and Folengo's *Baldus*, as well as dream narratives, such as *Le Roman de la rose* and the *Hypnerotomachia Poliphili*. See Clement, "Influence of the Arthurian Romances," 206–7. See also Abel Lefranc, *Les Navigations de Pantagruel, étude sur la géographie rabelaisienne*, and *Tiers Livre, édition critique*, xciv–ci.

against clandestine marriages, contracted without parental consent. M. A. Screech's masterly study of this diatribe in *The Rabelaisian Marriage* describes the problem as a conflict between civil and canon law: "At this time in France young persons, even children, could be betrothed *in verbis de futuro* or married *in verbis de parenti* without the consent or even the knowledge of their parents. These marriages did not depend on publicity in any form, and parental consent was simply irrelevant. The legal basis for this is in Ecclesiastical Law, which claimed precedence over Civil Law since marriage was held a sacrament and thus the exclusive preserve of the Church" (47–48). Gargantua sides with civil law against the church's claim to exclusive jurisdiction. This position is necessary and logical in terms of the narrative; Gargantua is a father and has his lineage to protect.[34] The logic of epic succession and aristocratic lineage converges, in Gargantua's discourse, with xenophobic nationalism, as he launches into a diatribe against "some unknown stranger, some barbarian, some rotten, poxy, cadaverous, penurious, and miserable cur" who would marry

"leurs [les dolens peres et meres] tant belles, delicates, riches et saines filles, les quelles tant cherement avoient nourriez en tout exercice vertueux, avoient disciplinées en toute honesteté,

[34]It was clearly in the aristocracy's interests to oppose church-approved marriages contracted without parental consent. The state vacillated between the two positions, at times supporting the breaking up of aristocratic strongholds, at times overiding canon law. In sixteenth-century France it seems for the most part that the state took precedence, as in the case of Francis I's request for an annulment of Jeanne D'Albret's marriage. Again, one wonders what the relation is between Gargantua's words and the use of marriage in royal political maneuvering, as illustrated by the case of Marguerite's daughter. For the relation between family and state in the sixteenth century, see Natalie Zemon Davis, *Society and Culture in Early Modern France: Eight Essays*, and her *Fiction in the Archives: Pardon Tales and Their Tellers in Sixteenth-Century France*; also Sarah Hanley, "Family and State in Early Modern France: The Marriage Pact."

esperans en temps oportun les colloquer par mariage avecques les enfans de leurs voisins et antiques amis, nourriz et instituez de mesmes soing, pour parvenir à ceste felicité de mariage, que d'eulx ilz veissent naistre lignaige raportant et haereditant non moins aux meurs et leurs peres et meres que à leurs biens meubles et haeritaiges." (Chap. 48, 321–22)

their [the grieving mothers and fathers] most lovely, delicate, rich, and healthy daughters. They had tenderly schooled the girls in all the virtuous arts and brought them up in all modesty, hoping in due course to marry them to the sons of their neighbours and old friends, who had been brought up and schooled with the same care. They had looked forward to the birth of children from these happy marriages, who would inherit and preserve not only the morals of their fathers and mothers, but also their goods and lands." (419)

Gargantua's aristocratic defensiveness against the threat of a (bourgeois) class of parvenus seeking economic and social advancement through "intermarriage" prefigures the concern of the gods relative to Pantagruel's family in chapter 51 (346). It also suggests a fundamental opposition between the "narrative progression" of his family and that of Panurge, who looks very much like the "unknown stranger" of chapter 48.

It is strange that Gargantua brings up the issue, which had not even occurred to the hero ("'Most gracious father,' replied Pantagruel, 'till now I had not given the subject a thought'" [318; 418]). With a simple declaration, the father eliminates the necessity for his son to pursue the proposed quest: "'During your absence I will set about choosing you a wife and preparing a feast. For I want yours to be a famous wedding, if ever there was one'" (325; 421). Yet in this scene there is absolute complicity between father and son; the hero's quest is rendered unnecessary from the start without any appearance of tension on the surface of the text.

The subtext to these chapters of the *Tiers Livre* recasts the issue in a somewhat different light and provides clues to the motivations at work in this meaningful moment between father and son. Again, as in *Pantagruel*, chapters 14–15, a hidden subtext shapes the Rabelaisian text that reveals the ideological swerve Rabelais makes when the question of woman is introduced. François Habert's *Songe de Pantagruel* (1542) is a work that seems to have first copied Rabelais and then served as a subtext for him.[35] The *Songe* is a dream narrative. Pantagruel holds a banquet at which are assembled wise and learned men. He consults them in the hope of gaining knowledge about the Truth. That night he dreams of his dead father, who delivers a diatribe against the pursuit of worldly wealth. He tells his son that Pan, the great shepherd and a figure of Christ, left a book containing a guide to true happiness. Then Gargantua disappears and Panurge appears in the dream, having just returned from the Orient, where he witnessed a tournament held by the Turkish sultan. The list of participants includes many heroes of medieval romance as well as gods and the kings of France and Spain. Panurge's association with Mercury and with rhetorical prowess as well as thievery is made explicit in the poem. He says he was skilled at "Forger monnoye, & en oster à ceulx / Qui la garder estoient trop paresseulx" (lines 531–32) ("Forging money, and taking it away from those / Who were too lazy to watch out for it"). The sultan imprisons him, but he escapes with the aid of the sultan's daughter Melusine, who also gives him a valuable ring. Suddenly Gargantua returns, crying out to Pantagruel that he must take a wife:

> En premier lieu que tu soys adverty
> Au monde bas de prendre ung bon party,

[35]*Le Songe de Pantagruel, avec la deploration de feu messire Anthoine du Bourg, chevalier, chancellier de France* (Paris: Adam Saulnier, 1542) has been published, with an excellent introduction by John Lewis, in *Etudes Rabelaisiennes* 18(1985): 103–62.

Et te lier par loyal mariage
Multipliant la terre davantage.
(*Songe de Pantagruel*, 148, lines 603–6)

First of all, may you be advised
To take an active interest in this world below,
And to settle down in loyal marriage
Increasing and multiplying the world.

Finally, through a series of negations ("Ne cherche point," "Do not seek"), Gargantua gives his son some practical guidelines concerning what sort of woman he should take as wife to "multipli[er] la terre."

The *Songe* strikingly brings together the themes of fatherhood, death, mourning, and marriage in its dedicatory epistles, one of which is addressed to a man whose father has died (Habert praises the son for being an admirable legacy to his father's name), another to a woman who has recently been widowed (129–30). An oedipal configuration emerges in the very juxtaposition of the dedicatory verses, while throughout the dream itself the dead father repeatedly returns.

The *Songe* reveals that Rabelais displaces the question of marriage from Pantagruel onto Panurge, as he did the original encounter with a woman as erotic object in *Pantagruel*; it also provides evidence that Rabelais's resurrection of Gargantua is by no means the accident of absentmindedness that many critics have supposed. Once again, as in chapter 15 of *Pantagruel*, it is as if the issue of the hero's marriage cannot be avoided, though there is an effort to displace it. And it seems important, in the case of both marriage and the quest, that the hero's father be there to sanction and to determine the actions of his son. Whereas for Panurge, whose lineage is unknown, the fear is that he will be cuckolded and that "his" son will not be his, for Pantagruel that fear (and desire) is the fear of usurping the father's place, of becoming a father in his own right. The books enact a filiation that, in the *Tiers Livre*, begins to confront the impossibility of succession as culmination, closure, or resolution, either because it will be a repetition (Pantagruel and *his* son, Pantagruel's son and his, etc.) or because, being this history, it will be severed from the past that the narrative claims has begotten it.

The scene between father and son forecloses the possibility of Pantagruel's involvement with a woman in the course of the narrative. Some of the reasons for avoiding this can be found in the near-hysterical debates of the *Tiers Livre*. The anxieties about cuckoldry and castration (both in part a displacement of incest) lie behind the evocation of Tobias's dog (chap. 35) from the Book of Tobit, where seven men have died in their attempt to consummate their marriage with Sarah.[36] The sacred is also at work here, as palimpsest. In *Pantagruel*, chapter 15, it was necessary to eliminate the courtship phase of Pantagruel's development so as not to compromise his status as an epic hero, his Aeneas-like adherence to a higher cause. Here, at the threshold of the quest, *La Queste del Saint-Graal* comes to mind. The necessary condition for revelation, in that work, is a knight's chastity; Galahad, Perceval, and Bors are virgins or near-virgins. Galahad is the most perfect of the three, he who receives the full revelation of the Grail:

> Galahad, alone capable of completing the Grail adventure, has himself transcended desire, since his perfection consists in a chastity that precludes even the wish for union. Thus, where Perceval seeks unsuccessfully to find the father, the Grail, and to escape the contingent nature of signs, Galahad, himself the product of an almost immaculate conception and a second Christ in Christ's line, eludes genealogy altogether. His is a faultless self-sufficiency connatural with the identity of engenderer and engendered as well as with the coincidence of signifier and signified. (Bloch, *Etymologies and Genealogies*, 210)

[36]*The Apocrypha: An American Translation*, 107–30.

Pantagruel betrays no desire to marry; his will perfectly matches the will of his father, their complicity also being emblematized briefly by the reference to Tobit, a story of absolute filial obedience where even the names of the father and son, Tobit and Tobias, are practically indistinguishable ("Tobit" and "Thobie" in French).[37] Pantagruel's chastity enables him studiously to avoid the oedipal problem of succession to the king (and Gargantua is called "king" throughout the *Tiers Livre*) in order to preserve the authority of the father (and so too of tradition).[38]

That Pantagruel is simultaneously obedient to the father and virgin presents a paradox, since it is the father's will that he marry. His obedience promises genealogical continuity, while his presence in the narrative disrupts that continuity so that, rather than succession, there is a harking backward in time, to the father and to origins.[39]

This father-son relation may be said to allegorize, as it has throughout the earlier books, the problems of succession inherent in the Renaissance myth about itself as a period in time. As the thematic allegory of a whole Renaissance problematics, the narrative both supports and interrogates the arguments made by Thomas Greene's *Light in Troy*, which describes Renaissance versions of imitation as replete with the ambivalence of (biological) filial succession. "The pathos of [the] incomplete embrace" between the humanist son and

[37] *Petit Robert 2: Dictionnaire des noms propres.* Homophonic resemblance in proper names is a common technique of medieval romance.

[38] Tobit neatly figures a reverse oedipal story: the father is blinded and the son restores his sight.

[39] Bloch writes of the epic: "The most tangible sign of an underlying tension in the narratively sequential and representationally integral universe of the epic is to be found in a certain closure to its own posterity. Indeed, so wholly fixated upon the past is the Old French *chanson de geste* as to produce a blindness to (repression of?) any possibility of the future" (*Etymologies and Genealogies*, 103).

the ancient father, the lack of verification or approval from the paternal figure, the absence of the other's voice forces the humanist's realization that "his dialogue with the past always remained finally constructed" (43). This recognition of contingency is at work in the parodies of succession in the first two books, while the ironizing of the parodic quest also signals a distance between the adoption of the structure and an adherence to its metaphysics.

Greene goes on to describe the humanist "movement": "The whole enterprise sustained conflicts between intuitions of intimacy and intuitions of separation, between the belief in transmission and a despair of transmission, between the denial of estrangement and the acceptance of estrangement, between reverence for the *maiores* and rebellion against them. Microcosmically the humanist text can be read as a reflection, an instance of these conflicts" (*Light in Troy*, 45). The paradox is one of authentication based on tradition as against the desire to supersede the past. Inheritor of the ancients— revered fathers—the Renaissance author finds himself in the position of ceding all greatness to the fathers or directly challenging their superiority. The same might be said of the narrative in relation to the Bible. If Pantagruel (and *Pantagruel*) derives his (its) genealogy from the Bible, then the will to superiority becomes sacrilegious. But the *Tiers Livre*'s predicament is not that of "heuristic" imitation, which Greene describes as the humanist ruse—"the double ruse of a myth of origin and a myth of modernist growth away from the origin"—and Pantagruel is not, in Greene's terms, the humanist poet who "like the son in a classical comedy . . . displaces his father at the moment of reconciliation" (41). Pantagruel's position brings growth to a halt, in the longing for and impossibility of return, while the narrative endlessly defers the designated path of continuation.

Greene goes on to delineate a "healthy" resolution to the imitative dilemma, what he calls "dialectical imitation"(45), an ideal relation between father and son ("a two-way current of mutual criticism"): "By exposing itself in this way to the destructive criticism of its acknowledged or alleged predecessors, by entering into a conflict whose solution is witheld, the humanist text assumes its full historicity and works to protect itself against its own pathos" (45). What Greene, in his dialectic that is really a synthesis, and others fail to account for is the radical negativity of the *Tiers Livre*'s "solution" to its own narrative continuation, a solution that I would argue is constitutive of the novel in its very negativity.[40]

[40]Even Richard Waswo, who generally criticizes the idealization of the past by present critics, lapses in his description of Renaissance imitation: "To see oneself as able to reenact the literary or imperial achievements of Rome, to take it as a model for 'imitation,' was not (as it later became) to impose limits but to expand possibilities. It was to assert the eventual equality required in adopting a role-model relationship, such as that of fathers and sons. We must feel ourselves, though immature, enough *like* them to believe that someday we can and will do what they have done, that their power will be ours" (*Language and Meaning in the Renaissance*, 140). David Quint offers a more straightforward example of the positivist school of Rabelais interpretation, in one of its most successful versions, Christian exegesis: "Rabelais ends his book, and now his entire five books, by depicting his characters in the possession of an apocalyptic foretaste, participating now as interpreters in a future closure of meaning—and then by drawing both those characters and his reader back into the incomplete, still open-ended processes of history. The quest for the Grail-like Dive Bouteille ends by urging the seeker to continue on the quest of human history" (*Origin and Originality in Renaissance Literature: Versions of the Source*, 204). In focusing on the negativity of the text, I am following in the footsteps of critics such as Beaujour, Cave, Glauser, Gray, Paris, and Rigolot; these critics, however, often self-consciously refrain from acting out the ideological totalization that is a trademark of the positivists (see Rigolot's "Cratylisme et Pantagruélisme" for a notable exception), rather than participating in the debate to find "the meaning" of Rabelais. I think it is important to engage the debate, not to show that there is a message, but to demonstrate that it cannot be one that synthesizes, or one that illustrates the artist's literary mastery, or one that triumphantly adopts bourgeois individualism as a solution to a crisis about meaning. For an important corrective to the notion that Renaissance imitation was a positive endeavor, see Margaret Ferguson, *Trials of Desire: Renaissance Defenses of Poetry*.

Critics have read the chapters describing Pantagruelion as the hope in the Pandora's box of the *Tiers Livre*, or even as a culminating vision of sorts, answering to their own as well as Rabelais's dream of a serene Renaissance ushering in the modern scientific age or Christianity's "divine mission" of conquest. David Quint argues, with regard to chapter 51 (346–47): "The assault of the Rabelaisian giants is an emblem of those apocalyptic events—the ascent of a restored Zion into the Kingdom of Heaven—which complete salvation history after progressive advances in human learning and technology have brought the evangelical mission of Christianity to its fulfillment" (*Origin and Originality*, 175). But in fact the image of progression outlined in chapters 49 through 52 suggests an encroachment of science, technology and human ingenuity upon the divine, a challenge to it whereby mortal man could attain through his own powers the status of a god (which is why, perhaps, readers are reminded at the end of chapter 51 that the gods have punished all previous attempts). Furthermore, the challenge that Pantagruel's heirs represent remains a potential one. This path of scientific progress is never pursued in the context of the narrative. Pantagruel remains single and childless, a monument to his progenitor but not a god. If the hope for such a future is expressed, there is little confidence in that hope: the gods are already preparing for its destruction.

The relationship of Pantagruel to Gargantua may be seen to personify the proper genealogical relation characteristic of the epic mode. The connection between the thematic father-son relationship and questions of signification—what constitutes the "proper" of language and of narration—was already thematically suggested by Gargantua's appearance at the moment when the Ockhamist philosopher disrupts the proper relation between question and answer, between language and communication. Howard Bloch traces how medieval language theory, incorporating language into the realm of nature, connected the idea of narrative order and its disruption to the natural order of genealogical succession and the "unnatural" paths of illegitimacy, adultery, sodomy, and other forms of generative and nongenerative sexual coupling.[41] He argues that the genre of epic was associated with the idea of the "natural" genealogical progression, or family as lineage (*Etymologies and Genealogies*, passim). Commenting on Alain de Lille's *De planctu naturae*, he writes: "In this way the satirist envisages two types of language coterminous with two principles of descent. The first is natural and correct, since Nature, Hymen's brother, is the guardian of grammar, the proper, and the paternal; the second, in contrast, transgresses the rule of natural genealogy and grammatical rectitude. It poses the possibility of a discourse divorced from property, and, as its name [Jocus] suggests, inscribed in the illegitimacy of play" (134). Alain's allegory of sexuality and language (and its extension, narrative) offers a suggestive image of the transfer of the quest from the (epic) protagonist to Panurge and the eventual direction Rabelais's narrative continuation takes. If in fact epic can only monumentalize the past, as Bakhtin suggests, then it is only the principle of transgression, of illegitimacy—Panurge—that will allow the narrative to continue. This occurs, but with a residue of anxiety: the references to filial obedience, the submerged signs of the oedipal conflict surrounding Pantagruel and his father, and in contrast, Panurge's newfound obsession with genealogical rectitude and narrative teleology. Gargantua's fear of miscegenation is displaced onto Panurge, the un-

[41]Michel Foucault, *The Order of Things: An Archaeology of the Human Sciences*, 35: "The great metaphor of the book that one opens, that one pores over and reads in order to know nature, is merely the reverse and visible side of another transference, and a much deeper one, which forces language to reside in the world, among the plants, the herbs, the stones, and the animals. . . . Language partakes in the world-wide dissemination of similitudes and signatures. It must, therefore, be studied itself as a thing in nature. Like animals, plants, or stars, its elements have their laws of affinity and convenience, their necessary analogies."

known stranger, who thereby expresses a fear of legitimate succession. Of course any filial succession, however legitimate, may only seem so from the son's point of view: for Pantagruel's sons, intermarriage with the gods is an achievement, it is progress. The gods, however, recognize it as a threat.

Panurge, as his name suggests and his behavior demonstrates, is all-desiring. He speaks in praise of expenditure and waste (*Tiers Livre*, chaps. 3 and 4) rather than conservation. Being parentless and homeless, he is free from the constraints that bind Pantagruel to the strict path of paternal inheritance. Panurge is also associated with the transgression of the proper, in language as in every other endeavor. His first meeting with Pantagruel (*Pantagruel*, chap. 9), his debate with Thaumaste (*Pantagruel*, chap. 13), his courtship of the "noblewoman of Paris" (*Pantagruel*, chap. 14), and his misinterpretations of the *Tiers Livre* debates all demonstrate the way he "distorts" language's communicative function to his own purposes.[42]

Yet in a curious reversal signaling the displacement of the question from Pantagruel to Panurge, he suddenly becomes concerned with propriety, with controlling and channeling his Panurgic nature within the lawful, ordering bonds of marriage. For all his transgressive behavior and his freedom from constraints, what he fears most is that his wife will transgress the rules of marriage and make him a cuckold with her all-desiring (chap. 9). The anxiety about genealogical rectitude, what is proper, is comically displaced onto Panurge and to the subject of cuckoldry.

Panurge, in his constant refusal to accept the signs proffered him in the *Tiers Livre*, enacts at the same time the

---

[42]Berrong points out that Panurge's interpretations in the *Tiers Livre* are not necessarily wrong, just as Pantagruel's are not necessarily right; he also provides a useful survey of other critics' opinions on Panurge's "misinterpretations" in the *Tiers Livre*. See *Every Man for Himself*, chap. 2.

endless and repetitive proliferations of desire and language and the search for a transcendent sign, the authentic sign to end all signs (and his search). This double movement away from and toward closure enables the narrative to continue, for Panurge's restless search is what generates most of the *Tiers Livre*'s discourse. In this sense Panurge is like Perceval, whose constant misinterpretations lead him to digress from the path of his quest.[43] *Le Songe* connects Panurge to the genre of romance: he is an errant wanderer from the East, witness to marvelous tournaments in which the illustrious knights of romance do battle. In the *Songe*, however, Panurge's errance has no direction; it is Pantagruel, rather, who is in quest of the Truth. By transferring the quest to Panurge the rhetor, Rabelais makes it a specifically semiotic problem as well. Panurge personifies and dramatizes the "scandal of language" (Cave, *Cornucopian Text*, 193), its duplicitous movement both toward a plenitude of meaning and toward a self-generating deviation or errance in infinite semiotic regression. As the principle of digression and generator of the quest, Panurge becomes the locus for Rabelais's parodic exploration of romance as the genre that puts into question its own process of narration.[44]

[43]One particularly humorous moment in *La Queste del Saint-Graal* stresses this aspect of Perceval that Chrétien de Troyes had already developed in *Perceval le Gallois, ou Le Conte du Graal*. After Perceval has barely escaped the irremediable loss of virginity that would have rendered futile his quest for the Grail, a holy man appears to him. Perceval begs the man to interpret the events that took place, at which point the man answers: "'Ah, Perceval,' sighed the other, 'you will ever be simple. So you have no idea who the young woman was that brought you to the verge of mortal sin, when the sign of the cross preserved you?'" *The Quest of the Holy Grail*, 131).

[44]Of *Le Conte du Graal*, Bloch writes: "Chrétien, like Perceval, himself seeks a poetic rectitude that is, in the telling of the tale, constantly disseminated—scattered and partial; and that accounts, ultimately, for the increasing incoherence of a bifurcated romance which cannot end" (*Etymologies and Genealogies*, 207).

The Grail romances, from *Le Conte du Graal* to the *Queste del Saint-Graal*, inscribe narration as the quest for the Grail, the search for a transcendental signifier and the impossibility of its attainment, as the story's movement toward a closure beyond words (the end of the story) denied it by the digressive paths of signification that defer the story's "death" and leave the romances open to successive continuations.[45] The quester in the Grail romances, as I mentioned earlier, seeks through the quest to reestablish a lost genealogical continuity and to return to a lost father. Panurge, on the contrary, seeks to establish a line of succession and quests for the word that will guarantee the legitimacy of his line, just as the word of the king legitimizes Rabelais's creation. His quest is arbitrary and absurd from the beginning; the *Tiers Livre* proves he will find no such guarantee.

Rabelais's narrative inscribes a temporal predicament into the relation between Pantagruel and Panurge, one that also brings into play the generic conflicts between epic and romance in what Bakhtin has called the "novelization of genres," the insertion of "indeterminacy, a certain semantic openendedness, a living contact with unfinished, still evolving contemporary reality (the openended present)" (*Dialogic Imagination*, 7). Critics have noted Panurge's resolute futurity, his denial of the viability and importance of the past (and his own unknown genesis reinforces this), while, as I have shown, Pantagruel's adherence to it produces an impasse in terms of the narrative's future movement. Marcel Tetel characterizes

[45] Among the continuations are, on the one hand, extensions and rewritings of the Grail story, such as Robert de Boron's *Le Roman de l'estoire dou Graal* (ca. 1200) and *La Queste del Saint-Graal* (ca. 1225–35), and on the other, continuations that focus on the specific quests of Perceval and Lancelot: the *Didot-Perceval* (ca. 1214), *Perlesvaus* (ca. 1220–25), the *Lancelot-Graal*, and the thirteenth-century prose *Lancelot*. See Charles Méla, *Blanchefleur et le sainte homme, ou La Semblance des reliques: Etude comparée de littérature médiévale*; also Bloch, *Etymologies and Genealogies*, and Dragonetti, *Vie de la lettre*.

the relationship nicely: "Panurge represents anxiety about the past, the sources and the readings, and the desire to deny that past; Pantagruel, on the other hand, expresses an ambivalence towards the past and establishes himself as continuator of the past, the elect of the gods in the Platonic tradition" ("Rabelais et Folengo: *De patria diabolorum*," 210).

Bakhtin's formulation suggests, however, that it is somehow possible to "represent the present," a phrase that itself expresses the impossible contradiction of the endeavor, as Paul de Man has noted in his discussion of literature as complicating the relation between modernity and history.[46] Panurge's quest for the word of the Holy Bottle, like the assertion of modernity that "exists in the form of a desire to wipe out whatever came earlier, in the hope of reaching at last a point that could be called a true present, a point of origin that marks a new departure" ("Literary History and Literary Modernity," 148), strives for the place beyond language where no further interpretation will be necessary. But that quest is already defined in the work as a regressive quest, a return to a past already repeated in the earlier books and in the medieval quest itself. That past, the situating of the self as a product of history, brings Pantagruel to paralysis. When de Man writes that "the continuous appeal of modernity, the desire to break out of literature toward the reality of the moment, prevails and, in its turn, folding back upon itself, engenders the repetition and the continuation of literature" (162), he is describing the ambivalence of writing that "can be considered both an act and an interpretive process that follows after an act with which it cannot coincide" (152). The

---

[46]De Man, *Blindness and Insight*, 162: "The continuous appeal of modernity, the desire to break out of literature toward the reality of the moment, prevails and, in its turn, folding back upon itself, engenders the repetition and the continuation of literature. Thus modernity, which is fundamentally a falling away from literature and a rejection of history, also acts as the principle that gives literature duration and historical existence."

figure for that ambivalence, for "literature," is Rabelais's (ironic) quest.

At the end of the *Tiers Livre*, two possible continuations of Rabelais's narrative might be envisaged. One would trace the story of Pantagruel, developing the outline suggested in the Pantagruelion chapters of the *Tiers Livre*. The other, the continuation actually adopted, follows the company's vicissitudes as they quest for the word of the Holy Bottle. Panurge's quest proceeds under the guise of parody and satire: parody because the search for Truth is rendered comically futile by the character Panurge, and satire in that the *terre gaste* of the *Quart Livre* remains unconnected to any suggestion of potential restoration that might have been figured as the protagonist's redemptive quest.[47]

What gets displaced or masked in the narrative, however, is the residual dilemma posed by Pantagruel's relation to his father. With Pantagruel, as I said, the narrative reaches an impasse: the story has already been written by the father. The quest for a totalization of meaning, a will to mastery reflected in the father's exhortations of the early books, the son's gigantic feats, and the exposition of the miraculous powers of the herb Pantagruelion, finds no avenue of expression through its hero. The text's quest for its own meaning, in the impossibility of returning to an original meaning or source and in the desire to constitute another universe of meaning, moves the narrative forward to a resolution, however artificial and "inauthentic."[48] Thus, whereas the medieval Grail romance dramatizes its "inability to recapture a lost narrative continuity" in the process of narration itself,

---

[47]Galahad is figured explicitly as a redeemer in the *Queste*, and even Teofilo Folengo's *Baldus*, which is a parody of questing, provides an ostensibly redemptive purpose for the quest.

[48]I am referring, of course, to the attribution of inauthenticity that marks the *Cinquième Livre*. See Alfred Glauser, *Le Faux Rabelais, ou l'inauthenticité du "Cinquiesme Livre."*

Rabelais's text imposes a teleology whose impossibility is already presupposed. While parodying the very idea of quest, the narrative is impelled along its course. The desire for a stabilization of sense is still at work, *unparodied*, in Pantagruel's adherence to his father's path, just as the narrative that proposes lineal succession (the story of Pantagruel) implies closure or resolution, however deferred that closure might be.

The nostalgia for a past one cannot return to resurfaces in the *Quart Livre*, in chapters 25–28 about the island of the Macreons. Like the Rome Du Bellay will write about later in the century, these *antiquitez* are in ruins:

> Et par la forest umbrageuse et deserte, descouvrit plusieurs vieulx temples ruinez, plusieurs obelisces, pyramides, monumens et sepulchres antiques, avecques inscriptions et epitaphes divers. Les uns en letres Hieroglyphicques, les aultres en languaige Ionicque, les aultres en langue Arabicque, Agarene, Sclavonicque, et aultres. . . . Panurge dist à frere Jan: "Icy est l'isle des Macraeons. Macraeon, en grec, signifie vieillart, home qui a des ans beaucoup." (*Quart Livre*, Marichal ed., chap. 25, 128)

> In the shady and unfrequented forest, he pointed out several old ruined temples, several obelisks, pyramids, monuments, and ancient tombs, with different inscriptions and epitaphs. Some were in hieroglyphics, others in the Ionic tongue, others in Arabic, Hagarene, Slavonic, and other tongues. . . . Panurge said to Friar John: "This is the island of the Macreons. Macreon, in Greek, means old man, a man stricken in years." (505)

In the *Briefve déclaration* of 1552 Rabelais glosses hieroglyphs nostalgically, pointing again to the adequacy of representation to meaning that was the reason for their evocation in *Gargantua*, chapter 8: "Ainsi estoient dictes les lettres des

antiques saiges Aegyptiens,. . . par la nature et office desquelz estoit représenté ce qu'ilz vouloient désigner" (Demerson ed., 777) ("This is what the letters of the ancient Egyp-
tian sages were called, . . . by whose nature and function
were represented that which they wanted to designate").
They are accordingly "sacred sculptures," designated not as
"languaige" (language) but as "letres" (letters), traces of a past
not immediately interpretable by linguistic means. They
point to but do not speak about the past, which is thereby
rendered inaccessible. The ruined temples, obelisks, and
pyramids are monuments and tombs bearing inscriptions
and epitaphs, signs of an absolute past, not texts to be read as
Alcofrybas reads the unearthed book of Gargantua's genealogy.

In these chapters the passage of time has brought decay
and desolation. History is seen as regression; Macrobe describes his islands as "'once fertile, much visited, wealthy,
and populous. . . . Now, in the course of time and with the
world's decay, they have become poor and desolate, as you
see'" (129; 506). Death, not resurrection, is the focus of Pantagruel's story of Christ in chapter 28. It is interesting that
Epistemon mentions France in this context, although his os-
tensible reason for doing so is to eulogize Guillaume Du
Bellay:

> "Lequel vivant, France estoit en telle felicité que tout le
> monde avoit sus elle envie, tout le monde se y rallioit, tout le
> monde la redoubtoit. Soubdain après son trespas, elle a esté
> en mespris de tout le monde bien longuement." (chap. 26,
> 130)

> "Whilst he lived the fortunes of France were so great that the
> whole world envied her, the whole world sought her alliance,
> and the whole world dreaded her. Immediately after his death
> she became the scorn of the whole world, and has been so for
> a long time now." (507)

This passage suggests that the *Tiers Livre*'s irresolution and the *Quart Livre*'s satiric tone are related to a crisis of nationalist sentiment that renders untenable the earlier books' epic aspirations. Whereas the *Songe* can exhort to the son to read the book of Pan, the *Quart Livre* can only mourn the finality of the god's death.[49]

At the end of this series of anecdotes about how nature announces its sorrow at the death of heroes, Pantagruel gives two examples of evil tyrants who wanted to produce the effects of a cataclysm at their death, to make it seem as though the world were mourning (131–32). These examples ostensibly criticize tyranny and the production of signs that, "instituted by human imposition" (*Gargantua*, chap. 9, 71; 59), signify "falsely." From *Gargantua* on, the text worries the problem of the proper measure of authority and connects it to the author's own preoccupation with controlling the meaning and reception of his work. These examples demonstrate that signs *can* signify falsely. The death of the father (the Father) brings with it here the end of divine guarantee for the meaning of signs; whereas hieroglyphs, produced by and circulated among a closed group of elect, were adequate to what they represented, now no such adequation can be relied upon to guarantee meaning. Appropriately, chapter 27 invokes Plutarch's *On the Cessation of Oracles*.

Gérard Defaux has suggestively compared the *Quart Livre* to Exodus, based on the mention Panurge makes in chapter 56—"'I remember reading that, as they stood around the edges of the mountain on which Moses received the Laws of the Jews, the people palpably saw the voices'"(228; 568–69)—one of the two famous "parolles dégelées/parolles gelées"

---

[49]M. A. Screech's article "The Death of Pan and the Death of Heroes in the Fourth Book of Rabelais: A Study in Syncretism" concentrates on Rabelais's syncretic use of sources in these chapters. Defaux and Jeanneret both connect these chapters to the episode of the "parolles dégelées."

chapters of the *Quart Livre*.[50] Although he concludes his reading of these chapters by synthesizing Rabelais's message in the *Rabelais moralisé* tradition, his comparison does point to the exile without revelation of the *Quart Livre*'s quest: "But these resemblances are not what really matter. Their only function ultimately is to articulate the differences, to make the other spring forth from the same, to show to what extent the universe in which our voyagers travel is an absurd and fallen universe, an empty universe, deserted by God. Pantagruel can always think Presence, Word, and Revelation. A disenchanted and vanquished Moses, he will not have his theophany" ("A propos de paroles gelées et dégelées," 169). Chapters 55 and 56, like the chapters on the death of Pan, also meditate on history as decay, on the mysterious origins of words that "trickle down" to the present—traces, like the ruins in chapter 25, of a past inaccessible to the present. But these chapters replace pathos and nostalgia with parody and wordplay; Pantagruel's speculations on the source of the unfrozen words overinterprets, as Defaux has noted. There is, rather, in the two chapters a movement toward the reduction of the possibilities of meaning, as Jean-Yves Pouilloux's study of these chapters has so brilliantly shown ("Notes sur deux chapîtres du *Quart Livre*").

In chapter 26 signs might be counterfeited, abused by tyrants, yet there was no doubt that such portents from the divine could exist. Here the status of the signs themselves is reduced. Whereas Pantagruel wants generally to ascribe lofty and distant origins to the mysterious sounds—the manor of

[50]Jean Guiton, "Le Mythe des paroles gelées (Rabelais, *Quart Livre*, LV–LVI)"; Jean-Yves Pouilloux, "Notes sur deux chapîtres du *Quart Livre*, LV–LVI"; Michel Jeanneret, "Les Paroles dégelées (Rabelais, *Quart Livre*, 48–65)"; Tonino Tornitore, "Parole gelate prima e dopo Rabelais: Fortuna di un topos"; Gérard Defaux, "A propos de paroles gelées et dégelées (*Quart Livre* 55–56): 'Plus hault sens' ou 'lectures plurielles'?" and his "Vers une définition de l'herméneutique rabelaisienne: Pantagruel, l'esprit, la lettre et les paroles gelées."

Truth, Orpheus's head and lyre—they turn out to be the leftover traces, animate and inanimate, meaningful and meaningless, of a battle that had been fought the previous winter (chap. 56, 228). The demystification of origins occasions play: Defaux rightly notes that the reduction from the spirit in language (the "parolles voltigeantes" ["bounding words"] of Homer in chap. 55, 227; 568) to its letter (the "frozen words" of chap. 56) makes of it a concrete material to be freely and irreverently manipulated in the dizzying wordplays of chapter 56.

Defaux concludes that the "moral" of the story ("the lesson is highly exemplary here" [173]) is that "the 'more sublime sense' ['plus hault sens'], and the inestimable wealth it carries, are accessible only to those who have first learned to master the literal meaning" (173). But there is a contradiction between what the episode seems to say and what it does, two incompatible orders of signification that lead Pouilloux to suggest two meanings ("sens"), one internal to the episode itself and one in the context of the novel as a whole (92). Once the origins of these signs have been demystified they become things, and Pantagruel loses interest in their specificity; on the contrary, he would rather mystify silence: "'I'd rather sell you silence, though I should ask a higher price for it" (chap. 56, 229; 569). He rejects the narrator's desire to preserve the frozen "motz de gueule" ("gay words") on the grounds that Pantagruelists always have such words on hand. Pouilloux notes that "everything takes place as though we had an ensemble programmed in such a way as to neutralize its own capacities for production; a machine to make emptiness, that is to say, silence" (92). Panurge, in contrast, persists in believing that "the word of the Holy Bottle" will be an end point, a sacred and reified symbol that will end the proliferating wordplay that destroys him in chapter 56. Until then, his phrase suggests, the narrative will continue, in spite of the allegory of the frozen words. Thus, Pouilloux concludes, "The 'frozen words' narrate a misrecognition ['méconnaissance'], but this misrecognition alone makes possible the existence of the *novel* ['roman']" (94).

But the *méconnaissance* is not Panurge's, as Pouilloux would have it. Nor can the contradiction described be resolved in the movement between figurative and literal, since the passage from one to the other is itself rendered ironic by the terms of the narrative. In the movement from sound to sight, in the literalization of the words and their redeployment as both literal and figurative (in the wordplays), there is also a passage into writing: the wordplay in the final paragraph of chapter 56 can only be read, not enacted or heard in the exchange between Frère Jean and Panurge. The predicament that presents itself sequentially in the episode of the "paroles dégelées/paroles gelées" is an allegory of writing as well, a "rhetoric of temporality" that recognizes the illusion of narrative extension even as it resumes a teleological quest.[51]

The quest, in Rabelais, takes the form of a teleological narrative that both is and is not parodic. Likewise, its failure is and is not ironic. In presenting the quest as superfluous even before it has begun, Rabelais parodies the mystifications of romance, figuring the futility (in comic terms) of pursuing a quest that cannot, a priori, arrive at a revelatory goal. In the Grail romances, particularly in continuations of

[51]Paul de Man, "The Rhetoric of Temporality," in *Blindness and Insight*. Two points de Man makes are particularly relevant to the irony of the *Quart Livre*: "The ironic language splits the subject into an empirical self that exists in a state of inauthenticity and a self that exists only in the form of a language that asserts the knowledge of this inauthenticity" (214); also: "The act of irony, as we know [*sic*] understand it, reveals the existence of a temporality that is definitely not organic, in that it relates to its source only in terms of distance and difference and allows for no end, for no totality" (222). About the "illusion of narrative extension," de Man writes: "The fundamental structure of allegory reappears here in the tendency of the language toward narrative, the spreading out along the axis of an imaginary time in order to give duration to what is, in fact, simultaneous within the subject" (225).

Chrétien's *Le Conte du Graal* such as *Le Queste del Saint-Graal*, there is confidence that the signs of revelation point in a particular direction—the divine—whether or not the quester can arrive at that revelation. This confidence is shared by a community of readers in the text. The failure of the quest is limited to its goal, the sense in which the quest is "doomed by the impossibility of . . . a transcendence identifiable with the Grail itself" (Bloch, *Etymologies and Genealogies*, 207), and to the failure of the individual quester to correctly interpret the signs of the sacred.

In Rabelais's text, however, the signs themselves are confused. The quest is doomed not only by the impossibility of arrival but also, and more radically, by the impossibility of reliably interpreting any given sign. There are no longer any divine guarantees, and narrative proliferation is repetitive in the sense that it is play indulging in the illusion of direction. None of this, of course, accounts for the satire of the *Quart Livre*; a more historically contextualized reading of the work would be needed, one that goes beyond the scope of this book. My aim here is to understand the quest as a thematic and structuring principle in the narrative's continuation—to learn why, in fact, the quest is so compelling that the history of Rabelais's reception includes a fifth book that, though apocryphal for most critics, is nevertheless canonical for translators, students, and lay readers of Rabelais.

The *Quart Livre* does not end so as to make continuation impossible, nor is the quest so forgotten that the Holy Bottle, as icon, might become irrelevant. David Quint's conviction that the last chapters of the *Cinquième Livre* were indeed written by Rabelais is telling in this regard (*Origin and Originality*, chap. 6). Waswo's notion that the later Renaissance and the rise of scientific empiricism brought back reference theories of meaning suggests the interesting speculation that arrival at the oracle became necessary as a way of imposing closure on this radically unfinished text. A Renaissance predecessor of Rabelais, Teofilo Folengo, also parodies the quest and figures the failure of his parody in a way that clearly underscores the impasses of the model and the attempts to overthrow it and yet arrive at closure. Folengo's magnum opus in macaronic Latin, later dubbed the *Baldus*, delineates a quest linguistically, thematically, and structurally similar to that of Rabelais's final books. In his case as well, the quest is cast in the satiric or comic mode, parodying, as Marcel Tetel has noted, the descent to the underworld in search of the father of the *Aeneid*, book 6, which in turn forms part of the genealogy of Rabelais's father-son relationship. Again, as Tetel notes, the Virgilian paradigm proposes a successful movement of departure, descent, and return; the *Baldus* and the books of Rabelais both adhere to the paradigm and seriously question it in their "negative" quests.[52]

In book 12 Baldus and his companions embark upon a voyage, the first two incidents being an encounter between the trickster figure Cingar (Panurge's prototype) and a sheep merchant and a storm at sea. Expanded versions of both episodes occur in the *Quart Livre*, constituting chapters 5–8 and 18–22. The reappearance, in Rabelais's text, of the key passages in the chapter that announces a quest reinforces, along with other evidence of borrowing, the suggestion that Rabelais is following the course of Folengo's adventurous journey.[53]

Although the description of Baldus's infancy and early exploits humorously sketches the portrait of an antihero, the

---

[52]Marcel Tetel, "Rabelais et Folengo; *De patria diabolorum*," 204: "The classical Virgilian model remains idealized and represents, as well, an ideal world. When Folengo seizes upon it, he materializes and vulgarizes it; he does not denigrate it, but he puts it into question in order to test himself against it, in order better to mold it to the exigencies of his epoch, with a satiric and transfigurational goal."

[53]For Rabelais's use of Folengo, see Marcel Tetel, "Rabelais and Folengo," and his "Rabelais et Folengo: *De patria diabolorum*"; Louis Thuasne, *Etudes sur Rabelais*; Michel Jeanneret, "'Ma patrie est une citrouille': Thèmes alimentaires dans Rabelais et Folengo."

latter half of the poem approaches, in its tone, the high seriousness of epic; the quest, an incredible voyage and a har-
rowing of hell, is endowed with a (quasi-noble) moral purpose (to purge the world of witches) and sanctioned by
paternal authority (Guidone, Baldus's father, assigns him this
mission in book 18). Through a narrative deus ex machina (a
sudden earthquake), Baldus finds himself in a room full of
classical and medieval and Renaissance heroes. The mysterious "divine being . . . protector of paladins," Seràfo, seats
Baldus among them, whereupon another earthquake ensues,
and the vision disappears in smoke (book 18, lines 381–
501).[54]

Just before Baldus and his companions arm themselves for
the descent, they encounter the author of the text, Merlin
Cocaius (Folengo's most frequently employed pseudonym)
(Paoli ed., 36–37; book 22, lines 1–232). The (metatextual)
commentary provided by the author's persona betrays an
(ironic) embarrassment concerning the text's blasphemous
discourse at the threshold of a sacred world (here in its demonic aspect). The macaronic muse (who governs the lower
regions of the body and what pertains to the human or demonic rather than to the divine) has been chosen because
Homer and Virgil have exhausted the supply of the most
precious poetic materials.[55] Here genealogical descent implies decay and decadence. The quest affords the possibility
of redemption—Merlin has awaited for one-hundred years,
six months, eight days, and fourteen hours the moment
when Baldus, as a degraded Christ figure, will rout the de-

---

[54]Teofilo Folengo, *"Baldus" e le altre opere latine e volgari*, ed. Ugo E.
Paoli, "Sommaria espozione del 'Baldus,'" 32.

[55]The following is a translation from the *Baldus* by P. L. Jacob, *Histoire
macaronique de Merlin Coccaie, prototype de Rabelais*, 312: "Phoebus, thinking
deeply about this matter, finally gave this response: 'There are different
metals that I have become accustomed to distributing to different Poets. . . . Our store is full of such materials, except for the box of gold
which has been completely used up by Homer and Virgil.'"

mons of hell.[56] In a final act of purification, the heroes are forced to confess their sins. Baldus, now an exemplary hero, volunteers first, swearing fealty to God while Cingar, in his reluctance to confess, becomes the scapegoat for the text's (previous) recalcitrance (Paoli ed., 37).

The quest fails, however, in both its redemptive and its parodic aims. The confrontation with Lucifer is never realized. The failure of the proposed redemption presents itself as ironically self-conscious: at the bottom of hell sits a gourd (or pumpkin) in which astrologers, poets, and all who tell lies are condemned and tortured.[57] There, of course, the author of the work is forced to remain, leaving Baldus's fate in the hands of some future poet who will ensure his safe return. In this sense the quest is always already a failure; the author of such self-conscious blasphemy cannot but be condemned on his own terms. As a parody the quest also fails, for it cannot escape the (Christian) teleology it seeks to undermine. Unlike Rabelais, of course, Folengo's epic can have no serious nationalist thrust; there is no "Italy" to unify under a monarch, while Folengo's language, macaronic Latin, exiles the writer, a priori, from the possibility of such an enterprise. The sacred model loses none of its authority. The final lines of the poem:

---

[56]For this use of the term "degraded" see Paolo Valesio, "Il seggio e l'ombra: Da un romanzo spagnolo del quattrocento," 84: "The concept of 'degradation' is here understood in a gnoseological or truly technical sense, not in a moral way: that is, it involves studying the theologemes present, in indirect and fragmented form, in literary texts (in all important literary texts—this is the project of a longer work). It is an indirection that varies, from the simplicity of brutal foreshortenings to refined allusion, to contradiction. The task of the semiotician is to illuminate and reconstruct these theologemes, in all their (complex) relations with their contexts."

[57]See Michel Jeanneret's "'Ma patrie est une citrouille'" for the importance of food, and the pumpkin in particular, in these two texts.

Tange peroptam, navis strachissima, portum,
tange, quod amisi loginqua per aequora remos:
he heu, quid volui, misero mihi, perditus Austrum
floribus et liquidis immisi fontibus apros[58]

Touch that most yearned for shore, O weary ship,
arrive, for I have lost my oars in the immense waters:
Alas, what have I wished, poor fool: destroyed,
I have sent the Auster onto the flowers
and boars into clear springs

—demystify the work and condemn it for having defiled its sources. At the same time, the author despairs of the work's capacity to offer a viable (if demonic) alternative (here expressed in the conceit of a boat without its guiding oars) to the divine telos it satirizes.

As its precedent, Folengo's text illuminates aspects of the failure of the Rabelaisian quest, a failure that the continuator renders explicit in his (?) depiction of the company's arrival at Bacbuc's temple. The ironic self-condemnation of the Italian poet is unimaginable in an author with Rabelais's national success and royal patronage and in a country with imperialist aspirations, however ambivalent Rabelais might have been about those aspirations. At the same time, the narrative leaves undemolished (though it is residual) the paradigm of history figured in the father-son relationship, "of history as a temporal hierarchy that resembles a parental structure in which the past is like an ancestor begetting, in a moment of unmediated presence, a future capable of repeating in its turn the same generative process" (de Man, "Literary History," 164). This paradigm was shared by the Renaissance in its myth about itself and has been accepted by the European

[58]These lines are rendered doubly ironic, since the last two come from Virgil, *Eclogue* 2, lines 58–59.

descendants of the Renaissance. Given such a model, it is not surprising to think that Rabelais would have continued the quest to the point of arrival—Mireille Huchon's work on the "archaeology" of the *Cinquième Livre* suggests that it was there at least in potential—and that a continuator did so.[59] The failure of the quest is its inability to unify a community under a transcendent symbol that will confer, with its universal truth, the silence of an "authentic" closure; its triumph, in the centuries of interpretation that have enlisted a *Rabelais moralisé* for their cause, is individualism.

The Holy Bottle, successor both to the popular tradition incarnated in Folengo's pumpkin, carnival, and Bakhtin's grotesque and to the elite pre-Christian and Christian traditions of divine inspiration, sacred blood, and Communion, seems to bring the entire range of a civilization's semiotic possibilities together in one collective symbol. There is an attempt to create a communality of meaning through the use of the onomatopeic word "trinch," which, however, must be explained as such, since the literary text cannot call sound into presence: "'Elle est,' s'escria Panurge, 'par la vertu Dieu, rompuë, ou feslée, que je ne mente: ainsi parlent les bouteilles cristalines de nos pays, quant elles près du feu esclattent'" (Jourda ed., chap. 44, 452) ("'By God almighty,' cried Panurge, 'it's broken or cracked, I'll swear. That is [how] glass bottles [speak] in our country when they burst beside the fire'" [703]). Panurge, of course, does not understand, and in a further reference to a physical action rendered impossible in the literary medium, he is encouraged to drink. The interchangeability of wine and the book, which seems to confer a greater immediacy on the text—

> "Les philosophes, prescheurs et docteurs de vostre monde vous paissent de belles parolles par les aureilles; icy, nous

---

[59]Mireille Huchon, *Rabelais grammarien: De l'histoire du texte aux problèmes d'authenticité*; see also her "Archéologie du Ve Livre."

realement incorporons nos préceptions par la bouche. Pourtant je ne vous dy: Lisez ce chapitre, voyez ceste glose; je vous dy: Tastez ce chapitre, avallez ceste belle glose. Jadis un antique Prophète de la nation Judaique mangea un livre, et fut clerc jusques aux dens" (chap. 45, 453)

"The philosophers, preachers, and doctors of your world feed you with fine words through the ears. Here we literally take in our teaching orally, through the mouth. Therefore I do not say to you: Read this chapter, understand this gloss. What I say is: Taste this chapter, swallow this gloss. Once upon a time an ancient prophet of the Jewish nation swallowed a book, and became a learned man to the teeth" (704)

—serves instead to emphasize the absence of an immediate transformation.[60] Panurge drinks, but he continues to question. Finally Bacbuc provides an interpretation, claiming for "trinch" a universally agreed-upon meaning, as in the case of the word "sac." This gesture of glossing, as well as the lack of unanimous response by the characters, thematizes the impossibility of assuming that a universal semiotic code exists with-

[60]See Richard Lanham, *The Motives of Eloquence: Literary Rhetoric in the Renaissance*, 175–76: "Fundamental to Rabelais's narrative strategy—and I think to Spenser's—is the impossibility of direct, non-symbolic experience. Both try to re-create it self-consciously, but this obviously cannot be the same thing as a primitive, participative, 'unscientific' reality. . . . They want to invoke a reality they cannot address directly. Direct address would destroy it, translate it into concepts, allegorize it . . . such language can only remind us that what it points to, by the nature of language, it cannot describe." See also Jacques Derrida, *Writing and Difference*, 280: "Henceforth, it became necessary to begin thinking that there was no center, that the center could not be thought in the form of a present-being, that the center had no natural site, that it was not a fixed locus but a function, a sort of nonlocus in which an infinite number of sign-substitutions came into play. This was the moment when language invaded the universal problematic, the moment when, in the absence of a center or origin, everything became discourse." Terence Cave also discusses this feature of discourse in Rabelais in *Cornucopian Text*.

in the text itself and between the text and its readers, whereby words (such as "trinch") and symbols (such as the bottle) can be immediately understood. Every discourse, every sign, requires interpretation and means different things to different individuals, including the all-encompassing substance, wine:

> "Si avez noté ce qui est en lettres Ioniques escrit dessus la porte du temple, vous avez peu entendre qu'en vin est vérité cachée. La dive Bouteille vous y envoye, soyez vous mesmes interprètes de vostre entreprinse." (Jourda ed., chap. 45, 454)

> "If you have noticed what is written in Ionic characters above the gate of the temple, you may have understood that the truth lies hidden in wine. The Holy Bottle directs you to it. You must be your own interpreters in this matter." (705)

Shortly thereafter the characters begin to rhyme, in one of the few avenues available to narrative prose for approximating actual transformation. But Frère Jean, employing once again the rhetoric of deflation, casts into final doubt this Bacchic enthusiasm: "Va, vieil fol, dist Frère Jean, au diable! Je ne saurois plus rithmer, la rithme me prent à la gorge; parlons de satisfaire icy" (chap. 46, 459) ("'Go to the devil, you old fool,' said Friar John. 'I can't rhyme anymore. The rheum has got me by the throat. Let's talk of giving satisfaction here'" [709]).[61] The quest fails to provide a unified code of meaning that will, in retrospect, render the search meaningful to a community of questers. Whereas the Folenghian quest rejects the possibility of a divine revelation in favor of a demonic vision that turns against the author himself, the Rabelaisian quest results in a final skepticism about the possibility of finding a meaning that extends beyond the bound-

---

[61]See Frère Jean's interpretation of the "enigme en prophétie," *Gargantua*, chap. 58.

aries of the individual quester.[62] It is no wonder then that within the same century a later compatriot of Rabelais will impose, without embarrassment, just such a limit on the relevance of his text.[63]

If the Rabelaisian novel is read as concluding with the *Quart Livre*, then it may be said that the quest fails as a means of achieving narrative resolution. Like its medieval predecessors, the Rabelaisian romance fragments into a series of disjointed episodic adventures that lead nowhere. This fragmentation is figured thematically; the companions drift from one island to another. Each episode reflects a darker version of the *terre gaste*; few signs are decipherable, and no redemption is in sight. The quest for the Grail and its more earthy version, the Holy Bottle, dissipates once and for all in the confusion and chaos of an unredeemable world.

In the "Ancien Prologue du Quart Livre" of 1548, Rabelais reminds his readers that he had asked them, at the beginning of the *Tiers Livre*, to reserve their laughter "for the seventy-eighth book" (289). The suggestion is that the quest will continue indefinitely and that, after all, "the adventure of meaning (*sens*), where the Holy Bottle is the sublime avatar of the holy Grail (or 'Sangréal,' precious blood di[of] . . . vine of

---

[62]This inability to share a common vision is dramatized in the Prologue to the *Quart Livre*—"But where are you? I can't see you" (11; 439)—and in the series of unanswered questions that constitute the Prologue to the *Cinquième Livre* (Jourda ed., 277–84; 601).

[63]Michel de Montaigne, *Essais*, "Avis au lecteur," 35: "C'est icy un livre de bonne foy, lecteur. Il t'advertit dès l'entrée, que je ne m'y suis proposé aucune fin, que domestique et privée" ("This is a book of good faith, reader. It warns you from the beginning that I have proposed for myself no other goal than a domestic and private one"). I am not saying that Montaigne means what he says here, only that there is no embarrassment about the assumption that an individual's own musings and meditations could have universal application.

the mass), becomes, by a wave of the magic codpiece, the grotesque misadventure of an overly inflated object" (Méla, "Pour un retour au Moyen-Age," 59). But if the parodic claim of the text is that the quest for a transcendent signifier is an overvaluation of signs and their capacity to totalize, then the same is not true of the narrative quest for meaning. Like Chrétien de Troyes's *Conte du Graal*, Rabelais's books contain the story of their reading, which is realized in the continuations of both works. The Grail continuations allegorize Chrétien's story of reading by becoming absorbed in the digressive paths deviating from the holy road of the Grail. The *Cinquième Livre*, however, brings the questers to revelation in a manifest sign, which is both fetishized and rendered ironic.[64] The revelation, this sign, points the questers back along the path of the quest to their point of origin—"'La dive Bouteille vous y envoye, soyez vous mesmes interpretes de vostre entreprinse'"—says Bacbuc (Jourda ed., 454) ("'The Holy Bottle directs you to it. You must be your own interpreters in this matter'" [705]). The reading the Rabelaisian text produces is a story of reading whereby the end serves purely to situate the beginning and the direction of the narrative. The continuator, as reader of the Rabelaisian books, supplies an ending that in fact assigns an origin to the quest. What the continuator of Rabelais's text reveals in his "fiction of a conclusion" (Cave's phrase), is that the meaning of the quest, rather than being a divine revelation from above, is the quest for individual meaning. Beginning, quest, and ending thus become the inevitable fictions of narration, of writing and of reading, and of the construction of meaning itself—here ambivalently, later as defensively and triumphantly bourgeois.

[64]What I am arguing is that the authorship, in the strict sense, of the *Cinquième Livre* is a relatively unimportant factor in the outcome of the quest, the point being that the nature of the quest is such as to compel the outcome realized by the *Cinquième Livre*.

# Bibliography

Alberti, Leon Battista. *Opere volgari*. Ed. C. Grayson. Bari: Later-za, 1960.

Angoulême, Marguerite d'. *L'Heptaméron*. Ed. M. François. Paris: Garnier, 1967.

*The Apocrypha: An American Translation*. Trans. Edgar Goodspeed. Intro. Moses Hadas. New York: Vintage, 1959.

Aristotle. *Poetics*. Trans. I. Bywater. New York: Modern Library, 1954.

Armitage, R. H. "Is *Gargantua* a Reworking of *Pantagruel* I?" *PMLA* 59(1944): 944–51.

Auerbach, Erich. *Mimesis: The Representation of Reality in Western Literature*. Trans. Willard Trask. Princeton: Princeton University Press, 1953.

Bakhtin, Mikhail. *The Dialogic Imagination: Four Essays*. Trans. C. Emerson and M. Holquist. Austin: University of Texas Press, 1981.

———. *Rabelais and His World*. Trans. Hélène Iwolsky. Cambridge: MIT Press, 1968.

Baraz, Michaël. *Rabelais et la joie de la liberté*. Paris: José Corti, 1983.

Bauschatz, Cathleen. "'Une Description du Jeu de Paulme Soubz Obscures Parolles': The Portrayal of Reading in *Pantagruel* and *Gargantua*." *Etudes Rabelaisiennes* 22(1988): 57–76.

———. "Montaigne's Conception of Reading in the Context of

Renaissance Poetics and Modern Criticism." In *The Reader in the Text: Essays on Audience and Interpretation*, ed. I. Crosman and S. Suleiman, 264–91. Princeton: Princeton University Press, 1980.

Beaujour, Michel. *Le Jeu de Rabelais*. Paris: Editions de l'Herne, n.d.

Béné, Charles. "Erasme et le chapître VIII du premier *Pantagruel* (Novembre 1532)." *Paedagogica Historica* 1(1961): 39–66.

Berrong, Richard. *Every Man for Himself: Social Order and Its Dissolution in Rabelais*. Saratoga, Calif.: ANMA Libri, 1985.

———. *Rabelais and Bakhtin: Popular Culture in "Gargantua and Pantagruel"*. Lincoln: University of Nebraska Press, 1986.

Berry, Alice Fiola. "Apollo versus Bacchus: The Dynamics of Inspiration (Rabelais's Prologues to *Gargantua* and to the *Tiers Livre*)." *PMLA* 90, 1 (January 1975): 88–95.

———. "'Les Mithologies Pantagruelicques': Introduction to a Study of Rabelais's *Quart Livre*." *PMLA* 92(1977): 471–80.

———. "The Mix, the Mask, and the Medical Farce: A Study of the Prologues to Rabelais's *Quart Livre*." *Romanic Review* 71, 1 (1980): 10–27.

———. *Rabelais: "Homo Logos"*. Studies in the Romance Languages and Literatures. Chapel Hill: University of North Carolina Press, 1979.

Blanchot, Maurice, *L'Espace littéraire*. Paris: Gallimard, 1955.

Bloch, R. Howard. *Etymologies and Genealogies: A Literary Anthropology of the French Middle Ages*. Chicago: University of Chicago Press, 1983.

Bloom, Harold. *The Anxiety of Influence: A Theory of Poetry*. New York: Oxford University Press, 1973.

Bouwsma, William J. "Anxiety and the Formation of Early Modern Culture." In *After the Reformation: Essays in Honor of J. H. Hexter*, ed. B. Malament. Philadelphia: University of Pennsylvania Press, 1980.

Boxer, Marilyn, and Jean Quataert, eds. *Connecting Spheres: Women in the Western World, 1500 to the Present*. New York: Oxford University Press, 1987.

Brault, Gérard. "'Un Abysme de Science': On the Interpretation of Gargantua's Letter to Pantagruel." *Bibliothèque d'Humanisme et Renaissance* 28(1966): 615–32.

Brownlee, Kevin, and Marina Brownlee, eds. *Romance: Generic*

*Transformation from Chrétien de Troyes to Cervantes*. Hanover, N.H.: University Press of New England, 1985.

Burke, Kenneth. *The Rhetoric of Religion: Studies in Logology*. Berkeley: University of California Press, 1970.

Burke, Peter. *The Renaissance Sense of the Past*. New York: St. Martin's, 1969.

Busson, Henri. "Les Eglises contre Rabelais." *Etudes Rabelaisiennes* 7(1967): 1–81.

————. "Rabelaisiana: 'Science sans conscience,' *Pantagruel* Ch. VIII." *Humanisme et Renaissance* 7(1940): 238–40.

Cassirer, Ernst, Paul O. Kristeller, and John H. Randall, Jr., eds. *The Renaissance Philosophy of Man*. Chicago: University of Chicago Press, 1948.

Castiglione, Baldassare. *Il libro del cortegiano: Opere di B. Castiglione, G. Della Casa, B. Cellini*. Ed. C. Cordié. Milan: Riccardo Ricciardi, n.d.

Cave, Terence. *The Cornucopian Text: Problems of Writing in the French Renaissance*. Oxford: Clarendon, 1979.

Charles, Michel. *Rhétorique de la lecture*. Paris: Seuil, 1977.

Chesney, Elizabeth A. *The Countervoyage of Rabelais and Ariosto: A Comparative Reading of Two Renaissance Mock Epics*. Durham, N.C.: Duke University Press, 1982.

Chrétien de Troyes. *Perceval le Gallois, ou Le Conte du Graal*. Ed. Mario Roques. Trans. Lucien Foulet. Paris: Nizet, n.d.

Clement, Nemours H. "The Influence of the Arthurian Romances on the Five Books of Rabelais." *University of California Publications in Modern Philology* 12(1925–26): 147–257.

Colie, Rosalie. *Paradoxia Epidemica: The Renaissance Tradition of Paradox*. Princeton: Princeton University Press, 1966.

Costa, Dennis. *Irenic Apocalypse: Some Uses of Apocalyptic in Dante, Petrarch and Rabelais*. Saratoga, Calif.: ANMA Libri, 1981.

*Critical Inquiry*. Special Issue on Metaphor 5.1 (Autumn 1978).

Davis, Natalie Zemon. *Fiction in the Archives: Pardon Tales and Their Tellers in Sixteenth-Century France*. Stanford, Calif.: Stanford University Press, 1987.

————. *Society and Culture in Early Modern France: Eight Essays*. Stanford, Calif.: Stanford University Press, 1975.

"Debats." *Revue d'Histoire Littéraire de la France* 86, 4(1986): 709–22.

Defaux, Gérard. "A propos de paroles gelées et dégelées (*Quart*

*Livre* 55–56): 'Plus hault sens' ou 'lectures plurielles'?" In *Rabelais's Incomparable Book: Essays on His Art*, ed. Raymond La Charité. Lexington, Ky.: French Forum, 1986.

———. "Au coeur du *Pantagruel*: Les deux chapitres IX de l'édition Nourry." *Kentucky Review Quarterly* 21, 1(1974): 59–96.

———. *Le Curieux, le glorieux et la sagesse du monde dans la première moitié du XVIe siècle: L'exemple de Panurge (Ulysse, Démosthène, Empédocle)*. Lexington, Ky.: French Forum, 1982.

———. "De Gorgias à Socrates: L'itineraire de Pantagruel." *Travaux de Linguistique et Littérature* 14, 2(1976): 7–20.

———. "D'un problème l'autre: Herméneutique de l'"altior sensus' et 'captatio lectoris' dans le prologue de *Gargantua*." *Revue d'Histoire Littéraire de la France* 85, 2(1985): 195–216.

———. "Un 'Extrait de haulte mythologie' humaniste: Pantagruel, Picus Redivivus." *Etudes Rabelaisiennes* 14(1977): 219–64.

———. *Pantagruel et les sophistes: Contribution à l'histoire de l'humanisme chrétien au XVIème siecle*. The Hague: Nijhoff, 1973.

———. "Rabelais et son masque comique: *Sophista loquitur*." *Etudes Rabelaisiennes* 11(1974): 89–136.

———. "Vers une définition de l'herméneutique rabelaisienne: Pantagruel, l'esprit, la lettre et les paroles gelées." *Etudes Rabelaisiennes* 21(1988): 327–37.

De Grève, Marcel. *L'Interprétation de Rabelais au XVIe siècle*. Geneva: Droz, 1961.

De Man, Paul. *Blindness and Insight: Essays in the Rhetoric of Contemporary Criticism*. 2d ed. Minneapolis: University of Minnesota Press, 1983.

Demerson, Guy. *Rabelais: Une Vie, une oeuvre, une époque*. Paris: Balland, 1986.

Derrida, Jacques. *Of Grammatology*. Trans. Gayatri C. Spivak. Baltimore: Johns Hopkins University Press, 1976. Originally published as *De la Grammatologie*. Paris: Minuit, 1967.

———. "Signature Event Context." *Glyph* 1(1977): 172–97.

———. "White Mythology: Metaphor in the Text of Philosophy." In *Margins of Philosophy*, trans. Alan Bass, 207–71. Chicago: University of Chicago Press, 1972. Originally published as *Marges de la philosophie*. Paris: Minuit, 1972.

———. *Writing and Difference*. Trans. Alan Bass. Chicago: University of Chicago Press, 1978.

Descombes, Vincent. *Modern French Philosophy*. Trans. L. Scott-Fox and J. M. Harding. Cambridge: Cambridge University Press, 1980. Originally published as *Le Même et l'autre*. Paris: Minuit, 1979.

Desonay, Fernand. "En relisant 'L'Abbaye de Thélème.'" In *François Rabelais: Ouvrage publié pour le quatrième centenaire de sa mort, 1553–1953*, 93–103. Geneva: Droz, 1953.

Dieckmann, Liselotte. *Hieroglyphics: The History of a Literary Symbol*. St. Louis: Washington University Press, 1970.

Dragonetti, Roger. *La Vie de la lettre au Moyen Age*. Paris: Seuil, 1980.

Dubois, Claude-Gilbert. *Problèmes de l'utopie*. Paris: Archives des Lettres Modernes, 1968.

———. *Mythe et langage au seizième siècle*. Bordeaux: Ducros, 1970.

Dujarric, G. *Précis chronologique de l'histoire de France*. Paris: Albin Michel, 1975.

Duval, Edwin. "Interpretation and the 'Doctrine Absconce' of Rabelais's Prologue to *Gargantua*." *Etudes Rabelaisiennes* 18(1984): 1–17.

———. "The Medieval Curriculum, the Scholastic University, and Gargantua's Program of Studies (*Pantagruel*, 8)." In *Rabelais's Incomparable Book: Essays on His Art*, ed. Raymond La Charité, 30–44. Lexington, Ky.: French Forum, 1986.

———. "Pantagruel's Genealogy and the Redemptive Design of Rabelais's *Pantagruel*." *PMLA* 99(1984): 162–78.

Edinger, Edward. *Ego and Archetype: Individuation and the Religious Function of the Psyche*. New York: Putnam's, 1972.

Eisenstein, Elizabeth. *The Printing Press as an Agent of Change: Communications and Cultural Transformations in Early Modern Europe*. 2 vols. Cambridge: Cambridge University Press, 1979.

Erasmus, Desiderius. *The Enchiridion*. Trans. and ed. Raymond Mimelick. Gloucester, Mass.: Peter Smith, 1970.

———. *The Praise of Folly*. Ed. and trans. C. Miller. New Haven: Yale University Press, 1979.

Febvre, Lucien. *The Problem of Unbelief in the Sixteenth Century: The Religion of Rabelais*. Trans. Beatrice Gottlieb. Cambridge: Harvard University Press, 1982. Originally published as *Le Problème de l'incroyance au XVIe siècle: La Religion de Rabelais*. Paris: Albin Michel, 1942.

Ferguson, Margaret W. "Saint Augustine's Region of Unlikeness: The Crossing of Exile and Language." *Georgia Review* 29, 3–4(1976): 842–64.

———. *Trials of Desire: Renaissance Defenses of Poetry.* New Haven: Yale University Press, 1983.

Ferguson, Margaret W., Maureen Quilligan, and Nancy Vickers, eds. *Rewriting the Renaissance: The Discourses of Sexual Difference in Early Modern Europe.* Chicago: University of Chicago Press, 1986.

Ferguson, Wallace. *The Renaissance in Historical Thought.* Cambridge, Mass.: Riverside, 1948.

Folengo, Teofilo. " *Baldus" e le altre opere latine a volgari.* Ed. Ugo E. Paoli. Florence: Felice le Monnier, 1953.

———. *Histoire macaronique de Merlin Coccaie, prototype de Rabelais.* Trans. P. L. Jacob. Paris: Garnier Frères, 1876.

———. *Le opere maccheroniche di Merlin Cocai.* Ed. A. Portioli. 2 vols. Mantua: G. Mandovi, 1882–83.

Foucault, Michel. *The Archaeology of Knowledge and the Discourse on Language.* Trans. A. M. S. Smith. New York: Harper, 1972. Originally published as *L'Archéologie du savoir* and *L'Ordre du discours.* Paris: Gallimard, 1969, 1971).

———. "Nietzsche, Genealogy, History." In *Language, Counter-Memory, Practice*, ed. D. Bouchard, 139–64. Ithaca: Cornell University Press, 1977.

———. *The Order of Things: An Archaeology of the Human Sciences.* New York: Random, 1970. Originally published as *Les Mots et les choses.* Paris: Gallimard, 1966.

———. "What Is an Author?" In *Textual Strategies: Perspectives in Post-Structuralist Criticism*, ed. Josué Harari, 141–60. Ithaca: Cornell University Press, 1979.

Fradenburg, Louise. "Criticism, Anti-Semitism, and the *Prioress's Tale.*" *Exemplaria: A Journal of Theory in Medieval and Renaissance Studies* 1, 1 (Spring 1989): 69–115.

*François Rabelais, ouvrage publié pour le quatrième centenaire de sa mort, 1553–1953.* Geneva: Droz, 1953.

Freccero, Carla. "Damning Haughty Dames: Panurge and the 'Haulte Dame de Paris' (*Pantagruel* 14)." *Journal of Medieval and Renaissance Studies* 15, 1 (Spring 1985): 57–67.

———. "1527: Margaret of Navarre." In *A New History of French*

*Literature*, ed. Denis Hollier, 145–48. Cambridge: Harvard University Press, 1989.

———. "The 'Instance' of the Letter: Woman in the Text of Rabelais." In *Rabelais's Incomparable Book: Essays on His Art*, ed. Raymond La Charité. Lexington, Ky.: French Forum, 1986.

———. "The Other and the Same: The Image of the Hermaphrodite in Rabelais." In *Rewriting the Renaissance: The Discourses of Sexual Difference in Early Modern Europe*, ed. Margaret W. Ferguson, Maureen Quilligan, and Nancy Vickers. Chicago: University of Chicago Press, 1986.

———. "Rabelais's 'Abbaye de Thélème': Utopia as Supplement." *L'Esprit Créateur* 25, 1 (1985): 57–67.

Freccero, John. *Dante: The Poetics of Conversion*. Ed. Rachel Jacoff. Cambridge: Harvard University Press, 1986.

Freud, Sigmund. *Beyond the Pleasure Principle*. Trans. James Strachey. New York: Liveright, 1950.

———. *On Creativity and the Unconscious: Papers on the Psychology of Art, Literature, Love, Religion*. Ed. Benjamin Nelson. New York: Harper, 1958.

———. *Totem and Taboo*. Trans. James Strachey. New York: W. W. Norton, 1950.

Frye, Northrop. *Anatomy of Criticism: Four Essays*. Princeton: Princeton University Press, 1957.

———. *The Secular Scripture: A Study of the Structure of Romance*. Cambridge: Harvard University Press, 1976.

Gaignebet, Claude. *Le Carnaval: Essai de mythologie populaire*. Paris: Payot, 1974.

Gasbarra, Shane. "The *Dialecticae Disputationes* of Lorenzo Valla: Book One." Unpublished paper, Yale University.

Gates, Henry Louis, Jr. "The 'Blackness of Blackness': A Critique of the Sign and the Signifying Monkey." *Critical Inquiry* 9, 4 (June 1983): 685–723.

Girard, René. *Violence and the Sacred*. Trans. Patrick Gregory. Baltimore: Johns Hopkins University Press, 1977.

Girault, François. *Les Grandes et Inestimables Chronicques du grant et enorme geant Gargantua* (1532). In *The Tale of Gargantua and King Arthur by François Girault*, ed. Huntington Brown. Cambridge: Harvard University Press, 1932.

Glauser, Alfred. *Le Faux Rabelais, ou L'Inauthenticité du "Cinquiesme Livre."* Paris: Nizet, 1975.

———. *Fonctions du nombre chez Rabelais.* Paris: Nizet, 1982.

———. *Rabelais créateur.* Paris: Nizet, 1966.

Gray, Floyd. "Ambiguity and Point of View in the Prologue to *Gargantua.*" *Romanic Review* 56(1965): 13–21.

———. *Rabelais et l'écriture.* Paris: Nizet, 1974.

———. "Rabelais's First Readers." In *Rabelais's Incomparable Book: Essays on His Art,* ed. Raymond La Charité, 15–29. Lexington, Ky.: French Forum, 1986.

———. "Structure and Meaning in the Prologue to the *Tiers Livre.*" *L'Esprit Créateur* 3, 2 (Summer 1963): 57–62.

Greene, Thomas M. *The Light in Troy: Imitation and Discovery in Renaissance Poetry.* New Haven: Yale University Press, 1982.

———. "Petrarch and the Humanist Hermeneutic." In *Italian Literature, Roots and Branches: Essays in Honor of Thomas Goddard Bergin,* ed. G. Rimanelli and K. J. Atchity, 201–24. New Haven: Yale University Press, 1976.

———. *Rabelais: A Study in Comic Courage.* Englewood Cliffs, N.J.: Prentice-Hall, 1970.

———. "Resurrecting Rome: The Double Task of the Humanist Imagination." In *Rome in the Renaissance: The City and the Myth,* ed. P. A. Ramsey, 41–54. Medieval and Renaissance Texts and Studies. Binghamton, N.Y.: State University of New York, 1982.

———. "The Unity of the *Tiers Livre.*" *Etudes Rabelaisiennes* 21 (1988): 293–300.

———. *The Vulnerable Text: Essays on Renaissance Literature.* New York: Columbia University Press, 1986.

Guiton, Jean. "Le Mythe des paroles gelées (Rabelais, *Quart Livre,* LV–LVI)." *Romanic Review* 31(1940): 3–15.

Habert, François. "Le Songe de Pantagruel." Intro. John Lewis. *Etudes Rabelaisiennes* 18(1985): 103–62.

Hallyn, Fernand. "Le Paradoxe de la souveraineté." *Etudes Rabelaisiennes* 21 (1988): 339–45.

Hanley, Sarah. "Family and State in Early Modern France: The Marriage Pact." In *Connecting Spheres: Women in the Western World, 1500 to the Present,* ed. M. Boxer and J. Quataert, 53–63. New York: Oxford University Press, 1987.

Harari, Josué, ed. *Textual Strategies: Perspectives in Post-Structuralist Criticism*. Ithaca: Cornell University Press, 1979.

Hay, Denys. *The Italian Renaissance in its Historical Background*. Cambridge: Cambridge University Press, 1961.

Higman, F. M. *Censorship and the Sorbonne: A Bibliographical Study of Books in French Censured by the Faculty of Theology of the University of Paris, 1520–1551*. Geneva: Droz, 1979.

Holland, Norman N. *The Dynamics of Literary Response*. Oxford: Oxford University Press, 1975.

Hoyt, Robert S., and Stanley Chodorow. *Europe in the Middle Ages*. 3d ed. New York: Harcourt, 1976.

Huchon, Mireille. "Archéologie du Ve Livre." *Etudes Rabelaisiennes* 21(1988): 19–28.

————. *Rabelais grammarien: De l'histoire du texte aux problèmes d'authenticité*. Etudes Rabelaisiennes 16. Geneva: Droz, 1981.

Hugo, Victor. *Oeuvres complètes: Critique*. Vol. 12. Ed. Jean-Pierre Reynaud. Paris: Laffont, 1985.

Huguet, E. E. A. *Dictionnaire de la langue française au 16e siècle*. Paris: Champion, 1925.

Jameson, Fredric. "Magical Narratives: Romance as Genre." *New Literary History* 7, 1 (Autumn 1975): 135–63.

————. "Of Islands and Trenches: Neutralization and the Production of Utopian Discourse." *Diacritics* 7, 2 (Summer 1977): 2–21.

————. *The Political Unconscious: Narrative as a Socially Symbolic Act*. Ithaca: Cornell University Press, 1981.

Jeanneret, Michel. *Des mets et des mots: Banquets et propos de table à la Renaissance*. Paris: José Corti, 1987.

————. "'Ma patrie est une citrouille': Thèmes alimentaires dans Rabelais et Folengo." *Etudes de Lettres* 2(1984): 25–44.

————. "Les Paroles dégelées (Rabelais, *Quart Livre*, 48–65)." *Littérature* 17(1975): 14–30.

Jung, Carl G. *Aion*. Princeton: Princeton University Press, 1970.

————. *The Archetypes and the Collective Unconscious*. Princeton: Princeton University Press, 1969.

Kaiser, Walter. *Praisers of Folly: Erasmus, Rabelais, Shakespeare*. Cambridge: Harvard University Press, 1963.

Kelly, Douglas. "*Translatio Studii*: Translation, Adaptation, and Allegory in Medieval French Literature." *Philological Quarterly* 57(1958): 287–310.

Kennedy, William J. *Rhetorical Norms in Renaissance Literature.* New Haven: Yale University Press, 1978.

Ker, W. P. *Epic and Romance: Essays in Medieval Literature.* 2d ed. London: Macmillan, 1908.

Kermode, Frank. *The Sense of an Ending: Studies in the Theory of Fiction.* New York: Oxford University Press, 1967.

Kline, Michael B. *Rabelais and the Age of Printing.* Etudes Rabelaisiennes 4. Geneva: Droz, 1969.

Koenigsberger, G., and G. Mosse. *Europe in the Sixteenth Century.* London: Longman, 1968.

Kristeller, Paul Oskar. *Renaissance Thought: The Classic, Scholastic, and Humanist Strains.* New York: Harper, 1961.

Kritzman, Lawrence. "The Allegory of Repression." *Substance* 28(1981): 72–85.

———. "Rabelais's Comedy of Cruelty: A Psycho-allegorical Reading of the Chiquanous Episode." In *Rabelais's Incomparable Book: Essays on His Art,* ed. Raymond La Charité. Lexington, Ky.: French Forum, 1986.

Kuhn, Thomas S. *The Structure of Scientific Revolutions.* 2d ed. Chicago: University of Chicago Press, 1962, 1973.

Lacan, Jacques. *Ecrits.* Paris: Seuil, 1966.

———. *Ecrits: A Selection.* Trans. Alan Sheridan. New York: Norton, 1977.

———. *Le Séminaire de Jacques Lacan: Livre XX encore.* Ed. Jacques-Alain Miller. Paris: Seuil, 1975.

———. "Seminar on the Purloined Letter." Trans. Jeffrey Mehlman. *Yale French Studies: French Freud* 48(1973): 38–72.

La Charité, Raymond. "Gargantua's Letter and *Pantagruel* as Novel." *L'Esprit Createur: A Rabelais Symposium* 21, 1 (Spring 1981): 26–40.

———. ed. *Rabelais's Incomparable Book: Essays on His Art.* Lexington, Ky.: French Forum, 1986.

———. *Recreation, Reflection and Re-creation: Perspectives on Rabelais's "Pantagruel."* Lexington, Ky.: French Forum, 1980.

Lanham, Richard. *The Motives of Eloquence: Literary Rhetoric in the Renaissance.* New Haven: Yale University Press, 1976.

Lefranc, Abel. *Les Navigations de Pantagruel, étude sur la géographie rabelaisienne.* Paris: Leclerc, 1905.

———. *Rabelais: Études sur "Gargantua," "Pantagruel," le "Tiers Livre."* Paris: Albin Michel, 1953.

Loomis, Roger Sherman, ed. *Arthurian Literature in the Middle Ages.* Oxford: Clarendon, 1959.

———. *Arthurian Tradition and Chrétien de Troyes.* New York: Columbia University Press, 1949.

Lydgate, Barry. "Going Public: Rabelais, Montaigne and the Printed Word." Paper presented at the New England Renaissance Conference at Mount Holyoke College, October 1978.

———. "Mortgaging One's Work to the World: Publication and the Structure of Montaigne's *Essais.*" *PMLA* 96(March 1981): 210–23.

———. "Printing, Narrative and the Genesis of the Rabelaisian Novel." *Romanic Review* 71, 4 (November 1980): 345–73.

McKinley, Mary. "Bakhtin and the World of Rabelais Criticism." *Degré Second* 11(September 1987): 83–88.

Marin, Louis. *Utopiques: Jeux d'espaces.* Paris: Editions de Minuit, 1973.

Méla, Charles. *Blanchefleur et le saint homme, ou La Semblance des reliques: Etude comparée de littérature médiévale.* Paris: Seuil, 1979.

———. "Pour un retour au Moyen-Age." *L'Ane* 1(1981): 10, 59.

———. "La Reine et le graal." *Ornicar?* 22–23(1981): 301–4.

———. "Romans et merveilles." In *Précis de littérature française du Moyen Age,* ed. Daniel Poirion, 214–35. Paris: Presses Universitaires de France, 1983.

Montaigne, Michel de. *Essais.* Ed. Pierre Villey. 3 vols. Alcan, 1930–31.

Moody, Ernest A. *Truth and Consequences in Mediaeval Logic.* Amsterdam: North-Holland, 1953.

More, Saint Thomas. *Utopia.* Ed. Edward Surtz. New Haven: Yale University Press, 1964.

Morris, Edward. "Rabelais, Romances, Reading, Righting Names." In *Romance: Generic Transformations from Chrétien de Troyes to Cervantes,* ed. Kevin Brownlee and Marina Brownlee, 155–77. Hanover , N.H.: University Press of New England, 1985.

Napoli, Giovanni di. *Lorenzo Valla: Filosofia e religione nell'umanesimo italiano.* Rome: Edizioni de Storia e Letteratura, 1971.

Nelson, William. *From Fraud to Fiction*. Cambridge: Harvard University Press, 1973.

Nietzsche, Friedrich. *Basic Writings of Nietzsche*. Ed. Walter Kaufmann. New York: Modern Library, 1968.

Nykrog, Per. "Thélème, Panurge, et la Dive Bouteille." *Revue d'Histoire Littéraire de la France* 65, 3(1965): 385–97.

Ockham, William of. *Ockham: The Philosophical Writings*. Ed. Philotheus Boehner, O. F. M. New York: Nelson, 1962.

Ong, Walter. *Interfaces of the Word: Studies in the Evolution of Consciousness and Culture*. Ithaca: Cornell University Press, 1977.

Ozment, Steven. *The Age of Reform, 1250–1550: An Intellectual and Religious History of Late Medieval and Renaissance Europe*. New Haven: Yale University Press, 1980.

Paris, Jean. *Rabelais au futur*. Paris: Seuil, 1970.

Palmieri, Matteo. *Della vita civile*. Ed. F. Battaglia. Bologna: N. Zanichelli, 1944.

Paris, Jean. *Rabelais au futur*. Paris: Seuil, 1970.

Parker, Patricia. *Inescapable Romance: Studies in the Poetics of a Mode*. Princeton: Princeton University Press, 1979.

―――. *Literary Fat Ladies: Rhetoric, Gender, Property*. London: Methuen, 1987.

*Petit Robert 2: Dictionnaire des noms propres*. Paris: Le Robert, 1967; rpt. 1983.

Plattard, Jean. *L'Oeuvre de Rabelais: Sources, invention et composition*. Paris: Honoré Champion, 1967.

Poirion, Daniel, ed. *Précis de littérature française du Moyen Age*. Paris: Presses Universitaires de France, 1983.

Pouilloux, Jean-Yves. "Notes sur deux chapîtres du *Quart Livre* LV–LVI." *Littérature* 5(1972): 88–94.

―――. "Notes sur l'abbaye de Thélème." *Romantisme* 1–2(1971): 200–208.

*La Queste del Saint-Graal*. Ed. Albert Pauphilet. Paris: Champion, CFMA, 1949.

*The Quest of the Holy Grail,*. Trans. P. M. Matarasso. Middlesex, England: Penguin, 1969; 1976.

Quint, David. *Origin and Originality in Renaissance Literature: Versions of the Source*. New Haven: Yale University Press, 1983.

Rabelais, François. *L'Abbaye de Thélème*. Ed. Raoul Morçay. Paris: Droz, 1934.

————. *Gargantua: Edition critique*. Ed. R. Calder, M. A. Screech, and V. L. Saulnier. Geneva: Droz, 1970.

————. *Gargantua and Pantagruel*. Trans. J. M. Cohen. Harmondsworth, England: Penguin, 1955.

————. *Oeuvres de François Rabelais: Edition critique*. Ed. Abel Lefranc. 6 vols. Paris: Honoré Champion, 1913–55.

————. *Oeuvres complètes*. Ed. Guy Demerson. Paris: Seuil, 1973.

————. *Oeuvres complètes*. Ed. Pierre Jourda. 2 vols. Paris: Garnier Frères, 1962.

————. *Pantagruel: Edition critique*. Ed. V. L. Saulnier. Geneva: Droz, 1965.

————. *Le Quart Livre: Edition critique*. Ed. Robert Marichal. Geneva: Droz, 1947.

————. *Le Tiers Livre: Edition critique*. Ed. M. A. Screech. Geneva: Droz, 1964.

Ragland-Sullivan, Ellie. "The Myth of the *Sustantificque Mouelle*: A Lacanian Perspective on Rabelais's Use of Language." *Literature and Psychology* 34, 3(1988): 1–19.

Regosin, Richard. "The Artist and the *Abbaye*." *Studies in Philology* 68, 2 (1971): 121–29.

————. "The Ins(ides) and Outs(ides) of Reading: Plural Discourse and the Question of Interpretation in Rabelais." In *Rabelais's Incomparable Book: Essays on His Art*, ed. Raymond La Charité. Lexington, Ky.: French Forum, 1986.

Richards, I. A. *The Philosophy of Rhetoric*. Oxford: Oxford University Press, 1936, rpt. 1979.

Ricoeur, Paul. *The Philosophy of Paul Ricoeur: An Anthology of His Work*. Ed. Charles E. Reagan and David Stewart. Boston: Beacon, 1978.

————. *The Rule of Metaphor: Multi-disciplinary Studies of the Creation of Meaning in Language*. Trans. Robert Czerny. Toronto: University of Toronto Press, 1979. Originally published as *La Métaphore vive*. Paris: Seuil, 1975.

Rigolot, François. "Cratylisme et Pantagruélisme: Rabelais et le statut du signe." *Etudes Rabelaisiennes* 13(1976): 115–32.

————. *Les Langages de Rabelais*. Etudes Rabelaisiennes 10. Geneva: Droz, 1972.

————. *Le Texte de la Renaissance: Des rhétoriqueurs à Montaigne*. Geneva: Droz, 1982.

————. "Vraisemblance et narrativité dans le *Pantagruel*." *L'Esprit Createur* 21, 1 (Spring 1981): 53–68.

Rigolot, François, and Sandra Sider. "Fonctions de l'écriture emblématique chez Rabelais." *L'Esprit Créateur* 28, 2 (1988): 36–47.

Said, Edward. *Beginnings: Intention and Method.* Baltimore: Johns Hopkins University Press, 1975.

Saulnier, Verdun. "Le Doute chez Rabelais?" *Etudes Rabelaisiennes* 14(1977): 1–21.

————. *Rabelais II. Rabelais dans son enquête: Etude sur le "Quart" et le "Cinquième" livre.* Paris: SEDES, 1982.

Schrader, Ludwig. "Panurge: Théories récentes—observations méthodologiques—conséquences possibles." *Etudes Rabelaisiennes* 21(1988): 145–56.

————. *Panurge und hermes: zum Ursprung eines Charakters bei Rabelais.* Bonn: Romanisches Seminar der Universitat Bonn, 1958.

Screech, M. A. "The Death of Pan and the Death of Heroes in the Fourth Book of Rabelais: A Study in Syncretism." *Bibliothèque d'Humanisme et Renaissance* 17(1955): 36–55.

————. "Emblems and Colours: The Controversy over Gargantua's Colours and Devices." In *Mélanges d'histoire du XVIe siècle offerts à Henri Meylan*, 65–80. Geneva: Droz, 1970.

————. *Rabelais.* Ithaca: Cornell University Press, 1979.

————. *The Rabelaisian Marriage: Aspects of Rabelais' Religion, Ethics and Comic Philosophy.* London: Edward Arnold, 1958.

————. "The Sense of Rabelais's Enigme en Prophétie (*Gargantua* LVIII)." *Bibliothèque d'Humanisme et Renaissance* 18(1956): 392–404.

Sebillet, Thomas. *Art poétique françoys.* Ed. Felix Gaiffe. Paris: Edouard Cornély, 1910.

Smith, Paul J. *Voyage et écriture: Étude sur le "Quart Livre"* de Rabelais. Etudes Rabelaisiennes 19. Geneva: Droz, 1987.

Spitzer, Leo. "The Works of Rabelais." In *Literary Masterpieces of the Western World*, ed. Francis Horn. Baltimore: Johns Hopkins Univ. Press, 1953.

Stephens, Walter. *Giants in Those Days: Folklore, Ancient History, and Nationalism.* Lincoln: University of Nebraska Press, 1989.

Telle, Emile. "Thélème et le paulisme matrimonial erasmien: Le Sens de l'enigme en prophétie." In *François Rabelais: Ouvrage publié pour le quatrième centenaire de sa mort, 1553–1953*, 104–19. Geneva: Droz, 1953.

Tetel, Marcel. "Rabelais and Folengo." *Comparative Literature* 15(1963): 357–64.
———. "Rabelais et Folengo: *De patria diabolorum*." *Etudes Rabelaisiennes* 21(1988): 203–12.
Thuasne, Louis. *Etudes sur Rabelais*. Paris, 1904.
Tillyard, E. M. W. *The Elizabethan World Picture*. New York: Random, 1959.
Tobin, Patricia. *Time and the Novel: The Genealogical Imperative*. Princeton: Princeton University Press, 1978.
Tornitore, Tonino. "Parole gelate prima e dopo Rabelais: Fortuna di un topos." *Etudes Rabelaisiennes* 22(1988): 43–56.
*Les Utopies à la Renaissance*. Colloque international, Université Libre de Bruxelles. Brussels: Presses Universitaires de Bruxelles, 1963.
Valesio, Paolo. "Genealogy of a Staged Scene (*Orlando Furioso*, V)." *Yale Italian Studies*, n.s., 1, 1 (1980): 5–31.
———. *Novantiqua: Rhetorics as a Contemporary Theory*. Bloomington: Indiana University Press, 1980.
———. "Il seggio e l'ombra: da un romanzo spagnolo del quattrocento." *Scienze Umane* 2(1979): 73–88.
Valla, Lorenzo. *Opera omnia*. Ed. Eugenio Garin. 2 vols. Turin, 1962.
Vinaver, Eugène. *The Rise of Romance*. Oxford: Clarendon, 1971.
Waswo, Richard. *Language and Meaning in the Renaissance*. Princeton: Princeton University Press, 1987.
———. "The 'Ordinary Language Philosophy' of Lorenzo Valla." *Bibliothèque d'Humanisme et Renaissance* 41(1979): 255–71.
———. "The Reaction of Juan Luis Vives to Valla's Philosophy of Language." *Bibliothèque d'Humanisme et Renaissance* 42(1980): 595–609.
Weinberg, Florence M. *The Wine and the Will: Rabelais's Bacchic Christianity*. Detroit: Wayne State University Press, 1972.
Wolf, Eric R. *Europe and the People without History*. Berkeley: University of California Press, 1982.
Woodward, William Harrison. *Studies in Education during the Age of the Renaissance, 1400–1600*. Cambridge: Cambridge University Press, 1924.
Wunenburger, Jean-Jacques. *L'Utopie, ou La Crise de l'imaginaire*. Paris: Jean-Pierre Delarge, 1979.

# Index

Library of Congress Cataloging-in-Publication Data

Freccero, Carla, 1956–
    Father figures : genealogy and narrative structure in Rabelais / Carla Freccero.
        p.    cm.
    Includes bibliographical references and index.
    ISBN 0-8014-2554-9 (cloth : alk. paper)
    1. Rabelais, François, ca. 1490–1553?—Criticism and interpretation.
2. Fathers and sons in literature.    3. Father figures in literature.    4. Genealogy
in literature.    5. Narration (Rhetoric)    I. Title.
PQ1697.F38F7    1991
843¹.3—dc20                                                            90-55728